HONG KONG
1841-1862

HONG KONG UNIVERSITY PRESS REPRINT

This edition is reprinted from the original 1937 edition. No changes apart from minor typographical errors have been made to the original text, including its quotations from other works, and its original illustrations and index are also retained. The existence of a new Additional Note at the back of the book is indicated by a numbered reference in the margin of the text.

HONG KONG
1841-1862
BIRTH, ADOLESCENCE AND COMING OF AGE

GEOFFREY ROBLEY SAYER
*With new Introduction and Additional Notes
by D. M. Emrys Evans*

HONG KONG UNIVERSITY PRESS

© HONG KONG UNIVERSITY PRESS 1980

ISBN 962-209-012-5

This reprint has been authorized by
the original publisher, the Oxford University Press

Originally published in 1937 with the title
Hong Kong: birth, adolescence, and coming of age

Printed in Hong Kong by
LIBRA PRESS LIMITED
56 Wong Chuk Hang Road, Hong Kong

The Waterfall at Hong Cong

Frontispiece]

ADDITIONS TO THE 1980 REPRINT

Foreword	vi
Introduction to the 1980 Reprint..	vii
A Short Biography of G. R. Sayer	xx
Works referred to in the Text	xxiii
Selected Works which have appeared since the first publication of this Book..	xxv
Additional Notes *(at the end of the book)*	1

FOREWORD

IN PRESENTING this new printing, with a new Introduction and Additional Notes, of G. R. Sayer's *Hong Kong: birth adolescence and coming of age,* I would like to thank Oxford University Press for kindly making it possible by authorizing the reprint and the Hong Kong University Press Committee for their encouragement and support. A special debt is owed to Mr Y. K. Fung, Editor of the Hong Kong University Press, for his careful editorial assistance, and to those others who contributed information which I hope will have made the Additional Notes more useful to the modern reader. The fee agreed for this work has been donated to the English Schools Foundation of Hong Kong for the award of an annual 'G. R. Sayer Prize in History' which is intended for award to students at The Island School, Hong Kong.

D. M. EMRYS EVANS

INTRODUCTION
TO THE 1980 REPRINT

GEOFFREY ROBLEY SAYER'S *Hong Kong: birth, adolescence and coming of age* was first published in 1937 by the Oxford University Press. It has been difficult to come by for some time and, as it is one of the few general works on the history of Hong Kong, albeit ending with the events of the year 1861, its republication now will enable many to capture its period flavour and set it alongside the works which have appeared subsequently. It was the first of the two works by Sayer on the history of Hong Kong, the second being *Hong Kong 1862–1919: the years of discretion*, published by the Hong Kong University Press in 1975, some thirteen years after the author's death in 1962 and some thirty-seven years after his retirement from the service of the Hong Kong government in 1938.

Not many general historical works on the origin and development of Hong Kong had appeared before Sayer's offering, though more have appeared since. Sayer's two works do make a contribution to what we can now see as a wider canvas set against the background of traumatic change on the mainland of China. But Sayer was not a professional historian—he was a career civil servant. After a classical education at Highgate School and Queen's College, Oxford, he joined the Hong Kong government as a cadet officer in 1910 after a competitive examination. The description 'cadet' had originally been used, at the time when Governor Sir Hercules Robinson instituted his new scheme of recruitment of civil servants for Hong Kong in 1861, in its East India Company sense of a junior in the Company's service. But, by the time Sayer came to Hong Kong, the expression denoted an administrative officer, the highest grade of civil servant, and it remained in use officially until 1960 when it was replaced by the more prosaic 'administrative officer'.

Sayer was thus one of an élite, one of a highly selected group many of whom gave distinguished service both in Hong Kong and elsewhere.[1]

---

[1] For an account of the origin and development of the cadet grade in the Hong Kong Government, see H. J. Lethbridge, 'Hong Kong cadets, 1862–1941', *Journal of the Hong Kong Branch of the Royal Asiatic Society* (hereafter referred to as *JHKBRAS*) 10 (1970) 36–56, which has a reference to Sayer on p. 44 and in note 34.

INTRODUCTION

One of the first three cadets appointed in 1862, Sir Cecil Clementi Smith, was to become Governor of the Straits Settlements, and later cadets were to achieve recognition in Hong Kong and elsewhere as Governors and High Commissioners. Their contribution was not to be made, however, only to the quality of government but also to the development of British Sinology. Though they were, as Lethbridge puts it, 'gentlemen trained in the ideology of pre-war English public schools and older residential universities', and conformed to the mores and values of the upper middle classes from which they were drawn, not all allowed 'their curiosity and intelligence to slumber in a sub-tropical climate'.[2] Many of the Hong Kong cadets were men of letters who brought to bear on their everyday administrative duties a scholarly and literary approach, which found intellectual outlets in areas far beyond the dutiful or even imaginative discharge of their duties, and further cultivated their intellects by turning to what was to them a new culture lying but a short distance across the border in China. The sojourn in Canton required of them by their terms of service served also to whet their appetites for a good deal more than learning the Chinese language, and many were to embark on a voyage of discovery through the language and civilization of China. Some were to achieve scholarly attainments in these fields which lay far beyond the confines of their official duties: mention here need only be made of Sir James Stewart Lockhart and Sir Reginald Fleming Johnston (the latter in 1931 became Professor of Chinese at what is now the University of London's School of Oriental and African Studies after climaxing his public career as Commissioner of Weihaiwei).

Sayer too was of this breed though he never fully ventured into Sinological studies. He was, nevertheless, definitely a scholar administrator, a man of letters who brought to the execution of his duties a scholarly concern for the history and culture of the place which he helped to administer. But, perhaps, *coelum, non animum, mutant*[3], a feature

[2] Lethbridge, op.cit., p. 50.

[3] In his later work, *Hong Kong 1862–1919,* Sayer quotes (p. 25) from a despatch from Governor MacDonnell of Hong Kong to the Secretary of State for the Colonies in which MacDonnell suggests a motto to accompany the Colony's official coat of arms. This suggested motto was derived from an epistle of the Roman poet Horace and read: *coelum, non animum mutant.* The full quotation reads as follows: *coelum, non animum, mutant qui trans mare currunt* which, roughly translated, says that they who cross the sea may change the sky above them but their spirit is not changed. Ironically,

of the finest kind of colonial civil servant who, wherever he served in the Empire, maintained his intellectual traditions and enhanced the government of the particular colony where he was posted.

The republication of *Hong Kong: birth, adolescence and coming of age*, therefore, allows the reader of today to take another look at a flower of that tradition.

But what of his literary work? Doubtless, Sayer would have been modest about his first published work, a translation of some of Horace's *Odes* published privately in 1922, and his other published writings, apart from his two histories of Hong Kong, were two translations in his retirement of Chinese works on pottery—Lan Pin-nan's *Ching-te-chen T'ao Lu*[4] and Ch'en Liu's *T'ao Ya*[5] in 1951 and 1959 respectively, both works considered significant in the history of Chinese ceramics.

Sayer was thus one of the administrative élite and was probably conscious of this. Indeed, one of his contemporaries, Stephen Francis Balfour,[6] even as Sayer was engaged on his two historical works on Hong Kong as a British colony, was concerning himself with the history of Hong Kong before it became a British colony.[7] But what of Sayer's official business whilst he was engaged in his academic pursuits?

A review of his career[8] suggests that his historical inquiries may well have been a relief from the generally humdrum nature of the duties cast upon him. He was not destined to achieve the highest office in spite of his excellent showing in the Colonial Service examinations, which would have qualified him to opt for India had he wished (a contemporary, Norman Lockhart Smith, for example, was to become Hong Kong's Colonial Secretary in 1936, only two years before Sayer's retirement[9]),

---

though many cadets were to venture into new intellectual fields of inquiry, their intellectual traditions, nurtured in the English classics, as was that of Sayer, were to persist.

[4] London, Routledge, Kegan Paul & Co., 1951.

[5] London, Routledge, Kegan Paul & Co., 1959.

[6] Balfour joined the Government in 1929 and died in internment in Stanley during the tragic Allied air-bombing of the internment camp in 1944.

[7] The fruits of his research were originally published as 'Hong Kong before the British' in the Shanghai journal *T'ien Hsia Monthly* 11–12 (1940 & 1941) 330–352 and 440–464. This was reprinted in *JHKBRAS* 10 (1970) 134–179.

[8] For a summary of Sayer's career, see p. 15.

[9] Smith was fortunate enough to have retired just a few days before the Japanese assault on Hong Kong in December 1941.

and he filled a wide variety of positions which ranged from Assistant Superintendent of Police, Acting Private Secretary to the Governor, through Head of the Sanitary Department[10] until he reached his last position of Director of Education. It was a much-varied career which not only included service in the Great War but which took him through nine different facets of government in Hong Kong.

As a writer, his classical upbringing remains evident. His literary style was somewhat idiosyncratic, a fact which might be more readily discerned in *Hong Kong 1862–1919: the years of discretion* than in *Hong Kong: birth, adolescence and coming of age*. The former he considered ready for publication but it required considerable sub-editing to make it acceptable as a piece of continuous and readable prose. *Hong Kong: birth, adolescence and coming of age*, coming from the same pen at a not very much earlier date, must have received considerable editorial attention for, though it bears the unmistakable mark of Sayer's pen, it suggests also the influence of an unseen hand. So be it. It is the work as we have it that we must judge and from that and that alone we must attempt to evaluate Sayer's importance and the importance of the two historical writings which represent his contribution.

He classed himself modestly as a chronicler, a gleaner and assembler of facts. But, as has been said, 'reporting facts is the refuge of those who have no imagination' (Luc de Clapier, *Réflexions et maximes*). A cursory glance, however, at *Hong Kong: birth, adolescence and coming of age* reveals an active mind at work—there is here no mere recording of past events but we see colours on a palette, mixed and applied to his canvas to produce a view all his own. In retrospect, it must be said that Sayer was not a man of dazzling insight whose writings cause the scales to fall from our eyes and he would not have claimed as much. Unlike many, his writings reveal an innate modesty and appreciation of his own achievements which led him into unnecessary self-deprecation with which it is not possible wholly to agree. It is best today to see his historical writings in two different perspectives: first, against a backdrop of earlier historical accounts of Hong Kong and then in the context of our further developed views of today. The latter is a task which can best be left to the reader and not attempted in an introduction such as this,

---

[10] Curiously, Lethbridge, op.cit., p. 49, states that this was a Department which required a Head with 'specialist knowledge' rather than a cadet. Yet Sayer headed the Sanitary Department from 1920 to 1925 and from 1928 to 1934.

though it will be necessary to draw attention to some anomalous parts of the book.

Sayer was clearly heavily dependent on secondary sources for his introductory material concerning the ineluctable struggle between Britain and China which we have come to know pejoratively as the 'Opium War'. In particular, he drew heavily on Hosea Ballou Morse's *The chronicles of the East India Company trading to China,* an epoch-making work published in 1925 by the Oxford University Press. He also had the same author's *The international relations of the Chinese empire,* published in 1907. He was well served too by *The Chinese Repository* and by printed series of British Parliamentary papers on relations with China during the 1830s, to which he makes constant reference when dealing with events before and after the time when the East India Company's monopoly of trade was brought to an end in 1833 and events moved towards their climax in the years 1839 to 1842. It would be too easy today to dismiss Sayer as being unduly uncritical of the traumatic events of those days, but a reading of his presentation of the concatenation of events which eventually resulted in the Opium War shows an attempt to separate the diplomatic dilemma from the sordidness of one of the articles of trade involved. Perhaps Sayer does not go far enough in underlining the extent to which many of the prime actors in the drama themselves found the opium trade repugnant but sublimated this to what they perceived a greater principle: free trade and open and equal relations with the Chinese Imperial Government.

Pens will continue to scratch for many a year over the rights and wrongs of the Opium War and many will continue to disregard the expressions of doubt which were felt by many of the British merchants who could not be discarded into the popular category of pirates and smugglers beloved of the denigrators of British diplomatic conduct of the time. Sayer was writing for a public which he assumed would not necessarily have any great knowledge of the history of the events which culminated in the Opium War and the cession of Hong Kong. Indeed, when Sayer wrote this book, apart from the works of Morse, there were few accounts of the Opium War and of the foundation of Hong Kong. But in the last decade or so, a number of works have appeared, some popular, some scholarly. There are two popular works, Coates' *Prelude to Hong Kong* and Collis's *Foreign mud.* There is Inglis's more learned work, but still aimed at the popular market, *The Opium War,* and then scholarly works such as Beeching's *The Chinese Opium Wars* and Fay's *The Opium War*. But the classic is and will remain Fairbank's *Trade and diplomacy on the China coast*. Finally there is Hurd's *The Arrow War* dealing with the events surrounding what is sometimes called the 'Second Opium War'.[11] Sayer's sources were, of course, far more limited, both in terms of original sources and in terms of published accounts. By and large, except for periods when he took home leave, he would have been limited to the sources available to him in the Colonial Secretariat Library including, possibly, the correspondence of the Colonial Secretariat, and the University of Hong Kong Library. Today, of course, we have the advantage of many other works from which we can derive our source information. The Public Record Office of Hong Kong is now a treasure-house of primary material and adds to the wealth of the University of Hong Kong Library (though it must be pointed out that Sayer must presumably have had access to materials now long since destroyed during the Japanese occupation). Much of his historical speculation has now been overtaken by documented and scholarly works such as Lo Hsiang Lin's *Hong Kong and its external communications before 1842* and a multiplicity of micro-studies, which have appeared in the *Journal of the Hong Kong Branch of the Royal Asiatic Society*, re-established in 1960 shortly before Sayer's death in 1962. Sayer himself tended to use broad sweeps of the brush with periodic attention to fine detail, and his writing is within a certain classical tradition. He set himself an objective and, within the limits which he set, he achieved that objective.

Before Sayer wrote this book, there had been very few attempts at an overview of the historical antecedents and development of Hong Kong. As the question of China's relations with Britain came gradually to the forefront of the minds of Britain's literate classes in the 1830s, general descriptive works flooded onto the market to satisfy eager readers. The outbreak of hostilities, the Opium War, saw a large crop of personal reminiscences of experiences in China, possibly the first being Lord Jocelyn's *Six months with the Chinese expedition* (London, John Murray, 1841). In introducing his book Lord Jocelyn confessed that 'all opinions are hazarded with the greatest diffidence as, from the slight and imperfect knowledge those most acquainted with the country have been able to obtain, very little weight must be given to the remarks and

---

[11] See the supplementary bibliography, pp. 20–21.

suggestions of any private individual.' Indeed, he went on to confess further that each piece of 'slight information' gained served only 'to show the darkness under which we are still labouring; and the faint insight hitherto obtained'.

Jocelyn himself was a cautious and cultured writer but he was to be followed by a flood of literature, mostly produced by military men engaged in the campaign and they undoubtedly fed an eager popular imagination with their accounts of their encounters with the mysteries of the Orient and of the 'Celestials' (as the Chinese were popularly called at the time). The majority of these accounts were highly coloured by the popular prejudices of the day but the sheer number of volumes of this sort which poured off the presses in the 1840s showed that they had a ready market. Some of these works were undoubtedly serious and remain important reading today: see William D. Bernard's *Narrative of the voyages and services of the Nemesis* and Sir John Davis's slightly later work in two volumes (after his retirement from the Governorship of Hong Kong) *China during the war and since the peace*. Less important is Rev. G. N. Wright's *China illustrated in a series of views*, which is best known today for the 128 engravings which have now become popular collectors' items (the so-called 'Allom engravings'). Wright's accompanying letterpress is little more than a melange of plagiarism and prejudice but it found a ready market in its day. There were many others and Sayer does not, unfortunately, include a bibliography.[12]

But it is necessary to collate and examine the secondary works which would have been accessible to Sayer whilst he was writing his history. The Opium War writings and the contemporary newspapers can be taken for granted but these were sources and not in themselves 'historical writings'.

It was not until 1861 that there appeared for the first time a work which set out to be an historical treatment of the origins and development of early Hong Kong (even though it is largely an eyewitness account of contemporary events). This was William Tarrant's *Hong Kong, 1839–1844*, first printed in weekly instalments in Tarrant's newspaper, the *Friend of China* in 1861 and the early months of 1862.

Tarrant arrived in China for the first time in 1835 at about the age of eighteen and he was thus present through all those events which led

[12] A bibliography of the works to which Sayer refers and which he has not included in his 'Abbreviations used in the references' is given on pp. 18–19.

up to the outbreak of hostilities out of which Hong Kong emerged as a British Colony. Though he intended to cover the period 1839 up to 1862, personal circumstances cut short his account when he had dealt with the events of 1844. That he was unable to complete his work is unfortunate in that Tarrant had himself been caught up in the vicissitudes of the young colony and he suffered both from the ill-will of those whom he antagonized and from the self-inflicted wounds of his undoubtedly indiscriminate pen. His account of the infant colony and of its early struggles was based on his own observations as well as on documentation and he did attempt to create a perspective which would enable the reader to evaluate the events which he recounted. It was a work of history in spite of the personal spleen which punctuates his writing and his invaluable reportage is not totally obscured.

Tarrant probably intended the work in its completed state to be an apologia for himself and his troubled career, much of it reads as a vindication of his character and reputation. Even if completed, it would never have been a great work of scholarship and Hong Kong had to wait some years before another history, entitled *Europe in China* by Dr E. J. Eitel, emerged in 1895. Eitel had access to a good deal of source material (as did Sayer, of course) which no longer exists for the use of modern researchers (some of it was lost during the Japanese occupation of Hong Kong), but Eitel's inherent approach to the subject mars his extensive work in many ways. Eitel himself first came to Hong Kong with missionary intentions though his career in Hong Kong made him a Government Inspector of Schools. The moral prejudices evident in the book led a later writer, Sir Charles Collins (below, p. 9) to say that the book had the reputation of being the 'book of the bad governors', and the bias with which he interpreted events and the colours chosen by him for the broad sweeps of his brush are almost everywhere evident. But he was a painstaking author and there is much fact in his pages which is not now obtainable readily, if at all, elsewhere. Eitel certainly has his value, therefore, as a secondhand source. But he has to be read as a creature of his own time and taken for what he would undoubtedly have held himself out to be and no more.

In 1898, a few years after Eitel's work appeared, James Norton-Kyshe, then Registrar of the Supreme Court, produced his painstakingly all-embracing *History of the laws and courts of Hong Kong*. Norton-Kyshe wrote a number of books on legal subjects (including the highly esoteric

The law and customs relating to Gloves), which he assiduously drew to the attention of the Secretary of State for the Colonies in the vain hope that they would gain him preferment in the judicial side of the Colonial Service. London was not impressed and he left Hong Kong in 1904, a disappointed man, and on reading his *History* it is not difficult to see why. The man was a chronicler and nothing more. But Norton-Kyshe had, as did Eitel, the advantage of having access to many records now, alas, destroyed and his two-volume work, though nothing more than an unselective compilation of names and events in chronological order and in no way a work of history, is a most useful and fascinating collection of data, personalities and events with an attraction all its own and to which Sayer admits resorting.

Sayer was the next to make a serious attempt to give a real historical impress to the forces which shaped and guided the Colony, and to put in some order the principal happenings of moment by completing this present volume and when he wrote its successor volume, *Hong Kong, 1862–1919: the years of discretion.*

In 1952 there appeared a work entitled *Public administration in Hong Kong,* an account of the development of public administration in Hong Kong from the earliest days until the period just after the end of the Japanese occupation. The author, Sir Charles Collins, treated Eitel's *Europe in China* and Sayer's *Hong Kong: birth, adolescence and coming of age* as 'the standard works of reference for the earlier part of Hong Kong history' (he was, presumably, unaware of Sayer's later and then unpublished work) and commented that Sayer covered the same ground as Eitel 'though not so minutely, with greater judgment'. Nicely put!

To complete the picture, we have G. B. Endacott's three works: *A history of Hong Kong, Government and people in Hong Kong* and the posthumously published *Hong Kong eclipse,* edited by A. Birch, which is concerned with the events leading up to the fall of Hong Kong in 1941 and with the years of the Japanese occupation. Endacott's works have the great virtue of solidity and dependability though his style is turgid and his manner of dealing historically with his subject is not calculated to inspire his readers to an eager exploration through the pages of Hong Kong history. But Endacott's own purposes were probably achieved by his books and, even if they are uninspired, they are meticulous. They do give the modern reader a solid factual standpoint from which to assess the idiosyncrasies of earlier writers and to detect their fanciful or sometimes wilful deviations from the plain truth or historical fact. But history is little without the judicious intrusion of the historian's own psyche into his professionally objective assessments and judgments. It is well to bear this in mind when taking a modern view of Sayer and we should remember that our view of the events which he describes has been influenced by many works published later. Certainly, our view of the diplomatic events which he investigates must necessarily be affected by later works such as Gerald S. Graham's *The China Station* which covers roughly the same ground as Sayer's account of the early years of Hong Kong and the diplomatic role of its early Governors (though Graham does approach his subject from a naval and military standpoint).

Why, then, should it be felt worthwhile to republish Sayer's work at a time when attitudes have moved on, when more detailed scholarship is available to us in published form?

In republishing a work in the form in which it appeared some forty years ago, there should be the implicit assurance that it is as worthy of attention *now* as it was when it first appeared. The work may represent a stage in the intellectual development of a man whose life's works are themselves worthy of critical examination, or the work itself may represent an historical point of view which contributes both to our understanding of particular historical events and our perception now of the underlying reasons of others' attitudes in time now past to those events. In other words, the work itself may have become a piece of history.

Sayer describes succinctly his own view of the historian's task in his Preface to this volume. He said that 'the business of the historian is not simply to record a sequence of events . . . but to select and to draw inferences.' It should be emphasised that he said this by way of an apology for not quoting chapter and verse to support all the statements which the book contains. Occasionally, he admitted, he allowed himself the luxury of jumping what he called a 'yawning gap' in the factual record, sometimes having the satisfaction or suffering the mortification of finding 'an ample bridge close at hand'. He even admitted that he shut his eyes on occasion to the possibility of such bridges existing though, he continued, 'I suppose several of my guesses are capable of easy confirmation or refutation by reference to official documents.' That he did not do so is a damaging admission but at least his candour may disarm to a certain extent the critic who is able to reveal the fallibility of some of his guesses and, as will be seen from the Additional Notes to this reprint, his readable prose is not free from fallibility. It must be said, unfortunately, that, having access to the sources to which he refers in his Preface but not all of which he used, he should not have allowed himself that luxury of guesswork which, if indulged in by a historian, should at least take refuge behind the cloak of drawing legitimate inferences!

Considering Sayer and his work in this light, *Hong Kong: birth, adolescence and coming of age* in many ways cannot be seen as a part of a continuum of scholarship and writing. The work was published but one year before retirement ended his career of public service to Hong Kong and comes, therefore, more as a wave of farewell than as a casting off upon an intellectual odyssey. His second historical work about Hong Kong, covering the period 1862 to 1919, was all but finished when he left Hong Kong in 1938 and reached what he himself considered its final form the following year. The Second World War delayed its publication for some time and Sayer had some difficulty in finding a publisher for what he was content to leave as a work deliberately not brought up to date (it contains many references—as does the present work—to a Hong Kong familiar only to those who lived in Hong Kong during the term of Sayer's career in Hong Kong from 1910 until 1938). He left the manuscript substantially as it was and it remained unpublished at the time of his death in 1962. It was finally published by the Hong Kong University Press in 1975 and it represents Sayer's final statement on Hong Kong. It is unfortunate that he chose not to leave a record of his own time in Hong Kong for it was a period of immense change on the mainland of China, a period which did not leave Hong Kong untouched. Sayer undoubtedly played a significant part in the administration of Hong Kong during the troubled times of the nineteen-twenties and nineteen-thirties, but we cannot now know his views on the events which he witnessed since he wrote purely as an historian of past events.

He took a bland, if not a neutral, and certainly forthrightly simple view of the history of relations between China and Britain. Our perspectives are different, no doubt, today and we would now probably attach more significance in the long term to the Opium War and the Arrow War than the long-popular notion that both of those wars represented sordid gunboat diplomacy in the aid of a despicable trade. Those who take that view and that view only betray their own lack of familiarity with the broader sweeps of the history of China's diplomatic, cultural and political contact with the West and Hong Kong's role in it. Sayer's wider concern is perhaps evident in the space which he devotes to the long series of incidents and events leading up, over an extended period, to the Opium War. His work comes across, therefore, as a story both of the development of a new colonial settlement under peculiar circumstances and of trade and diplomatic relations. The most important period dealt with by him is probably that of the Arrow War and its diplomatic aftermath, the Treaty of Tientsin and the Convention of Peking.

But some features of the work as a whole do call for comment. First and perhaps foremost is his decision to build the work up chronologically in terms of 'birth, adolescence and coming of age'. This he accomplished, with the exception of the first three chapters, by treating his subject in chronological episodes tied, from Chapter IX onwards, to the periods of governorship of successive Governors of Hong Kong.

If Sayer's work were to be published for the first time today, Chapter I would be considered as directed at those unfamiliar with the geography of the region (and, in any event, it is concerned, as is the whole book to a large extent, with the *island* of Hong Kong as a whole). Chapter III is today not only unnecessary but contains a great number of inaccuracies. Sayer entitled it 'Introduction—Linguistic' and he sought to introduce his readers to the complexities of rendering Chinese expressions into the English language. This was, as he described it, 'an apology for the Chinese proper names and place-names liable to appear in the text'. It was, he said, 'a complicated subject and the reader who is unfamiliar with the Chinese language may find it bewildering.' But he also expressed the hope that the chapter would draw attention to 'the more general gulf, the immense difference in outlooks, ideals, modes of thought, habits of life, and beliefs between the two peoples who have settled side by side to make the history of the British Colony of Hong Kong' (p. 15). He drew attention, in this connection, to the role of the 'cadet' in bridging the gulf.

Whilst there are some interesting insights into the origin of otherwise obscure expressions (for example, the deriving of 'Ewo', the sobriquet of Jardine, Matheson & Co., from a Cantonese name, Ng I Wo, of How Qua, the old Hong merchant), the chapter fails to take into account or even mention the Wade-Giles system of romanization which is now doomed to extinction with the official and all-pervasive utilization of *Pinyin*, the comparatively new official romanization.

It should also be remembered that Sayer was describing a Hong Kong very much in its birth pangs: he indicated as much by his subtitle. He was seeking to describe the early struggles of an ill-equipped young colony facing an uncertain future, a colony which was left to work out its own internal problems at the same time as coping with the vicissitudes of uncertain relations with its vast neighbour. Sayer was speaking of a period of empirical government in which the few qualified to administer were forced to rely on a host of inferiors for whom civil service was a novel concept. The period he describes was one in which Hong Kong struggled for survival against a combination of political and economic uncertainty, and inefficiency and corruption within the government. It was a period of personalities who scarred public life with their animosities, yet it was a period which ended with the resolution of the problem of Hong Kong's relationship to China and the institution of a new system of more professionalized government in Hong Kong itself.

It was this period which Sayer chose to treat, a period which closed with the demise of the old and the tentative. Hong Kong was to 'come of age' in 1861 when Sir Hercules Robinson cleansed the Augean stables and, *inter alia,* instituted that new system of civil service recruitment of which Sayer himself was a part, the cadet system.

The date which he chose for the close of his narrative may have been a date of convenience but it was also a date of wider significance both internally in Hong Kong and externally in terms of China's relations with Britain and other nations. Hong Kong's diplomatic position was radically altered and it may be said that Sir Hercules Robinson, who had succeeded Sir John Bowring in 1859, had set in motion internal reforms which were to give Hong Kong a much better style of Government. A new era opened with his governorship and it was there that Sayer chose to close. His instinct, looking back, was right.

Sayer, as has been said, admitted his own fallibility. It is desirable to put the factual record straight and this is done in the Additional Notes. Doubtless there are other points which have not been picked up but the purpose of the notes is to clarify Sayer's references to a Hong Kong of 1937 with which the reader of today might not be familiar.

D. M. EMRYS EVANS

University of Hong Kong

A SHORT BIOGRAPHY OF G. R. SAYER

Born on 11 February 1887 in England, he was educated at Highgate School, London and Queen's College, Oxford University where he obtained an honours degree in Classics and philosophy and a 'Soccer' Blue. He was appointed to the Eastern Cadet Service in 1910 and posted to Hong Kong. He married in 1919 and had three sons and two daughters. He held various posts in the Hong Kong Government for 28 years and retired in 1938.

During the First World War he was released for military service in France as an officer in the Rifle Brigade and was severely wounded. He was then transferred to the Chinese Labour Battalion where officers with a knowledge of Chinese were urgently needed.

In Hong Kong, besides his official duties, he was a well-known cricketer and the Captain of the Hong Kong inter-port cricket team. He was also the Vice President of the Hong Kong Branch of the English Association, President of the Hong Kong Civil Service Cricket Club and an official Justice of the Peace.

During the Second World War after his retirement, he was in the Ministry of Food and in the Chinese section of the Censor's Office. He published a translation of Horace's *Odes* in 1922 and wrote the present work and its sequel on the history of Hong Kong. After retirement he continued his Chinese studies and published translations into English of Lan Pin-nan's *Ching-te-chen T'ao-lu* in 1951 and Ch'en Liu's *T'ao Ya, or pottery refinements* in 1959, both on Chinese ceramics.

He was also a connoisseur and his collection of paintings and drawings of Hong Kong, the Sayer Collection, is now in the Hong Kong Museum of Art.

He died in hospital after an operation in London on 27 January 1962, at the age of 74.

His career in the Hong Kong Government

1910, Oct. 24: Appointed Cadet Officer in Colonial Secretary's Department and Legislature with an annual salary of £225 and arrived in Hong Kong on 1911, Jan. 1.

1911, Jan. 9 : Sent to Canton to study Cantonese.

1912, Nov. 9 : Passed his final Cadet's examinations and became a Passed Cadet.

Nov. 18—1913, Feb. 16 and 1913, Mar. 21—Nov. 21: Acting Assistant District Officer for the Southern District of the New Territories.

1913, July 29: Passed Law Examination.
     Nov. 22: Acting Assistant Superintendent of Police.

1914, Oct. 12: Attached to the Official Receiver's Office and appointed Acting Deputy Official Receiver of Debtors' Estates on 1915, Jan. 29.

1915, Jan. 20—Dec. 15: Acting Private Secretary to the Governor in addition to his other duties.
     Apr. 1 : Attached to Attorney General's and Crown Solicitor's Office.
     July 13: Passed Final Examination in Hakka colloquial.
     Sep. 8 : Acting Chief Assistant to the Secretary for Chinese Affairs and appointed Deputy Registrar of Marriages.

1916, Feb. 18: Seconded for military service in France.

1919, May 8 — 1920, Jan. 22: On leave.

1920, Jan. 23: Acting Deputy Registrar and Appraiser of Supreme Court and appointed Commissioner to administer oaths and take declarations, affirmations and attestations of honour.
     Mar. 17: Acting Head of Sanitary Department.

1921, May 9 : Passed Final Examination in Mandarin colloquial.

1924, Mar. 8 — 1925, Jan. 7: On leave.

1925, Jan. 8 : Attached to the Treasury and appointed on 1925, Apr. 24 Assistant Colonial Treasurer and Assistant Assessor of Rates (the title was changed to Assistant Colonial Treasurer and Assistant Commissioner of Estate Duties after 1926).
     Oct. 31—Nov. 11: Acting Private Secretary to the Governor in addition to his other duties.

1927, Apr. 25: Appointed member of the Board of Examiners.
     May 28: Acting Superintendent of Imports and Exports.

1928, Apr. 28: Acting Postmaster General.
     Oct. 12: Head of Sanitary Department and Registrar of Births and Deaths.

1929, Aug. 2 — 1930, Jan. 2: On leave.

1933, Jan. 14—Dec. 14: On leave.

1934, Mar. 24: Acting Director of Education.
     Oct. 24: Appointed Cadet Officer, Class I; Director of Education.

1937, Mar. 6 — Dec. 22: On leave.

1938, Sep. 16 — Nov. 27: On leave.
    Nov. 28: Retired. His annual salary just before his retirement was £1,700.

Sources: *The Hong Kong Blue Book,* 1910–1938.
The Hong Kong Civil Service List, 1910–1938.
The Hong Kong Dollar Directory, 1936.
The Hong Kong Government Gazette, 1910–1938.
Sayer, G. R. *Hong Kong 1862–1919.* Introduction.
South China Morning Post, 'Obituary', 2 February 1962.
The Times, 'Obituary', 8 February 1962.

WORKS REFERRED TO IN THE TEXT

Sayer provided no bibliography and the following list does not include those works referred to by Sayer under the heading 'Abbreviations used in the references' nor does it include the contemporary newspapers to which he makes reference in the text and to which reference is made in his Preface. The correct titles are not always given in the text.

ABEL, CLARKE. *Narrative of a journey in the interior of China.* London, Longman, Hurst, Rees, Orme and Brown, 1818.

AUBER, PETER. *China.* London, Parbury, Allen & Co., 1834.

BELCHER, SIR E. *Narrative of a voyage around the world.* London, Henry Colburn 1843.

BERNARD, W. D. *Narrative of the voyages and services of the Nemesis.* London, Henry Colburn, 1844.

BINGHAM, J. ELLIOT. *Narrative of the expedition to China.* London, Henry Colburn, 1842.

BORGET, A. *La Chine et les Chinois.* Paris, Goupil et Vibert, 1842.

CUMMING, C. F. G. *Wanderings in China.* 1888.

CUNYNGHAME, A. A. T. *An Aide-de-Camp's recollections of service in China.* London, Saunders and Otley, 1844.

EITEL, E. J. *Europe in China.* Hong Kong, Kelly and Walsh Ltd., 1895.

ELLIS, SIR H. *Journal of the proceedings of the late embassy to China.* London, Murray, 1817.

HUNTER, W. C. *The 'Fan Kwae' at Canton before Treaty days, 1825–1844.* London, Kegan Paul, 1882.

JOCELYN, LORD. *Six months with the Chinese expedition.* London, John Murray, 1841.

LOCH, G. G. *Closing events of the campaign in China.* London, John Murray, 1843.

M'LEOD, J. *Narrative of a voyage in His Majesty's late Ship Alceste.* London, Murray, 1817.

MAXWELL, M. *A narrative of occurrences and remarks made on board His Majesty's late ship Alceste* (not published but a lithograph copy in the Admiralty Library).

MARTIN, R. MONTGOMERY. *China, political, commercial and social.* London, Madden, 1847.

MORSE, H. B. *The chronicles of the East India Company trading to China, 1635–1834.* Oxford, Oxford University Press, 1926.

———. *The international relations of the Chinese empire.* Shanghai, Kelly & Walsh, 1910–1918.

NORTON-KYSHE, J. W. *History of the laws and courts of Hong Kong.* Hong Kong, Noronha & Co., and London, T. Fisher Unwin, 1898.

OLIPHANT, L. *Narrative of the Earl of Elgin's mission.* Edinburgh, Blackwood, 1859.

OUCHTERLONY, J. *The Chinese war.* London, Saunders & Otley, 1844.

PARKER, E. H. (trans.). *Chinese account of the Opium War.* Shanghai, 1888.

SELECTED WORKS WHICH HAVE APPEARED SINCE THE FIRST PUBLICATION OF THIS BOOK

This selective bibliography is intended as a short guide to works written since Sayer's work first appeared and which might serve to assist the modern reader in putting *Hong Kong: birth, adolescence and coming of age* into perspective. It is not intended to be and is not a comprehensive bibliography. The *Journal of the Hong Kong Branch of the Royal Asiatic Society* (abbreviated here as *JHKBRAS*) and the Society's occasional collections of symposia papers may be taken as a wide source of miscellaneous information on the period covered by Sayer's book. Many of the works cited below themselves contain extensive bibliographies.

BALFOUR, S. F. 'Hong Kong before the British'. *T'ien Hsia Monthly* 11 (1940) 330–352, 12 (1941) 440–464.

BEECHING, JACK. *The Chinese Opium Wars*. London, Hutchinson, 1973.

BLAKE, CLAGETTE. *Charles Elliot, R.N.* London, Cleaver-Hume Press, 1959.

COATES, AUSTIN. *Prelude to Hong Kong*. London, Routledge, Kegan Paul, 1966.

COLLINS, SIR CHARLES. *Public administration in Hong Kong*. London and New York, Royal Institute of International Affairs, 1952.

CHANG HSIN-PING. *Commissioner Lin and the Opium War*. Cambridge, Mass., Harvard University Press, 1964.

COLLIS, MAURICE. *Foreign mud*. London, Faber, 1946 and 1969.

ENDACOTT, G. B. *An eastern entrepôt: a collection of documents illustrating the history of Hong Kong*. London, Her Majesty's Stationery Office, 1964.

———. *Government and people in Hong Kong*. Hong Kong, Hong Kong University Press, 1964.

———. *A history of Hong Kong*. London and Hong Kong, Oxford University Press, 1958, 2nd ed. 1973.

——— and DOROTHY E. SHE. *The diocese of Victoria, Hong Kong*. Hong Kong, Kelly & Walsh, 1949.

FAY, PETER W. *The Opium War, 1840–1842*. Chapel Hill, University of North Carolina Press, 1975.

FAIRBANK, JOHN K. *Trade and diplomacy on the China coast*. Cambridge, Mass., Harvard University Press, 1953 and Stanford, Stanford University Press, 1969.

GILES, H. A. *A Chinese biographical dictionary*. London, Bernard Quaritch and Shanghai, Kelly & Walsh, 1898.

GRAHAM, GERALD S. *The China station: war and diplomacy, 1830–1860*. Oxford, Clarendon Press, 1978.

HAO YEN-P'ING. *The comprador in nineteenth century China: a bridge between East and West.* Cambridge, Mass., Harvard University Press, 1970.

HAYES, J. W. 'The Hong Kong region'. *JHKBRAS* 14 (1974) 108–135.

History of Modern China Series, Compilation Group for. *The Opium War.* Peking, Foreign Languages Press, 1976.

HOLT, EDGAR. *The Opium Wars in China.* London, Putnam, 1964.

HUDSON, BRIAN J. 'Land reclamation in Hong Kong'. Ph.D. thesis, University of Hong Kong, 1970.

HUMMEL, ARTHUR W. (ed.). *Eminent Chinese of the Ch'ing period.* Washington, D.C., United States Government Printing Office, 1943.

HURD, DOUGLAS. *The Arrow War: an Anglo-Chinese confusion, 1856–1860.* London, Collins, 1967.

INGLIS, BRIAN. *The Opium War.* London, Hodder and Stoughton, 1976.

LIANG CHIA-PIN. *The thirteen Hongs of Canton.* 2nd ed. Taipei, Tunghai University, 1960. (in Chinese).

LO HSIANG-LIN. *Hong Kong and its external communications before 1842.* Hong Kong, Institute of Chinese Studies, 1963.

——. *The role of Hong Kong in the cultural interchange between East and West.* Tokyo, Centre for East Asian Cultural Studies, 1963.

SMITH, CARL T. 'The emergence of a Chinese élite in Hong Kong'. *JHKBRAS* 11 (1971) 74–115.

TARRANT, WILLIAM. 'Hong Kong, 1839–1844'. *Friend of China,* 1862.

WAKEMAN, FREDERICK, JR. *Strangers at the gate: social disorder in South China, 1839–1861.* Berkeley and Los Angeles, University of California Press, 1966.

WALEY, ARTHUR. *The Opium War through Chinese eyes.* London, George Allen & Unwin, 1958.

Although it was published thirteen years before the publication of *Hong Kong: birth, adolescence and coming of age,* reference should also be made to James Orange's *The Chater Collection: pictures relating to China, Hong Kong and Macao, 1655–1860* (London, Butterworths, 1924) since it is a valuable source of illustrative material related to the period covered by Sayer's work. Rev. G. N. Wright's *China illustrated in a series of views* (London and Paris, Fisher & Co., 1843) provides much illustrative material though many of the engravings were derived from earlier works. The text is of little value but the work was republished during the Arrow War in London by London Publishing and Printing Co. in 1858, and it is known now principally for the so-called 'Allom engravings' after the artist Thomas Allom, from whose drawings most of the engraved plates were prepared. Sayer makes specific reference to one 'Allom' (p. 96) as evidence for the existence of a British-held fort on the Kowloon shore named 'Fort Victoria'.

HONG KONG
BIRTH, ADOLESCENCE, AND
COMING OF AGE

HONG KONG

BIRTH, ADOLESCENCE, AND COMING OF AGE

By

GEOFFREY ROBLEY SAYER, B.A.
Cadet, Hong Kong Civil Service

OXFORD UNIVERSITY PRESS
LONDON   NEW YORK   TORONTO
1937

OXFORD UNIVERSITY PRESS
AMEN HOUSE, E.C. 4
LONDON EDINBURGH GLASGOW NEW YORK
TORONTO MELBOURNE CAPETOWN BOMBAY
CALCUTTA MADRAS
HUMPHREY MILFORD
PUBLISHER TO THE UNIVERSITY

PRINTED IN GREAT BRITAIN

PREFACE

IN the early part of this narrative—that is to say from the arrival of Napier in China until the cession of Hong Kong and the first few months of its settlement—when I am laying foundations, I have tried to quote chapter and verse, either in the text or by means of a footnote, for every statement of any consequence that I make. Subsequently, as the structure rises above ground and events become more humdrum (and sources multiply), I cannot always claim to be so precise, frequently contenting myself with quoting my authority only for the more striking.

The reader is thus left to speculate now and then as to whether for the intermediate material I have equally authentic sources in reserve or am drawing on my imagination. I make no claim to verbal inspiration for every statement. The business of the historian is not simply to record a sequence of events, much less a mere sequence of statements in the current press, but to select and to draw inferences. But, in point of fact, I fancy the reader would be able, without much trouble, to trace the justification for nearly every assertion made to some contemporary source, whether it be the weekly press—I am particularly indebted to the *Canton Press*, and in a lesser degree to the *Friend of China*—or the monthly review (I refer, of course, to the *Chinese Repository*); or the official publications, such as the early Hong Kong Government Gazettes or the invaluable Parliamentary White Papers; or unofficial chronicles and memoirs of the period; and, last but not least, to contemporary prints and pictures.

Occasionally I indulge in the luxury of jumping to a conclusion; and occasionally, having jumped a yawning gap, I have had the satisfaction, or the mortification, of finding an ample bridge quite close at hand.

Sometimes I deliberately shut my eyes to the possibility of such bridges existing, especially in connexion with the crucial period 1840–1, though I suppose several of my guesses are capable of easy confirmation or refutation by reference to official documents.

In thus claiming to base myself on contemporary records I may seem to do less than justice to writers like Dr. Eitel, Mr. Norton Kyshe, and Mr. H. B. Morse who have traversed much of the ground before and left us with the benefit of their selections; and I hasten to acknowledge my obligations to these authors respectively of *Europe in China*, *The History of the Laws and Courts*, and *International Relations*. I hasten at the same time to tender my apologies to the last-named for the company in which he finds himself; for, while Dr. Eitel proves a somewhat romantic guide to the early and crucial period of the Colony's foundation and Mr. Norton Kyshe, seeking to uphold the dignity of the law, contrives to defeat his object in two pompous volumes, Mr. Morse approaches his task with a critical eye, 'proving all things'.

G. R. SAYER

154 THE PEAK.

May 1937

CONTENTS

I. INTRODUCTION—GEOGRAPHICAL . . .	1
II. „ —HISTORICAL . . .	5
III. „ —LINGUISTIC . . .	15
IV. EARLY CONTACTS	21
V. NAPIER	34
VI. ELLIOT, 1836 TO 1839	49
VII. ELLIOT, 1840 AND 1841	67
VIII. THE BIRTH OF VICTORIA, 1841 . .	90
IX. POTTINGER, 1841–1844	116
X. JOHN F. DAVIS, 1844–1848 . . .	142
XI. SAMUEL G. BONHAM, 1848–1854 . .	162
XII. DR. JOHN BOWRING, 1854–1859 . .	173
XIII. HERCULES ROBINSON, 1859–1862 . .	186

APPENDIXES

I. Elliot's Original Proclamation of 2nd February 1841 .	201
II. First Gazetteer and Census, May 15th, 1841 . .	203
III. Original Marine-lot Purchasers, June 14th, 1841 .	204
IV. Extract from the *Canton Press*, February 1842 . .	206

CONTENTS

V. The First Government House	211
VI. Article III of the Treaty of Nanking	215
VII. Pottinger's Proclamation	216
VIII. Hong Kong Names: The Derivation of Street-names and Place-names in early Hong Kong	217
IX. A Short Glossary of Anglo-Oriental Terms	218
X. Population 1841–62	220
XI. Ships entering and clearing 1841–62	221
MAP OF THE CANTON DELTA	223
INDEX	225

LIST OF ILLUSTRATIONS

The Waterfall at Hong Cong (*sic*): original water-colour drawing made from the deck of H.M.S. *Alceste*, July 1816 . . . . . *Frontispiece*

Forcing the Passage of the Bocca Tigris on 7th and 9th September 1834 by H.M.S. *Imogene* and *Andromache*: lithograph in colour from a drawing by W. Skinner, R.N. . . . . . *facing p.* 41

Pedder's Hill and Harbour Master's House, Hong Kong: woodcut. *Illustrated London News*, 1857 ,, 113

View on the Queen's Road looking East from the Canton Bazaar, August 1846: lithograph M. Bruce—A. Maclure . . . . . . ,, 153

View of Spring Gardens, August 1846: lithograph M. Bruce—A. Maclure . . . . ,, 174

Victoria Peak, Hong Kong: woodcut. *Illustrated London News*, 1857 . . . . . ,, 195

ABBREVIATIONS USED IN THE REFERENCES

D.N.B.	*Dictionary of National Biography.*
P.R.O.	*Public Record Office.*
Corr. rel. China.	*Correspondence relating to China* (Parliamentary White Paper).
Comm. Rel.	*Report of the Select Committee on Commercial Relations with China 1847* (Parliamentary White Paper).
Addl. Corr. rel. China.	*Additional Correspondence relating to China* (Parliamentary White Paper).
Insults.	Parliamentary White Paper, 1857.
Naval forces.	Parliamentary White Paper.
Corr. rel. Operations, 1857.	*Correspondence relating to Operations, 1857* (Parliamentary White Paper).
Chin. Rep.	*The Chinese Repository.*

CHAPTER I
INTRODUCTION—GEOGRAPHICAL

THE island of Hong Kong—I speak for the benefit of those who have not been there and possibly do not know that it is an island—lies within the tropics, a degree or more south of the tropic of Cancer and a mile or so east of the one hundred and fourteenth meridian east of Greenwich.

This places it just off the southern coast of China from which it is separated by a stretch of water which, at its narrowest point, barely exceeds a quarter of a mile.

For its shape I refer the reader to the map of the Canton estuary on p. 223, for there he can see at a glance what words fail me to describe. He can also test for himself my calculation that the superficial area of the island is a bare thirty square miles, and my conviction that if a man set out to walk straight inland from any point on the coast he would strike the sea again before he had gone ten miles.

Such is Hong Kong island in the flat; a mere point, having position but no magnitude. But there are, I imagine, few places in the world less capable of reduction to terms of two dimensions. The beauty of Hong Kong lies in her high hills and the virtue in the depth of her sheltered waters.

The island, in fact, rises steeply from every part of its irregular coast-line to an equally irregular sky-line; the ridge averaging a thousand feet in height and culminating in a peak eighteen hundred feet sheer above the sea.

A few exiguous plains at sea-level offer scope for cultivation, but the rest is hill-side—barren, treeless slopes strewn with loose boulders and covered with a mat of coarse grass, or sheer cliffs of naked rock.

On the mainland opposite a parallel range of much the same height rises no less steeply, though at a distance of a mile or so from the shore, and hangs poised like a wave petrified in the very act of breaking.

Behind this range other ranges fold themselves, and a little to the westward two noble peaks, one broad-based on the mainland, the other rising abruptly from the sea, exceed three thousand feet in height. Forty miles off on the western horizon lies the Portuguese settlement of Macao. On the north-west the Pearl river debouches, leading, via the Bogue, to Canton, ninety miles away. In the middle of its broad estuary a gaunt, lone peak rises, Lin Tin, isle of ill fame. To the south and the south-west a score of small islands—the Ladrones—lovely in the variety of their shapes, lead out to the open sea.

n. 1

By what violent convulsion of nature these islands have emerged from the water or become submerged to their present level; by what sudden stroke of lightning or by what gradual attrition of sun and rain these rocks and boulders have attained their present shape I know not and do not pause to ask. For me they constitute merely the background of a human drama and I take them as I find them.

n. 2

And thus far I conceive those of my readers who have not seen Hong Kong have the advantage over those who have. For the former regard her rightly as merely one of a number of picturesque but unimportant islands off the coast of China; the resort of fishermen and stone-cutters; the hiding-place of smugglers and pirates; the home perhaps of a handful of tillers of the soil.

But the latter must first banish from their minds the close-packed roofs rising tier upon tier on her northern slopes; the noise and bustle of the water-front; ponderous merchant ships lying at the buoys; rakish junks cutting across the fairway; assiduous sampans; river-steamers on their marks awaiting the daily race to Canton; and ferry-boats plying incessantly to and fro between island and mainland.

It is not an easy task; and I offer, as an aid to reconstruction, the case of any one of these neighbouring islands, and in particular the island of Lantao. Lantao, though somewhat bigger and designed on even more majestic lines than Hong Kong, bears much the same relationship to the mainland; and (I assert it as axiomatic) differs from Hong Kong in no essential respect—except for the introduction of a foreign body therein. Consequently if the reader wishes to recall what Hong Kong was like at the time my chronicle opens he need look no farther than Lantao; and conversely if he wishes to imagine what Lantao would look like to-day if (as was once suggested) Hong Kong's role had fallen to her, he has only to look back at Hong Kong.

The contrast can be observed in comfort from the deck of a river steamer plying to Canton, and as he exchanges the multitudinous sights and sounds of a great harbour for the quiet beauty of an unravished shore he will be able to reflect, according to his mood, on the achievements of modern civilization.

But if, in this respect, the resident is at a momentary disadvantage he is compensated in another. The effect of climate on human conduct has not yet been reduced to an exact science. But it cannot be entirely disregarded in considering the history of Hong Kong or, for that matter, of any place in the tropics administered by Europeans. I am not thinking of typhoons or similar extravagant outbursts of the weather, but of the ordinary routine of the year; the regular range of temperature and rainfall; the change of the monsoon; the invariable sequence of the seasons.

As regards these things one may point out that the thermometer in Hong Kong rarely exceeds ninety degrees and rarely falls below forty-five; that the average rainfall in the year is about one hundred inches (and thirty in July), and so forth; but one cannot convey the real atmosphere of the place. The capabilities of the 'wet-bulb' in June; the first breath of the north-west wind in October—these must be experienced *in corpore vili*; and I do not doubt that those who have lived in Hong Kong will extract from the narrative a flavour which the stranger will miss.

CHAPTER II

INTRODUCTION—HISTORICAL

IT is clear that two alternative historical prefaces might be written to an account of the British occupation of Hong Kong, the story of British intercourse with China before the occupation and the story of the island before the occupation.

With the latter I have little concern, except for previous English contacts to which I devote a separate chapter. It is sufficient to be able to point out that when this island passed into English hands it was a barren and sparsely inhabited spot; and had been so for a century and more.

But in point of fact the matter can be very briefly dismissed. No historical monument has been discovered on the island: nor is there any tradition among local Chinese of stirring events having been enacted here or any suggestion that the island had in the past attained a state of greater prosperity and importance than that in which Englishmen found it. The sole reference, so far as I am aware, to the island in Chinese historical records is the account in the Tsing dynasty annals of the cession to Great Britain and its immediate preliminaries.

n. 1

On the mainland—I refer to that part which now forms part of the Colony—there are two historical monuments, and two only, unless the Kowloon City itself is so regarded—the Sung Wong T'oi, 'platform of the Sung Emperor', near Kowloon City; and the Wong Kwu Fan, 'Grave of the Emperor's aunt', a mile or so along the road beyond Tsun Wan in the New Territory.

n. 2

The former, consisting of a conspicuous granite boulder

incised with Chinese characters (Sung Wong T'oi),[1] is well known, and has been preserved for some thirty years as an ancient monument by the Government of Hong Kong. It is recorded in the standard Chinese histories that the fleet of the last emperor of the Sung dynasty was wrecked off Ngai Mun, which is identified with Wang Mun across the Canton river estuary. And the incised rock is traditionally said to mark the temporary lodging-place of the emperor before he embarked to meet his fate.

The Wong Kwu Fan is less well known, and perhaps makes a greater demand upon our credulity. It consists of a stretch of hill-side sloping to the sea, having for boundary stones two granite pillars set some fifty yards apart. Here lies, according to tradition, not only the aunt of an emperor of the Sung dynasty (the same, one surmises, who left his mark near Kowloon City); but the spouse of a member of the Tang family, seignors of the village of Kam Tin, lying ten miles or so away across the hills.

n. 3

Only one other claim deserves mention—namely that of Dr. Eitel, that on the eve of the collapse of the Ming dynasty, four hundred years later, the remnants of the Ming forces took refuge 'in the forests of Hong Kong'.

n. 4

I must confess that I find nothing to support this beyond the briefest reference in the Annals of the Tsing dynasty to encounters with the Ming troops at San On, the district of which Hong Kong forms an outlying member, and Kong Mun across the delta.

I turn now to Anglo-Chinese intercourse before the occupation; and I propose to separate the foreground, which will

[1] It is curious that Eitel gives this as T'ong = a hall.

INTRODUCTION—HISTORICAL

be treated in another chapter, from the background which will be sketched in here.

My actual starting-point is (as my title indicates) the year 1841, but I have paced back through the years until I have found a foothold sufficiently firm to ensure that I am well in my stride for the years that count. Such a place I find in the year 1834—the year of Lord Napier's arrival in Canton; and the seven years between 1834 and 1841 I call my foreground.

The background stretches back to the beginnings of foreign intercourse with China. The motive which, in the sixteenth century, led the ships of the maritime states of Europe—Portugal, Spain, Holland, and England—into Far Eastern waters was the hope of establishing a direct trade by sea with the Moluccas or Spice Islands; spices, which then occupied a much more important place in European economy than they do now, being hitherto introduced to Europe precariously by overland routes. n. 5

n. 6

It was, in fact, in the course of their search for condiments that the merchants discovered in China a far more important commodity, 'that elegant and popular beverage Tea'.

It is, however, a legitimate surmise that, whatever the attractions of cinnamon, ginger, nutmeg, mace, and pepper, the spice of romance made an appeal no less piquant to the merchant adventurers of Elizabethan times. It was surely this that in 1596 sent Richard Allot and Thomas Broomfield to China armed with the Queen's commendation addressed to the emperor in these stately terms:

'Elizabeth by the grace of God Queen of England, France, and Ireland, the most mightie Defendresse of the true and Christian faith, againste all that falsely profess the name of Christ.

'To the most high and sovereign prince, the most puissant Governor of the great kingdom of China, the chiefest Emperor in those parts of Asia, and the islands adjoining and the great monarch of the oriental regions of the world; wisheth health, and many joyful and happy years, with all plenty and abundance of things most acceptable.

'Whereas our honest and faithful subjects which bring these letters unto your highness, Richard Allot and Thomas Broomfield, merchants of the city of London, have made most earnest suite unto us, that we would commend their desires and endeavours of sayling to the regions of your empire for traffiques sake; whereas the fame of your kingdom so strongly and prudently governed being published over the face of the whole earth, hath invited these, our subjects, not only to visit your highnesses dominions, but also to present themselves to be ruled and governed by the laws of your kingdom during their abode there, as it becometh merchants, who for exchanges of merchandize are desirous to travel to distant and unknown regions, having this regard only, that they may present their wares and musters of diverse kind of merchandize, wherewith the regions of our dominions do abound, unto the view of your highness and of your subjects, that they may endeavour to know whether there be any other merchandize with us fit for your use, which they may exchange for other commodities, whereof in parts of your empire there is great plenty, both natural and artificial: We yielding to the most reasonable regards of these honest men, because we suppose that by this intercourse and traffique, no loss, but rather most exceeding benefits, will redound to the princes and subjects of both kingdoms, and thus help and enrich one another. And we do crave of your most Sovereign Majesty, that these our subjects, when they arrive at any of your ports or cities, they may have full and free liberty of egress and regress, and of dealing with your subjects, and may by your clemency, enjoy all freedoms and privileges as are granted to the subjects of other princes; and we on the other side, will not only perform all the offices of a well and willing prince unto your highness, but also for the greater increase of mutual love and commerce between us and our subjects, by these present letters of ours, do most willingly grant unto all and every of your subjects, full and entire liberty into any of the parts of our dominions to resort there, to abide and traffique, and then return as it seemeth best to them.

'All and every of which premises we have caused to be confirmed, by annexing herewith our royal seal. God most Merciful and Almighty, the Creator of heaven and earth, continually protect your Kingly Majesty.

'Given at our palace at Greenwich the 11th of July, 1596 and 28th of our reign.' n. 7

The ship was lost without trace before accomplishing her voyage; and it is idle to speculate on the effect which this document would have produced upon the Emperor had it survived the perils of the sea, and, be it added, the difficulties of translation. But nothing can rob the Queen of the credit for an expansive gesture of amity and goodwill.

By the beginning of the seventeenth century, following the custom of the time, a monopoly of the East Indian trade had been created in favour of 'The Governor and merchants of London trading in the East Indies'.

Intent upon spices they established their first trading-station at Bantam in Java. But they soon began to explore the possibilities of extending their sphere of action to Japan and China.

The potentialities of China as a market were especially intriguing. The following is an extract from a letter written by one of the Company's captains to the Company in 1622:

'Concerning the trade of China three things are especially made known unto the world. The one is, the abundant trade it affordeth. The second is that they admit no strangers into their country. The third is that trade is as life unto the vulgar which, in remote parts, they will seek and accomodate with hazard of all they have.... It requireth no more care than to plant in some convenient place whither they may come, and then to give them knowledge that you are planted. This condemneth the Dutch their long, continued roamings upon the coast....'

And the following comes from another letter written five years later in reply to a questionnaire:

(*Question*) 'Whether merchants strangers may not be permitted to bring in commodities... coming peaceably like friends?' (*Answer*) 'In no part of the main is either trade or stranger admitted: yet, in some places, as in islands bordering on the main, is trade allowed.'

The story of the East India Company during the next half-century is one of severe and ruthless struggle with their great rivals the Dutch, both in the Malayan Archipelago and also in the China Seas.

The Portuguese settlement of Macao, which had been founded in 1557 via Malacca, and which was the only place in China where European merchants had established a *pied-à-terre*, suggested one possible method of access. And it seems probable that it was its proximity to Macao that tended to concentrate foreign attention on Canton.

In point of fact it was left to a rival company, the Courteen Association, of which little else is known, to test this route for the first time; Captain Weddell entering the port of Macao in 1637 and thence, after an exchange of shots at the Bogue forts, forcing his way to Canton.

In 1664 and again in 1674 the East India Company made abortive attempts upon Macao; and actually it was at Amoy that they first gained a footing.

From Amoy they were, in due course, evicted; but their tenure there may have directly led to the modification of the discouraging attitude of Canton. In any case the Company secured a house in Macao in 1681 and, a year or so later, a precarious footing in Canton itself.

In 1689 the East Indiaman *Defence* entered Whampoa, the port of Canton; the first Company's ship to do so. By 1715 a regular seasonal trade had been established; and by 1770 the 'supercargoes', hitherto the sea-going staff in charge of the merchandise, had become shore-staff and resided during the season in 'factories' in Canton; and during the summer in the Company's premises in Macao. Meanwhile the Dutch and the French had come in on the back of the English Company; and by 1784 a number of American merchants, trading on private account but responsible for good behaviour to a merchant consul, gained admission. Private Englishmen and Scotsmen also began to dribble in about the beginning of the nineteenth century and to contrast their lot with the American free-traders. They were precluded, by the Company's monopoly, from direct trade with England; but carried on the 'Country' trade, mainly to India, under the Company's licence. In matters of conduct they were subject to the rules laid down by the Company's Select Committee which, in turn, was subject to the orders of the Cantonese authorities as conveyed to them by the approved merchant body known as the Co-Hong.

These standing orders were severe—extremely so to our present-day notions. Foreign women were not permitted in the factories; native servants were not permitted; access to the city was not permitted; exercise was limited to a weekly walk with an interpreter in the Fa Tei gardens across the river; and the journey to and from Macao could be undertaken by licence only. The factories themselves were the property of the Chinese merchants rented out to the foreigners; and though it is true that the accommodation was generally spacious and the fare luxurious, they have been justly called 'gilded cages'.

In 1800 the trade in opium from India, which before then had been carried on in a comparatively small way, was prohibited by Imperial edict and the Company thenceforward declined to carry opium in its ships. This, however, did not stop the trade but merely drove it into the hands of the private traders and the 'Country' ships. For the first twenty years after this edict the trade continued more or less openly at Whampoa; but in 1820, the volume of business having increased by leaps and bounds, a further edict appeared requiring the Hong merchants to certify that the ships coming to Whampoa brought no opium; and it was deemed expedient that all ships carrying opium should discharge at Lin Tin in the 'outer seas' instead of proceeding to Whampoa. The next stage was the establishment of floating hulks at Lin Tin, which thus from being a mere anchorage became a depot from which vessels proceeding to the east coast replenished their supplies. And finally (when all were receiving their ration before Canton itself) came the introduction of 'fast-boats', both foreign and native, which ran the gauntlet of the river and even introduced the drug into the factories themselves.

Among much that is confused and controversial I venture to think that one point at least plainly emerges in regard to this traffic—its great attractiveness. Legitimate trade was loaded with arbitrary and irregular charges and hedged about with galling restrictions. Respectable merchants were subjected to severe restraints. But opium, being prohibited, could not be taxed; nor could it be paid for (the opium-vessels being forbidden the port) except by hard cash in advance, or at least on delivery. Moreover being eagerly demanded it commanded high prices. It presented, therefore, a tempting way of escape out of the gilded cage.

The Company was, of course, concerned solely with the 'petty affairs of commerce' and the good behaviour of the merchants. Two attempts had been made to establish official relations with China, by Lord Macartney in 1793 and by Lord Amherst in 1816; but without result, except in so far as the refusal literally to 'kowtow' to the Emperor had left any impression on the Court. The position, therefore, of His Majesty's ships, which appeared out of the blue from time to time, was left in the air. And perhaps the only rule which can be regarded as established by the date of Lord Napier's arrival was that war-vessels must remain outside the Bogue—a rule which Commodore Anson in 1741 and Captain Maxwell in 1816 had elected to break.

One last point remains. It will be obvious that, under such conditions of intercourse, occasions of friction, misunderstanding, altercation, and violence were not few. And it is only to be expected that, in the course of one hundred and fifty years, instances of homicide occur; and that among these instances there are some in which a European is charged with the death of a fellow European and some in which he is charged with the death of a Chinese.

The list, a short but poignant one, is out of place here. But it is essential that the situation created by these cases, as it stood on Lord Napier's arrival, should be understood. And I think it can be summarized only by saying that the list provided a precedent for almost any line of action between quietly slipping away with or without connivance and surrendering the accused to the Chinese authorities for strangulation.

And this is not surprising when it is realized that the Englishman's notions of the 'rule of law' or 'the independence of the judiciary from the executive' were wholly foreign to China. These matters were, in fact, governed by no law; and the outcome of particular cases depended very largely on the resolution of individual men.

In 1831 the Select Committee informed the Viceroy of Canton that the Company's monopoly would expire at the end of three years, and were instructed to apply to their Government for a chief manager to undertake the functions hitherto shouldered by themselves. In April 1834 the time ran out. A month before, the first free ship, *Sarah*, had been dispatched by William Jardine from Whampoa with tea for London.

CHAPTER III

INTRODUCTION—LINGUISTIC

ONE more preface has still to be written, an apology for the Chinese proper names and place-names liable to appear in the text. It is a complicated subject and the reader who is unfamiliar with the Chinese language may find it bewildering; but if he persists and derives from this chapter some sense of the great gulf which separates China from Europe linguistically, it will not have been written in vain. For it will serve to draw attention first to the manner in which this particular gulf has been bridged, in so far as it has been bridged, by 'linguist', 'comprador', missionary, interpreter, and 'cadet'; and secondly to the more general gulf, the immense difference in outlook, ideals, modes of thought, habits of life, and beliefs between the two peoples who have settled side by side to make the history of the British Colony of Hong Kong.

The first problem is the fundamental one—how to represent these Chinese names in terms of the English alphabet: for in their native state they are, of course, hieroglyphics, and, as such, they are not only not spelt but are not even uniformly sounded. In other words, they are pronounced differently in different places. But lest the European reader should begin to scoff, he should remember the scale on which we are dealing. This is no question of local dialects but of the language of provinces as large as European states. And the real point of remark is not the diversity of pronunciation in the several provinces but the uniformity of significance throughout a vast continent.

But as we deal in terms of sound this diversity necessarily forces a choice upon us. Clearly, if a particular hieroglyphic or character can be indifferently represented by 'Lam' according to the Cantonese, 'Lim' according to the Hakkas, 'Lin' according to Pekin (and so forth), we have got to decide which of these alternatives to use, and, having made up our minds, we must stick to our choice. We cannot have Lam in Chapter I, Lim in Chapter II, and so on. Moreover, having elected Lam *à la* Canton for our first proper name we can hardly choose Chên, according to Pekin, for our second, unless, indeed, we are to adopt the elaborate convention of signifying by this means the part of the country from which each individual comes.

And here, no doubt, the reader will start to get restless and point out that as Lam, Lim, and Lin and the rest convey no meaning whatsoever to him we might as well cut the knot and substitute A, B, and C forthwith. And there is no doubt much to commend the solution, for no sooner have we solved the question as to which part of the country to follow in the matter of pronunciation than we are faced with the problem how to spell the selected sound. If, for example, A's name starts with L and rhymes with 'mean' shall we spell it Lean or Lien, or Leen or Lin? And if B's name is pronounced like no known sound in the English language, what are we to do then?

Finally, even though we succeed in representing exactly the Chinese sound by means of English letters we have achieved little or nothing. For, in addition to the correct sound, it is essential that we pronounce it in the correct tone of voice; and, before a European can hope to do that, he must closet himself with a Chinese teacher (or at least a gramophone) and withdraw from the world for several months and possibly a year or so.

In point of fact the few Chinese characters which appear in my story have most of them achieved recognition and even familiarity in Europe in their Roman robes, and to that extent at least have attained the essential qualification of a proper name. Of such are Lin, the High Commissioner charged with the suppression of the opium traffic; and Yeh, the High Commissioner of the Second Chinese war. And, though the strain is thin, it is too valuable to reject. I have therefore adopted *en bloc* the familiar spelling which has its origin in the official dispatches; and which is in point of fact the Pekingese sounds 'romanized' according to the accepted system of the time. And I have followed the same principle in the more abstruse cases of the Manchu names—Keshen, Keying, Eleepoo, and so forth.

n. 1

n. 2

On grounds of familiarity I allow too the claims of those strange names Howqua, Mowqua, Hing Tai, Puankiqua, Shykinqua, and the rest, by which the Cantonese monopoly merchants were known in the old factory days. But, lest the English reader should imagine them to be Chinese words, or the Chinese reader assume they are English, I venture to pass a remark or two upon them in this preface.

n. 3

In the first place the recurring suffix 'qua' appears to be a corruption of the Pekingese 'kwan', an official, and signifies that these merchants had secured official rank by purchase.

n. 4

The 'ki' when it occurs—as in Puan*ki*qua—is clearly the familiar Chinese idiom (which we see in 'Shing Kei', 'Ming Kei', and a hundred other cases) which signifies, as near as

n. 5

may be, 'Puan Incorporated' or 'Puan and Sons'; the net result being, it will be noted, to make the dignity of 'qua' a family rather than an individual affair. The name Howqua incidentally conceals a point of especial interest. 'How' is a gross corruption of 'Wu', the Pekingese pronunciation of the name which, when spoken by a Cantonese and converted into English, produces the tongue-twister 'Ng'. Howqua is in fact Ng I Wo, whose business connexion with William Jardine is perpetuated in 'Ewo', by which name the firm of Jardine, Matheson is still familiarly known.

n. 6   Finally 'Hing Tai'—the firm which achieved notoriety by running deeply into debt to the foreign firms in 1837—means simply 'the brothers', the significant part of the firm name being wholly omitted.

I now pass on to the place-names; and here I would point out that different considerations enter in, for whereas Chinese proper names are mere labels, Chinese place-names are significant, and frequently very picturesque, descriptions. Hong
n. 7   Kong, for example, means 'the fragrant lagoon', Fan-Ling
n. 8   'the chalk ridge'; Pekin 'the northern capital', and so forth. Are we then to surrender the sense without an effort and perpetuate the empty sound? Should not Hong Kong be 'Fairhaven', and Fan Ling 'Chalk farm', and so forth? And if Sham Shui Wan is 'Deep Water Bay' why should not Sham
n. 9   Shui Po be 'Deep Water Reach'? The idea is tempting; but it has serious defects. It is surely not desirable that European and Chinese, living side by side, in a community like Hong Kong, should, instead of common place-names, have parallel and mutually unintelligible lists.

We are then driven back once more to Chinese sounds; and

once more have to decide which of a number of alternatives to select. Shall it be 'Heong Kong' in imitation of the Cantonese or 'Hsiang Chiang' in imitation of Pekin? And shall it be Pekin or Pak King? Have we indeed the choice? Can we, having settled on Pekingese sounds for our proper names, settle on others for our place-names?

n. 10

I apply two principles: first, many place-names have already won their way to acceptance in English ears. Some, like Hong Kong or Fanling, are obvious, though crude, attempts to reproduce the Cantonese sound. Others, like Deep Water Bay, are palpable translations of the Chinese name. Others, like Gin-drinkers Bay, Port Shelter, Repulse Bay, are plainly the efforts of Englishmen at nomenclature irrespective of the Chinese name, if any. And others, like Stanley and Aberdeen, are superimposed upon well-known Chinese place-names.

All these I accept simply because they are familiar. I accept too Pekin, not because it represents any particular dialect, but also because it is already familiar: and I accept Canton for the same reason, though actually it is an obvious attempt to reproduce the name of the province rather than the provincial city. On the same ground I accept Amoy (rather than the Cantonese Hamun), Swatow (rather than Shantow), Swabue (rather than Shan Mi); and I accept the Portuguese Macao as well as the Chinese O Mun, Lamma as well as Pok Liu Chow, Lantao as well as Tai Yu Shan.

n. 11

For the rest I convert place-names into alphabetic terms according to the local pronunciation; or as near as may be.

That at least is true of my own narrative text. But when I quote, I generally endeavour to preserve the spelling of the original; for the original spelling frequently lends point to the quotation. The reader must therefore be prepared to meet a variety of spellings; and may rest assured that Kowlung, Kow Lung, Kau Lung, Cow Lung, Cow Loon, and even Kiulung are, in fact, one and all none other than the more familiar Kowloon.

CHAPTER IV

EARLY CONTACTS

THE distinction of having been the first English ship to visit Hong Kong has been claimed for the East India Company's ship *Defence*.[1] *Defence* reached Canton in 1689 and anchored *en route*, to quote the words of her master reporting to his employers, '15 leagues to the eastward of Macao'.

That, so far as distance and direction are concerned, would certainly bring her into Hong Kong waters; but nevertheless I suppose many will reject the claim.

Some will do so on the ground that, if such evidence is sufficient, we must not reject earlier visits, of which the evidence is no more but no less substantial. We have, for example, the case of the Company's ship *Carolina* which, in 1683, went from Macao 'to Lanto aleus Backelow', and, having stayed two months, on September 17th 'stood out from the islands'[2] and proceeded to Lampeco.

Others will prefer to wait for something more circumstantial. And if they turn to p. 29 of vol. i of (Mrs.) C. F. G. Cumming's *Wanderings in China*, dated 1888, they will not be disappointed. For, in reference to the harbour now familiarly known as Aberdeen on the south side of Hong Kong island, the following remarks will be found: 'It was to a great banyan tree on a small island in this harbour that Commodore Anson fastened his ship to haul her over for repair.'

A link with Anson, just a century before the British occupa-

[1] Morse, *E. I. Coy.*, vol. i, p. 78.   [2] Ibid., p. 52.

tion! This was worth waiting for. Unhappily the writer is silent as to the source of her information. Unhappily, also, the contemporary account of the Commodore's voyages in H.M.S. *Centurion*, though entering into considerable detail as to the ship's movements in the Canton estuary, is silent as to this particular incident. On the other hand, curiously enough, we find another chronicler, Captain Cunynghame, who wrote in 1843, some forty years earlier, describing this self-same small island in the following terms:

'Chuk-Pi-Wan... a land-locked, deep harbour towards the south. ... On a small island facing this town is a "joss-house" ... frequent rendez-vous of picnic parties.... The temple contains various relics ... amongst which ... a species of incense-vase supported by two figures dressed precisely in the costume of Europeans of the 17th century.' (*An Aide-de-camp's Recollections of Services in China* [1844]).

Is it possible that the authoress of *Wanderings* read this account and, by the aid of a vivid imagination, linked the story with a romantic naval figure? Or is it possible that this precise statement of an eyewitness had already degenerated into a vague and unreliable legend which, falling in due course upon receptive ears, ultimately reached the printed page?

The claims of *Centurion* must, I fear, be rejected. But in Captain Cunynghame I detect a reliable witness describing what he has seen with his own eyes. True, he may have been mistaken as to the period of the costume. What he saw may have belonged to the eighteenth and not the seventeenth century. But it is improbable: for, in the first place, the transaction which left these relics in the hands of the temple-keeper of Aplichau (Aberdeen) plainly occurred at a date sufficiently remote from 1843 to be wholly shrouded in mystery by that year; and secondly the eyewitness of an exhibit so entirely unexpected would surely have made certain of his dates before committing the strange facts to record. I am therefore willing to accept the statement as positive evidence not merely of an early but actually of a seventeenth-century contact between Hong Kong and England.

But whether the ship was *Defence* or *Carolina* or some other of a limited number of possible claimants, I am not prepared to guess.

The reader will perhaps inquire whether this temple and these costumes still survive; for here surely lies the obvious way of putting the witness's credibility to the test. The temple does; though reclamation has joined the small island to its larger neighbour Aplichau. Of the costumes I have found no trace. And the presumption would seem to be that they had not survived until 1888; for otherwise they would surely not have been supplanted by the banyan tree in *Wanderings*.

It is clear that Captain James Horsburgh, hydrographer to the East India Company, who surveyed the China Sea during 1806–19, spent some considerable time in Hong Kong waters. This may be inferred from his chart of the Canton estuary (of which a reduced print is to be found in Auber's *China*) on which the Chinese names of islands and other features of the seascape now familiar to Hong Kong residents have been transcribed with painstaking care, and still form the basis of local nomenclature. But the plainest evidence lies in his report to the Foreign Office in which he enumerates, among the abundant safe harbours near Canton, 'Toong Kwu bay, as well as Cap Sing Mun . . . together with the south-west side of Lin Tin in the north monsoon'; 'Tay Tam bay on the south of Hong Kong island affords shelter in all winds: Mirs' Bay or Ty-Po-Hoe in lat. 22° 30' presents a good anchorage....'

It is curious to find Tai Tam Bay (Stanley) selected, but Aberdeen passed by in silence. The Ty-Po-Hoe is, of course, none other than Tai Po, familiar to all visitors to the New Territories. Captain Horsburgh's verdict on its value as a harbour was subsequently to be confirmed by His Majesty's ships *Plover* and *Starling*, which left their names respectively in Plover Cove and Starling Inlet.

Thus far, it must be admitted, all our 'contacts' have, to some extent, been a matter of surmise or inference; but we now come to a naval occasion which is documented sufficiently to convince even the most sceptical; the visit of His Majesty's frigate *Alceste*.

His Majesty's Government, encouraged perhaps by the successful issue of the war with France, had in 1816 determined to make another attempt to open diplomatic relations with Pekin. Lord Amherst was chosen for the role of ambassador, with Sir George Staunton (a member of the East India Company's Select Committee at Canton) and Sir Henry Ellis as second and third members of the embassy.

The duty of conveying the embassy to China fell to His Majesty's frigate *Alceste* (Captain Murray Maxwell); the brig *Lyra* (Captain Basil Hall) and the Company's ship *General Hewitt* acting as consorts.

In due course the flotilla reached Anjeri roads in Java on June 9th, 1816, where *Lyra* was sent ahead to effect a junction with Sir George Staunton, then in Canton. On July 10th *Alceste* and *Lyra* met again at the agreed rendezvous off

EARLY CONTACTS 25

Lemma island; and thence proceeded to Hong Kong to pick up Sir George, and to water.

Sir George, incidentally, had left behind clear instructions as to where he was to be found if required, and, as it happens, these instructions are extant: for the East Indiaman *Thomas Grenville*, homeward bound, is recorded as being

'ordered to proceed to the eastward to communicate with Sir G. Staunton who was to be found at one of the two following places of rendez-vous:

'(i). Malihoy Bay, abreast the Waterfall at Hong Kong, in the channel between Hong Kong and the North end of Lamma Island.

'(ii). Northward of and within two or three miles of the Great Lema.'[1]

This is believed to be the first specific mention of Hong Kong in the records of the East India Company. Malihoy is easily identified with Ma Liu Ho, by which name Waterfall Bay is still known to the Chinese.

Here I will leave Sir Henry Ellis, who in 1817 published a diary under the title *Journal of proceedings of the late embassy to China*, to take up the story:

'10th July. In the evening the ships weighed and proceeded to the island of Hong Kong for the purpose of watering. We hope that we shall be enabled to pursue our voyage on the morning of the 12th.

'The situation of the watering place is picturesque. A stream of water falls down the mountain forming the island and the casks may be filled, when the tide serves, close to the beach.

'Surrounding projections of the land enclose a small bay, the resort of fishing vessels. . . .

'So many European vessels were probably never before collected together in this bay and the whole scene from the shore was highly animated. At night the number of fishing-boats, each with a light, presented the appearance of a London Street well-lighted.'

n. 1

n. 2

[1] Morse, *E. I. Coy.*, vol. iii, p. 260.

Dr. Clarke Abel, physician to the embassy, has also left his version of the visit; from which I extract the following:

'In the evening the squadron weighed and stood for Hong Kong, one of the Ladrone Islands, distant from the Great Lemma 16 miles in a N.E. direction off which it anchored at 10 o'clock in the evening. Looking from the deck of the "Alceste" early in the following morning I found that we were in a sound formed by some small islands by which it was land-locked in every direction, and of which Hong Kong is the principal.

'As seen from the deck this island was chiefly remarkable for its high, conical mountains rising from the centre; and for a beautiful cascade which rolled over a fine blue rock into the sea.'

Dr. Abel also provides a charming mezzotint of 'Waterfall Bay, Hong Cong'. It is still plainly recognizable mid-way between Mt. Davis and Aberdeen. Indeed I declare, as a matter of record, that, as I write one hundred and twenty-five years later, the scene remains substantially unchanged.

n. 3

John M'Leod, surgeon of the *Alceste*, has also contributed his quota:[1]

'We joined them at anchor near the Grand Lemma on the following day, and found along with the *Lyra*, the *Discovery*, and *Investigator*, two surveying-ships belonging to the Company, having on board Sir G. Staunton, and some other gentlemen belonging to the factory, whose knowledge of the Chinese language rendered them necessary as interpreters.

'Circumstances occasioning the delay of a day or two, the ships passed on to an anchorage among the Hong Kong islands; where the Anjeri water, not being deemed good, was changed for that which fell from the rocks, and was certainly uncontaminated by any vegetable matter, for few places present a more barren aspect

---

[1] J. M'Leod, *The Voyage of the Alceste* (1817).

than these islands. They are called the Ladrones, from being the haunt of pirates....'

It will, no doubt, at once be concluded that the waterfall of Staunton's rendezvous, the waterfall of Ellis's account, the waterfall described by Dr. Abel, the water which fell from Surgeon M'Leod's rocks, and the waterfall of the print are one and the same; and that the anchorage described is Waterfall Bay.

This, however, involves two difficulties: first, in the earliest maps of Hong Kong (for example Belcher's, which is reproduced in Bernard's *Nemesis*) the name 'Waterfall' is reserved not for what we know as Waterfall Bay, but for a rocky stream discharging within the heart of Aberdeen Harbour; and secondly there is Ellis's description of the anchorage which surely can refer to Aberdeen, and Aberdeen only.

The matter is, however, settled beyond all doubt by yet another contemporary account, namely the official log of H.M.S. *Alceste*,[1] and more especially by the account in Captain Murray Maxwell's own privately published narrative. The log is brief, recording under date of July 10th, 1816:

'At 7.30 (p.m.) Weighed and made sail: squadron in co.
'At 10.15 Shortened sail and came to on the S.W. side of Low Kow in 17 fathoms: the watering place N.N.E $\frac{1}{2}$ E $\frac{1}{2}$ a mile.'

But Captain Maxwell supplements this as follows:

'On the evening of the 9th of July, we spoke His Majesty's Ship ORLANDO, returning from China: next morning at day-light, we saw the great Ladrone, and then steered for the appointed Rendezvous, off the Great Lema, where we arrived and anchored at four P.M.,

[1] P.R.O., Admiralty Records Ad. 51/2105.

Great Lema bearing S.E. by S., one mile distant, we found here the LYRA and Hon^le Comp^s Cruizers DISCOVERY and INVESTIGATOR they had arrived the preceding day, from Macao Roads with Sir George Staunton and several Gentlemen to join the Embassy.

'As the Imperial Edict of permission to land at the Pai-ho had not yet been received from Pekin, it was deemed advisable to wait a day or two, in the hope of being furnished with so essential a document, and that no time might be lost in stopping at Chusan, or elsewhere for Water, I proposed that the Squadron should go to the neighbouring Island of Hong Kong and complete up that necessary article, a proposition most readily acceded to by the Ambassador, and immediately put in execution. We anchored then in 17 fat^ms about eleven the same night when the Boats were hoisted out and watering directly commenced.

'Although the Soundings are very irregular in the Bay of Hong Kong, yet the ground is perfectly clear and good, the great irregularity of depth would indicate rocky bottom, instead of which it is all a stiff blue and very tenacious clay: the bearings of the water-fall N.N.E. $\frac{1}{2}$ E. distance quarter of a mile. Whilst there we were joined by the Hon^le Comp^s Ship GRENVILLE bound for England.

'We sailed at Noon of the 13th with the Squadron from Hong Kong in high spirits, and resolved to proceed with all alacrity to our ultimate destination. This Bay and excellent watering place, is formed by the Islands of Lama, and Hong Kong, which extend parallel to each other four or five miles, forming a narrow channel at the eastern entrance and gradually opening to a spacious Bay where a stream of water falls over a precipitous cliff in such abundance as would supply the largest Fleets. We had to turn out of the Bay and found the shores on each side steep to and bottom everywhere composed of mud and blue clay. By nine at night we had got to the eastward of the Great Lema and clear of all the islands, when we shaped a course for Pedro Branca. . . .'[1]

[1] Extract from *A Narrative of Occurrences and Remarks made on board His Majesty's*

EARLY CONTACTS 29

Off Waterfall Bay, then, the ships came to anchor; and resident and non-resident of Hong Kong alike can, without much difficulty, reconstruct the scene: the green hill-side rising steeply from the blue sea; the crystal water leaping over the purple rocks, and white-winged *Alceste* gliding in among the brown sails of the Chinese junks—like a swan among the water-hens.

One can hear the anchor-chains being run out; and see the topsails furled, the boats lowered, and the delighted crew filling their barrels to the brim at the water's edge.

Here surely was the harbour of the sailing-shipmaster's dreams—deep, sheltered roads; an exit and entrance at either end; and a perennial stream of reliable water discharging thus conveniently within.

A mile or so away, at the top of terraced rice-fields, stood (and still stands) the little village of Hong Kong Wai—the village of the Fragrant Lagoon, plainly deriving its name from the delectable haven hard by.

It is easy to see how the name would be sought out and fixed in the log and, I daresay, passed on shrewdly by word of mouth to other English ships; how, when the island came into English hands twenty-five years later, it came already named; and how finally, as steam succeeded sail, the fragrant little haven on the south yielded to the great harbour over the hill.

In point of fact one can almost trace the individual sponsors; for among Lord Amherst's staff on board *Alceste* was Mr. J. F. Davis, destined thirty years later to be Governor of the

late Ship Alceste. By Captain Murray Maxwell, C.B. (Lithographed. Copy in the Admiralty Library.)

Colony; while the brig *Lyra* carried Mr. Midshipman Hall, subsequently to reappear, as Captain W. H. Hall of the Hon. Company's steam-vessel *Nemesis*, in the nick of time at the birth of the colony in 1841.

Moreover, is it not clear that while Dr. Clarke Abel, with the zeal of a botanist, tried to scale the adjoining hills in search of specimens, Sir George Staunton (who spoke Chinese) took a quiet stroll to Hong Kong Wai? For why, otherwise, should the early maps name this valley 'Staunton's' valley?

n. 4

On July 13th at noon the squadron (four ships and a brig) weighed anchor and proceeded to sea. And the curtain falls on a brilliant little episode.

In October of the same year there is record of an instruction to *Cornwall* to complete her water at 'Taypa, or at a more convenient place in Hong Kong Bay'.[1] But for the next thirteen years 'the rest is silence'.

Thereafter Hong Kong comes fairly frequently into the news. In 1829, following serious difficulties with the authorities in Canton, the East India Company undertake a close examination of anchorages outside the Bogue, including that 'within the north west point of the island of Hong Kong proceeding in an easterly direction towards the Lyeemoon passage'.[2]

Later in the year there is record of at least six East Indiamen anchored in Hong Kong harbour,[3] and the following year, 1830, the Company decide to divert the whole of the season's shipping from Whampoa to 'Cowloon'.[4]

The island and harbour are clearly becoming known.

[1] Morse, *E. I. Coy.*, vol. iii, p. 260.
[2] Ibid., vol. iii, p. 213.
[3] Ibid., vol. iv, p. 231.
[4] Ibid., vol. iii, p. 261.

EARLY CONTACTS 31

In 1832 we have a fleeting glance of that curious figure Dr. Gutzlaff effecting the 'passage of Lai Moon' and debating with his conscience whether he should pay toll to the keepers of the Buddhist temple in the passage, who demanded rice.

This is, of course, a reference to Ly-ee-mun, Hong Kong's eastern gateway; whence Dr. Gutzlaff was proceeding on one of his strange trips to the east coast, for which he secured a passage in return for his services as interpreter; and thereby got facilities, while others smuggled opium, for surreptitiously introducing something equally forbidden and much less eagerly sought after, the tenets of the Christian faith. n. 5

Two years later Lord Napier, first Superintendent of Trade, writing in discomfort in Canton, in a dispatch dated August 21st, 1834, to Earl Grey, urges the employment of 'A little armament ... which should take possession of the island of Hong Kong in the eastern entrance of the Canton river, which is admirably adapted to every purpose'.[1]

The following April Sir George Robinson, then holding the post of Superintendent, contemplates the withdrawal of the entire British community on to the merchant ships 'which might then take their station in some of the beautiful harbours of Lantao or Hong Kong'.

In January 1836—having by the previous July established himself at Lin Tin—Sir George discusses 'the occupation of one of the islands in the neighbourhood so singularly adapted by nature for commercial purposes',[2] and in April 1836 he once more 'names the lady' and declares his predilection for 'the safe and commodious basin or harbour of Hong Kong'.

Later in the same year the Viceroy of Canton (Tang) n. 6

[1] *Corr. rel. China*, p. 27.   [2] Ibid., 1840, p. 131.

reports to the throne, claiming to have taken steps to disperse the opium-ships which in past years had used Lantao and Kap Sui Mun as a regular anchorage:

'with regard to Lantao I ordered the officer-in-charge of Lymun station to start and cruise about';

and in December we hear of a party of Englishmen and Americans making an informal examination of anchorages and reporting as follows:

n. 7 'Proceeding in a S.E. direction from Lin Tin we pass through the safe anchorage named Urmston's Harbor, or Toon Kwu, and enter the anchorage of Kap Shing Mun, at the N.E. end of Lantao. Till 2 or 3 years past, the opium-laden vessels used to anchor here from July till October for shelter against typhons.... Lantao, in Chinese called Taseu, or Taeyu, "large island"... is in some parts well peopled, and a fort has been erected on it, under the apprehension that the English desired to possess it. The peak of Lantao is the loftiest summit in the neighbourhood; but foreigners have never yet been permitted to ascend to the top....

'Passing out of the Kap Shwuy Moon by the narrow channel... we find ourselves a few miles north of the eastern or Lantao passage by which we may at once communicate through the Lamma Channel. On the west of this is Lantao, with several islets, and on the east are Hongkong and Lamma. North of Hongkong is a passage between it and the main called Lyee Moon (Le-e Mun) with good depth of water close to the Hongkong shore, a perfect shelter on all sides. Here are several good anchorages. At the bottom of a bay on the opposite main is a town called Cowloon (or Kewlung): and a river is said to discharge itself here, a statement the correctness of which we are disposed to doubt.

On the S.W. side of Hongkong, and between it and Lamma are several small bays, fit for anchorage, one of which named Heäng Keäng, probably has given name to the island....'[1]

[1] *Chin. Rep.*, vol. iii, p. 348, Dec. 1836.

The next year—whether as a result of this informal survey or no I cannot say—witnessed a wholesale move to Hong Kong: 'Of 25 receiving vessels off Mo Tau island Kap Sing Mun—nineteen proceeded to Tseem Sha Tsui.'

In 1838, however, Lantao appears to come into its own again; and is described in April of that year in an official memorial on the condition of Kwang Tung province as 'the place of this contraband traffic whither the soldiers are bribed to let them go freely to and fro. Here they form, as it were, a village'[1]—and here—'upwards of 100 receiving ships lie'.

Hong Kong, however, cannot have been wholly deserted, for we find Captain Middlemist, commander of the good ship *Falcon*, writing in August from 'Heong Kong' to Captain Elliot in Canton.[2] Moreover, unless contemporary prints lie, the work of Auguste Borget dated 1838 (and published 1842) shows clearly that Hong Kong Bay was a considerable resort of foreign shipping in that year.[3]

The next year it is Hong Kong all the time; but the story must be told in another chapter.

[1] Ibid., vol. vi, p. 683.   [2] *Corr. rel. China.*
[3] *La Chine et les Chinois*, by Auguste Borget (1842).

CHAPTER V

NAPIER

As pointed out in a previous chapter[1] the Viceroy of Canton had, not unnaturally, requested the Select Committee of the East India Company to take steps to provide, before their dissolution, for the supervisory functions hitherto performed by themselves.[2]

It was, in any event, obviously desirable, request or no request, that the British Government should make provision for the altered circumstances consequent on the abolition of the monopoly. And, in point of fact, it decided upon the appointment of a Commission of three[3]—a Chief Superintendent of Trade and two colleagues—with powers which may be roughly described as ordinary 'Consular' and ordinary 'Trade Commissioner' powers combined. In addition provision was made for the establishment of a Court of Criminal and Admiralty jurisdiction for the trial of offences committed by His Majesty's subjects in China or on the high seas within one hundred miles of China, over which one of the Superintendents was to preside.

For the post of Chief Superintendent, William John, eighth Lord Napier, was chosen. He was forty-seven years of age and had spent his life so far either in commanding one of His Majesty's ships or in raising stock in Selkirkshire.[4] His particular instructions given by Lord Palmerston,[5] the Foreign Secretary, were that he should not establish the Court until,

---

[1] Chapter II, p. 14.   [2] Auber, *China*, p. 335.
[3] *Corr. rel. China*, pp. 1, 5.   [4] *D.N.B.*   [5] *Corr. rel. China*, p. 4.

after full consideration, he deemed it desirable to do so; that he must be careful not to jeopardize existing trade while missing no opportunity of extending it to other ports besides Canton; that he was to look round for a suitable harbour in the event of war, but to call upon the armed forces of the Crown only in the last resort; that he was, in addition to investigating the chances of making a survey of the China Seas, carefully to explore the possibility of establishing diplomatic relations with Pekin; and, last but not least, that he was to announce his arrival in Canton by letter to the Viceroy.

It was a fairly comprehensive task, and it is not very clear what special qualifications Lord Napier possessed for carrying it through. But at any rate he had the assistance of colleagues well acquainted with local conditions, for both William Chichely Plowden and John Francis Davis were ex-members of the East India Company's Select Committee[1] in Canton.

Lord Napier reached Macao in His Majesty's frigate *Andromache* (Captain Chads) on July 15th, 1834, and, having completed his arrangements, including the substitution of Sir George Best Robinson, Bart., also a member of the Select Committee, for Mr. Plowden, who had left for home, and the appointment of Captain Charles Elliot to be Master Attendant, proceeded on the 23rd in *Andromache* to the Bogue and thence, in company with his colleagues and the Rev. Robert Morrison, his official interpreter, in the cutter *Louisa* to Whampoa, and in the boat of a merchantman[2] to Canton; where he arrived, without the customary passport, at the unconventional hour of 2 a.m. on the morning of the 25th.

Meanwhile the Viceroy of Canton, perceiving that, what-

[1] *Corr. rel. China*, p. 7.   [2] *Chin. Rep.*, Jan. 1835.

ever the status of the new-comer, it was not that of the familiar *taipan*, or general business manager, and having early intelligence of the arrival of 'the Chads' (as he persisted in calling the frigate) in Chinese waters, provided for all eventualities by sending the senior Hong merchants to Macao to intercept him and instruct him to await there the Imperial will; and, simultaneously, the Hip Tai, a military official of considerable rank, to the Bogue, doubtless with the same object.

Both merchants and official arrived too late; unless, indeed, the curious salute of three guns which Napier, in his official dispatch, tells us he received at the Bogue (and which is otherwise difficult to explain) was in fact the Hip Tai's greeting, or summons to halt.

The following day—July 26th—when putting the final touches on his letter to the Viceroy announcing his arrival, Lord Napier was confronted by the Hong merchants, who sought to serve him now with the Viceroy's edict which they had failed to deliver in Macao.

Lord Napier declined to accept service[1] and proceeded with his intention of delivering his letter to the Viceroy. For this purpose he detailed the Secretary[2] to the Commission to proffer it at the city gates, where it was refused by a succession of officials (though an offer by the Hong merchants and the Hip Tai jointly to ascertain the Viceroy's disposition is recorded) on the grounds that the character 'pin' or 'petition' was omitted, and that the proper intermediary was the body of the Hong merchants.

On the following days, 27th, 28th, 30th, 31st, the Hong merchants, spurred on by a fire of edicts from the Viceroy,

[1] *Corr. rel. China*, p. 8.   [2] Ibid., p. 8.

endeavoured to induce Lord Napier to admit the designation 'petition', or alternatively to withdraw to Macao.[1] In the course of these conversations the Hong merchants, having occasion to write Lord Napier's name, went out of their way to borrow (in order to represent the sound) two Chinese characters meaning, literally, 'laboriously vile'[2]—a device designed to bring the stranger into contempt in the eyes of the native scholars, and one which, but for Dr. Morrison's knowledge of the Chinese written language, would have escaped notice. This, in point of fact, was the interpreter's last service to the Commission, for he died on August 1st.[3]

Lord Napier persisted in his refusal to treat with the Chinese merchants, and matters remained in this posture until August 10th.

On August 10th the Hong merchants, having failed with Napier, invited the British merchants to a conference, giving no reason; but Napier, suspecting an attempt to undermine his position, himself called his nationals together and with the assistance of Davis persuaded them to decline the invitation.[4] The Hong merchants then served the Viceroy's edicts requiring Napier's departure on the leading British merchants, W. Jardine and others, and, having exhausted all other methods, on the 17th took the critical step of stopping the loading of cargoes on British ships.[5]

On the 18th, the *Andromache* having returned to the Bogue after a short cruise bringing with her her sister ship *Imogene*,[6] the Hong merchants in alarm came to inquire what was afoot

[1] *Corr. rel. China*, p. 17.   [2] *Chin. Rep.*, Aug. 1834.   [3] Ibid.
[4] *Corr. rel. China*, 1840, p. 11.   [5] Ibid., p. 15.
[6] The published dispatches do not indicate whether *Andromache* met *Imogene* by chance or by arrangement.

and received from Napier the reply that 'it was a secret to be divulged to the Viceroy only'. At the same time he offered to waive the delivery of the letter and communicate his arrival by word of mouth to the Viceroy.

Next day the merchants brought from the Viceroy a flat refusal to meet him and a further edict threatening the end of British trade if Napier did not forthwith depart. The challenge had been accepted.

It was at this juncture that Napier, writing on August 21st to Earl Grey, advocated taking possession of Hong Kong.[1]

On August 22nd, however, there came a message from the Viceroy proposing a visit by three officials, two civil and one military (with the object, one surmises, of assessing just how far it was safe to go in this interesting game of bluff).

Napier accepted the proposal and the meeting was arranged for the following day. In due course, after having objected to an arrangement of the seats, which carried out exactly the Chinese notion of the situation, and insisted on substituting one which carried out exactly his own; and having rapped the Chinese officials heavily over the knuckles for arriving late,[2] Lord Napier inquired the purpose of their visit.

He was told it was to ascertain first why he had come to Canton, second what his functions were, and third how soon he proposed to return to Macao; and he replied to the first by reminding them of the request of the previous Viceroy in 1831 that some one should be sent to manage the trade; to the second by referring to his letter which still remained undelivered; and to the third that, in that matter, he would suit his own convenience.

---

[1] *Corr. rel. China*, 1840, p. 27.   [2] Ibid., p. 30.

Three days later, August 26th, Lord Napier took the remarkable step of issuing a proclamation in Chinese in which he called the Viceroy ignorant and obstinate, and hinted that he was responsible for the ruin and discomfort of thousands of industrious residents of Canton by stopping the British trade.

This was a desperate throw; and it is astonishing to find no reference to it in his dispatch of August 28th[1] to Lord Palmerston—the last he was destined to write.

In this dispatch he announces that arrangements are on foot for a further meeting—this time with four officials; and the records show that on consecutive days he is being pressed by the Hong merchants to concede the point in the matter of the arrangement of the chairs.

As things turned out no meeting took place, and we are left guessing whether this was due to Napier's refusal to give way on the question of the chairs or to the fact that no such meeting was ever really intended by Chinese officialdom.

What is certain is that in response to Napier's manifesto an angry counter-proclamation promptly appeared roundly designating Napier a mad dog; while on September 2nd the Viceroy, suiting the action to the word, besides confirming the stoppage of trade and withdrawing servants and supplies, surrounded Napier's quarters with a guard of Chinese soldiers.

Events thereupon moved swiftly. On September 5th Napier sent for *Andromache* and *Imogene* to come to Whampoa for the protection of British life and property; Sir George Robinson himself conveying the message. On the 8th, having now no communication with the Hong merchants, he

[1] Ibid., p. 32.

addressed a long letter to the Secretary of the newly formed British Chamber of Commerce,[1] setting out his full case against the Viceroy and *inter alia* reminding him that he was dealing with 'a powerful monarch commanding armies of fine soldiers who have conquered wherever they went ... [and one who] is possessed of great ships of war, carrying even as many as 120 guns'.

The Hong merchants were invited (at second hand) to convey this reminder; and the threat was added that if (as expected) they declined, it would be published by proclamation in the streets.

The same day *Andromache* and *Imogene* forced the Bogue and, anchoring at Whampoa on the 11th, sent a small party of marines to the British factory.

On the 11th, too, the Viceroy duly replied,[2] in a public proclamation, *seriatim* to Lord Napier's points; and to the threat of force, backed as it was by the presence of men and ships, answered as follows:

'I cannot bear forcibly to drive him out. What [the Celestial Empire] values is the subjection of man by reason. It esteems not awing them by force.'

It was the *coup de grâce*. The surgeon, Dr. Colledge, and Mr. William Jardine were left to make such terms as they could; and on the 21st, while a chastened *Andromache* and *Imogene* retraced their steps through the Bogue,[3] still accompanied by the cutter *Louisa*, Napier, hostage for their good behaviour, was conveyed by the Broadway in an ordinary

---

[1] *Corr. rel. China*, p. 35; *Chin. Rep.*, Oct. 1834.
[2] *Corr. rel. China*, 1840, p. 37; *Chin. Rep.*, Oct. 1834.
[3] *Chin. Rep.*, Nov. 1834.

Forcing the Passage of the Bocca Tigris

Facing page 41]

passage-boat to Macao, by permission of the Chinese Government.[1] He reached his destination on September 26th and on October 11th died.

My various readers will no doubt assign various reasons for this unhappy ending. For my part I will limit myself to inviting attention to one point which hitherto seems to have escaped notice. It will be recalled that in 1637 Captain Weddell had forced the passage of the Bogue—the first Englishman to do so—and thus far the only English merchantman. Ever since then he had been regarded (and indeed still is) in popular estimation as a gallant figure who had successfully bearded the Cantonese lion in his den.

Lord Napier clearly shared the popular view, for we find him, in a semi-official dispatch to Palmerston of August 17th, quoting the case with evident approval[2] and a sly hint or two that he proposed to take him as his model.

Now if Napier had known his history he would have discovered that Weddell, like himself, merely placed his head in the Tiger's mouth and, like himself, had in the end humbly to request permission to depart.

But if this is a tragic instance of the failure of history to tell the truth, we have under our very eyes a more astonishing one.

I refer to the well-known contemporary lithographs depicting H.M.'s ships *Andromache* and *Imogene* pouring in their broadsides at the Bogue forts in response to Napier's summons; mementoes which clearly could never have been produced but for the firm determination on the part of all concerned to treat the affair as a glorious incident in English history and to forget the bitter sequel.

[1] Ibid., Oct. 1834. [2] *Corr. rel. China*, p. 14.

With the removal of Napier the trade at once resumed. The withdrawal of the embargo by the Viceroy was the natural step. He had imposed it to secure the withdrawal of an intruder and, having succeeded, he forthwith removed it.

But what of the British merchants? For them it was a case of exercising a choice, a difficult choice no doubt, for their livelihood was at stake. Moreover it would be misconceiving the essentials of the situation to regard them as a corporate whole or even a united body. They were now separate individuals competing with one another; and, while we may regret the lack of unity, we shall be slow to condemn too rigorously particular individuals, no matter how they exercised their choice. None the less, viewed as an incident in the international relations of England and China, the resumption of trade by British merchants at this juncture must clearly be regarded as the result of the exercise of a voluntary choice.

And the question which we naturally ask is—did they resume feeling that Napier had got no more than his deserts; or did they resume in the face of unmerited indignities and humiliations heaped upon the King's representative?

The Viceroy, polite and logical, suavely assumes the former, and (having, on October 19th, instructed the British merchants to write home for a business man—a *taipan* and not another superintendent—and meantime, to elect one of their own members to act)[1] in an edict of October 23rd[2] lavishes his unwelcome acknowledgements on the English merchants: 'It is now reported that Lord Napier has died. The said separate merchants have opened their holds—buying and selling—which shows a profound knowledge of the great

---
[1] *Corr. rel. China*, p. 47.   [2] Ibid, p. 55.

principles of dignity. It is altogether worthy of praise and esteem.'

But the merchants—or a portion of them, headed by William Jardine—stung by this, impinge themselves on the other horn of the dilemma; and, having opened their holds on September 29th, on December 9th, in a petition to the King,[1] loudly complain of the 'unprovoked stoppage of trade'; 'the wanton insults heaped upon the late Superintendent'; 'the insults offered by the Governor and the humiliating conduct pursued towards his Lordship'; adding that 'the most unsafe of all courses' is that 'of quiet submission to insult or unresisting endurance of contemptuous and wrongful treatment'.

Small wonder that Mr. J. F. Davis, who now automatically succeeded to the post of Chief Superintendent, characterized this petition as 'crude and ill-digested'.[2]

But what did the new Superintendent himself do in the situation with which he found himself confronted on Napier's death? What was his assessment of the position?

It can hardly be doubted that Mr. J. F. Davis knew full well that the unhappy Napier could not be supported by reasonable men. He puts it mildly in his dispatch of October 24th to the Governor-General of India: 'with regard to any measures of a coercive nature towards the local government (the policy and justice of which, except on the failure of an appeal to Peking, might be questionable)'; and he repeats it in reviewing the situation in a dispatch to the Foreign Secretary three months later. The decision, however, was not for him but for his Government, and accordingly the task which he found himself called upon to perform was that of quietly

[1] Ibid., p. 68.   [2] Ibid., p. 80.

awaiting further instructions without in any way committing his principals to any particular line of action. This attitude he described as one of 'quiescence'; or 'absolute silence'.[1] But its essential characteristic was that it had to be 'quiescence' without acquiescence. He must, in fact, do nothing to encourage the Viceroy to think the incident was closed—in case the British Government thought otherwise.

In this delicate task he acquits himself to admiration; and his 'Notice to British Subjects in China',[2] addressed from Macao on November 10th, 1834, is a brilliant response to the Viceroy's edict of October 23rd from which I have quoted above. The notice, too long to set out in full, claims to be a 'sedative' to the restless British merchants, to whom it is ostensibly addressed; but is at the same time calculated to play upon any feeling of uneasiness or suspense which the Viceroy might entertain as to the outcome of the recent affair.

He even takes the Viceroy upon his own ground by pointing out the incongruity, in one so versed in all the rules of propriety and dignity, of suggesting mere British merchants as the medium of conveying to their king his desire for the appointment of a new head manager. But in this he seems to have laid himself open to the retort that, after all, this was the medium which had produced not only Napier but himself.

Mr. Davis lay low in Macao for three months and then withdrew in accordance with his intention expressed before Napier's arrival. In one respect, however, he changed his plans, vacating his post instead of taking leave, so that Captain Charles Elliot, now Secretary, might succeed to the vacant post of third Superintendent.[3]

[1] *Corr. rel. China*, 1840, p. 44.   [2] Ibid., p. 56.   [3] Ibid., pp. 105, 144.

On January 22nd, 1835, Sir George Robinson stepped into Mr. Davis's shoes and readily accepted the legacy of the quiescent policy. Within a week, however, an incident occurred to show the limitations of that policy. The British ship *Argyle*, in distress off the China coast, had sent a boat ashore to seek a pilot. But instead of the ship's boat a native craft had appeared demanding ransom; and the Captain of *Argyle* had decided to proceed at once to Macao to report.

The safety of English seamen was at stake, and the Superintendents decided, at the risk of their dignity, to report the matter direct to the Viceroy of Canton—a task, in view of recent occurrences, obviously calling for tact, determination, and courage. For this task the third Superintendent, Captain Elliot, was selected, with the assistance of the Rev. C. Gutzlaff as interpreter.

The expected happened; and Elliot, roughly handled and thrown to the ground at the city gate, was contemptuously told, 'We only receive petitions.'[1] Elliot thereupon turned to Whampoa and was on the point of arranging for two armed British vessels to effect the release of the ship's crew, when he was checked by orders from the Chief Superintendent, fearful lest, if he persisted, the trade would once more be stopped. And in the end the authorities, stirring themselves, promptly recovered the missing seamen[2] and restored them to their ship.

In the following April, 1835, writing to Lord Palmerston, Sir George Robinson draws official attention for the first time to the dissensions among the British merchants, and actually makes the remarkable statement that 'the untoward reception at and disastrous removal of His Majesty's Commission from

[1] Ibid., p. 81. [2] Ibid., p. 85.

Canton was mainly to be attributed to the bitter party feeling which, I am sorry to assert, reigned at the very moment when general unanimity should have aided the efforts of its officers'.

He then proceeds to enunciate the proposition that so long as British merchants are hand in glove with Chinese in Canton the efforts of officials to establish on their behalf a satisfactory and dignified *modus vivendi* are inevitably undermined, 'counteracted by a strong undercurrent, if I may so express it', and for this reason urges that, before official approaches are made to the Cantonese authorities, the whole of the British community should be withdrawn from the bad influences of Canton together with British families resident at Macao and embarked on to merchant ships 'which might then take their station in some of the beautiful harbours of Lantao or Hong Kong'—a curiously prophetic proposition.

In July he reports the refusal of a British merchant (Mr. Keating) to recognize the jurisdiction of the Commission[1] in a small-debts case; and in November he persuades Mr. James Innes,[2] the 'stormy petrel' of the merchants, to desist from an obvious act of piracy, but only by promises of support which the British Government firmly declined to endorse. Immediately afterwards Sir George, still without instructions, takes upon his own responsibility the remarkable step of establishing himself on board the cutter *Louisa*, at the island of Lin Tin,[3] thereby obviating for British ships the inconvenience of calling at Macao for port clearances: a move not only welcomed by the British Chamber[4] in Canton but accepted without demur by the Cantonese authorities.

[1] *Corr. rel. China*, p. 95.
[2] Ibid., p. 102.
[3] Ibid., p. 104.
[4] Ibid., p. 109.

In January 1836 he argues, in a dispatch to the Foreign Secretary, for 'the destruction of one or two forts and the occupation of one of the islands in this neighbourhood so singularly adapted by nature, in every respect, for commercial purposes', as a measure more likely to put the relations of the two countries on a 'respectable, safe and becoming footing', than 'by forcing the Commission upon Canton'. The contingency which particularly haunts him is 'a case of homicide'. 'In the event of so unhappy a catastrophe occurring as the death of a Chinese we are helpless in Canton; we must give up a man....'[1] But he adds that there is no necessity for anything of the kind at the moment. All that is needed is 'a full and efficient control of shipping'—'No man can quit the country or evade just claims against him'; and (finding *Louisa*, 74 tons, somewhat cramped) he asks for a small merchant vessel of about two hundred tons.

The next month there is an illuminating allusion to the opium trade—which all this time had spread like a rank weed:

'On the question of smuggling opium, smuggling carried on actually in the Mandarin boats can hardly be termed such. Whenever His Majesty's Government direct us to prevent British vessels engaging in the traffic, we can enforce any order to that effect; but a more certain method would be to prohibit the growth of the poppy and manufacture of opium in British India.'

In April 1836, while again reporting tranquil conditions, he adds:

'If I could perceive more harmony among the British Community I should confidently address your Lordship on the advantages to be derived from a change in the position of the outside rendez-vous for

[1] *Corr. rel. China*, p. 106.

shipping, from the exposed and impracticable anchorage at Lin Tin, during the southerly monsoons, to the safe and commodious basin or harbour of Hong Kong. . . .'[1]

British society is, however, still divided and critical, and Sir George, alone in his cutter at Lin Tin, announces in November 1836 his intention of taking up his station permanently there.

A month later, however, he receives the dispatch dated June (and written on receipt of his January dispatches) curtly informing him that, in pursuance of a decision long arrived at to effect retrenchment, the post of Chief Superintendent had been abolished; and that the archives were to be handed over to Captain Elliot, who, with the withdrawal of Mr. Astell on April 1st, 1835,[2] had risen to Second Superintendent.

[1] *Corr. rel. China*, p. 131 (No. 74). [2] *Chin. Rep.*, vol. xi, p. 128.

CHAPTER VI

ELLIOT

1836–1839

ELLIOT (who had not followed his Chief to Lin Tin but on the contrary had, from his base at Macao, contrived to visit Canton) had in a letter to Palmerston already given his opinion that the arrival of a new viceroy Tang Ting Ching offered a favourable opportunity for reopening direct communication with Canton, and accordingly, when he himself became Senior Superintendent, observing that it would be difficult to explain any delay between his appointment and his first approaches towards recognition, determined to make the attempt forthwith.

Forewarned by Napier's failure, he stooped to conquer; and both designated the letter announcing his appointment to the Viceroy a 'petition' and entrusted it to the care of the Hong merchants for delivery. But at the same time he selected as the channel between himself and the Chinese merchants four British merchants, two belonging to the East India Company and two private traders, W. Jardine and L. Dent,[1] thereby taking the first step to ensure that unity the lack of which his immediate predecessor, segregated at Lin Tin, had so constantly deplored.

He was instructed to await the Emperor's pleasure in Macao,[2] and, this being signified after a delay of four months, he proceeded at once, having secured the necessary passport, to Canton, where he arrived on April 2nd, 1837.

[1] *Corr. rel. China*, 1840, p. 143.   [2] Ibid., p. 144.

The situation with which he was confronted was not an easy one. Ever since the tragedy of Napier the opium traffic had continued to expand, and in June 1836, in response to a memorial to the throne, an Imperial edict had been issued[1] calling upon the new Viceroy Tang to examine and report.

This he did, advocating some form of legalization, in September;[2] but in November, on receipt of a further Imperial edict, he had required W. Jardine, 'the iron-headed old-rat',[3] and other named British merchants to leave the country.[4] Chance, however, afforded Elliot the opportunity to herald his approach to Canton with the announcement of succour rendered to shipwrecked Chinese seamen by a British vessel; and he ventured, in a polite note, to express to the Viceroy the hope that this 'interchange of charities may strengthen the bonds of peace and good-will between the two nations'. But if Elliot had hoped to break the ice in this way he was disappointed. The Viceroy blandly replied that as between the Celestial Empire and the rest of the world there could be no question of peace and goodwill but merely of favours granted; and that in future Elliot must submit his remarks for examination by the Hong merchants before offering them to himself.[5]

Elliot at once, firm but polite, protested; and Tang, seeing that he had gone too far, yielded. This was obviously a severe blow to the Viceroy's pride, and it is clear as the story unfolds

---

[1] *Corr. rel. China*, p. 156; *Chin. Rep.*, July 1836.
[2] *Corr. rel. China.*, 1840, p. 161; *Chin. Rep.*, Jan. 1837.
[3] *Corr. rel. China*, p. 176; *Chin Rep.*, Nov. 1836.
[4] *Corr. rel. China*, p. 183. [5] Ibid., 1840, pp. 203, 208, 209.

that it rankled in his mind. Elliot lost no time in following up this success; and in June, while respectfully requesting a passport permitting his return to Macao, he applied for, and secured, permission to come and go in future in the cutter *Louisa* without passport.

The following September he was destined to secure a more important success still, the immediate release, 'pending trial according to the laws of my country', of four Lascars, members of a British ship's crew detained by the Chinese authorities on suspicion of wounding a Chinese villager. This he achieved under simple threat of hauling down his flag and retiring from Canton.

Never had the prospects of establishing a satisfactory relationship between the two countries looked so rosy. But this proved the peak of Elliot's diplomatic success.

In August and September the Viceroy, announcing the receipt of further Imperial instructions regarding the opium-ships, which had now moved 'from Kap Sing Mun eastward, to a place called Tseen Sha Tsuy',[1] called upon Elliot to send them away;[2] and Elliot (apart from insisting successfully on receiving such instructions through the hands of officials and not of merchants) could only reply that the 'outer seas' were beyond his jurisdiction; but 'he trusts some safe means of remedying a hazardous state of things may be found'. In point of fact the specific recommendation which he had made to the Foreign Secretary was for the appointment of a Special Commissioner to deal with opium.

In November he received Lord Palmerston's dispatch (dated June) giving him positive orders not to head his official

[1] Kowloon Point. [2] *Corr. rel. China*, 1840, p. 234.

communications with the Chinese authorities 'petition';[1] and, though he tried faithfully to induce the Viceroy to agree, he failed; and in December 1837 retired to Macao. As he did so he exchanged parting shots with the Viceroy; the latter issuing a manifesto embodying an Imperial Edict allowing Elliot one month to clear the outer seas of the opium-receiving ships,[2] while Elliot advised the British merchants to present direct to the Viceroy their claims for debt (amounting to the substantial total of two and a quarter million dollars) against 'Hing Tai', a bankrupt and absconding member of the Chinese merchants' association, the Co-hong.

During January and February 1838 Elliot is found reporting from Macao to the Foreign Office the existence of extensive opium-smuggling by armed British boats at Whampoa; and receiving from Lord Palmerston, in reply to his request, made a year before, for a naval ship, the intimation that 'Her Majesty's Government cannot interfere for the purpose of enabling British subjects to violate the laws of the country to which they trade'.

In April the public strangulation of a Chinese at Macao for complicity in some opium offence, the first example of the kind, served as a sharp reminder of the urgency of the situation; and Elliot, fearing that the Viceroy would attribute his withdrawal to Macao to a desire to assist the opium trade, made advances designed to reopen conversations with that official, pending the arrival of instructions from England. In this he was unsuccessful; and again in August another attempt —this time with the moral support of Rear-Admiral Maitland and a British man-of-war, H.M.S. *Wellesley*, anchored outside

---

[1] *Corr. rel. China*, 1840, p. 149.   [2] *Ibid.*, p. 250; *Chin. Rep.*, Nov. 1837.

the Bogue[1]—to proffer his co-operation in exchange for the dropping of the designation 'petition' equally failed.[2]

In December, however, following on the detection of Mr. James Innes in a glaring act of opium-smuggling[3] and his refusal to obey the Viceroy's peremptory order of expulsion from Canton, an attempt was made to strangle a Chinese, again for some opium offence, in the factory square. The attempt was stoutly resisted by the foreign merchants; a riot ensued;[4] and trade was forthwith stopped.

This brought Elliot hot-foot from Macao; and he did not hesitate, sinking his dignity, to petition the Viceroy, urging him publicly to declare against the opium-smuggler and to send officers in company with himself to clear the small opium-craft away from Whampoa. This he successfully achieved; and at the same time, while 'respectfully, but very earnestly, entreating the Viceroy to pardon the two coolies who were lately apprehended in the act of landing opium belonging to Mr. Innes',[5] seized the occasion to urge the assembled foreign merchants to steer clear of the dangerous traffic.[6]

In Canton, in January, he learnt from the senior Hong merchant the first news of the approach of Lin Tse Sü, the Imperial Commissioner, armed with plenipotentiary powers to eradicate the opium trade. In February he reported from Macao the 'continued stagnation of the opium traffic and the consequent locking up of the circulating medium producing great and general embarrassment'.

On February 26th a third Chinese victim was produced, and this time strangulation in the factory square was carried

n. 1

[1] *Corr. rel. China*, p. 311.   [2] Ibid., p. 310.   [3] Ibid., p. 323.
[4] *Chin. Rep.*, Dec. 1838.   [5] *Corr. rel. China*, p. 336.   [6] Ibid., p. 326.

through. This again brought Elliot hurrying to Canton; but beyond a carefully worded protest to the Viceroy he could effect nothing, and returned to Macao on March 10th, anticipating that the High Commissioner would first direct his attention to the 'outer seas'. At this juncture the 'iron-headed old rat' Jardine, scenting trouble with unerring instinct, slipped quietly away from the China coast.

On March 18th Lin issued in Canton his first manifesto, addressed directly to the foreign merchants,[1] demanding the delivery of all their opium in three days and the signing of bonds undertaking under pain of death never to import any more.

On the 22nd the proposal to seize Dent (one of the most senior merchants and head of one of the most important firms) once more spurred Elliot to swift action. Having formally left on record with the Chinese official at Macao a proffer of co-operation with the Commissioner[2] in giving effect to the Emperor's wishes, and having ordered 'all ships at the outer anchorages to proceed to Hong Kong, and be prepared to resist every act of aggression',[3] he himself passed the Bogue in H.M.S. *Larne* on the 24th and, at great personal risk, reached the factories in *Larne*'s gig at 6 p.m. He thereupon at once took Dent under his personal protection[4] and, 'moved by urgent considerations affecting the maintenance of peace between the two countries', demanded passports of the Viceroy on behalf of all the British merchants within three days: warning him of the consequences if he detained Her Majesty's officer and subjects against their will.[5]

---

[1] *Chin. Rep.*, April 1839; *Corr. rel. China*, p. 350.　　[2] *Corr. rel. China*, p. 362.
[3] Ibid., p. 363.　　[4] Ibid., p. 357.　　[5] Ibid., p. 367.

The Viceroy, in forwarding the demand to the High Commissioner,[1] was unable to resist a contemptuous comment on the expression 'the two countries', a sinister echo of that first encounter two years before when this same foreigner had caused him to 'lose face'.

The High Commissioner, having withdrawn servants and supplies, and cut off all communications in strict accordance with precedent, mounted an armed guard at the factories, and demanded first the delivery of the opium[2] and the signature of the bonds.

To the former demand Elliot acceded, proffering no less than 20,283 chests;[3] but the latter he utterly rejected,[4] and despite the helplessness of his situation contrived, by a conspicuous display of personal courage and determination, to secure an agreement with Lin under which, omitting all reference to the bond, the restrictions on personal liberty were to be withdrawn *pari passu*[5] with the delivery of the opium.

In another respect also he achieved a considerable tactical success. The High Commissioner had demanded that the several foreign merchants should provide his officers with signed orders enabling them to take delivery of the opium in the receiving ships lying at Lin Tin and elsewhere beyond the Bogue. This Elliot resisted, pointing out, with perfect reason, that now that the whole had been entrusted by the merchants to himself, his order, and his alone, could produce the opium. The importance of this lies in the fact that when subsequently the High Commissioner nominated individuals for expulsion[6]

[1] Ibid., p. 368.
[2] Ibid., p. 370.
[3] Ibid., p. 375.
[4] Ibid., p. 390.
[5] Ibid., 1840, p. 383.
[6] Ibid., p. 401.

he had to depend upon hearsay and suspicion only; and Elliot was thus able effectively to hold up Lin's guesses as a telling example of the risk of submitting oneself to Chinese justice.[1]

While still confined in Canton Elliot heard reports of Lin's intention to attack Macao and strongly urged the Foreign Secretary to consider the question of

'making some immediate arrangement either for the cession of the Portuguese rights or for the effectual defence' and 'its appropriation to British uses by means of a subsidiary convention.... The inner harbour', he proceeds, 'and the Typa are open to the objection of not being sufficiently roomy, or of depth enough to receive our large merchant ships. But this is not more than an inconvenience; for we are so completely the masters at sea that the large ships might remain in Hong Kong and send their cargoes over in smaller vessels as indeed is pretty much the case at present.'

The news also reached him that James Innes,[2] expelled in December from Canton, had been caught red-handed with opium in his possession in Macao; and he icily ordered him to leave the coast.[3]

On May 24th, the full quota of opium having been handed over, he asked for his passports, and on May 27th, with the remaining sixteen British merchants (who had been singled

---

[1] Elliot's dispatch to the Secretary of State written in confinement is too lengthy to repeat in full, but one comment in particular contained in it merits attention, namely that the Chinese Government had not the power to effect what they sought—the abolition of opium—and that the only alternative to intervention by Her Majesty's Government was 'a discreditable overthrow by lawless men'; and that there could be neither safety nor honour for either Government till 'Her Majesty's flag flies on these coasts in a secure position'. [2] *Corr. rel. China*, pp. 414, 420–7.

[3] *Chin. Rep.*, July 1841, p. 424: an order which this strong-minded gentleman appears to have disregarded, for he died and was buried at Macao on July 1st, 1841, aged 55.

out by name by the High Commissioner as security for the full delivery), reached Macao, after enjoining upon the commanders of British ships not to enter the port of Canton henceforth.[1]

The complete stoppage of the entire British trade followed. The gesture, though losing much of its effect by reason of the willingness, despite Elliot's representations, of the Americans to remain in Canton and risk those conditions which Elliot declared made residence there for foreigners neither 'safe nor respectable', was at least a signal proof of the tact and firmness with which he had handled his own countrymen. And it is pertinent to pause and contrast the resulting situation with that which ensued upon the withdrawal of the Superintendents from Canton four years and a half before.

A condition of stalemate followed; the High Commissioner having secured indeed the season's supply of opium, but, in the process, having lost the wherewithal to exercise further pressure upon the British merchants.

On the 7th July, however—the very day, curiously enough, on which Lin was making an ostentatious tour of the abandoned English factories—a collision took place at Tseem Sha Tsuy[2] between Chinese villagers and a party of seamen from the foreign merchant ships assembled in Hong Kong Bay, in the course of which a Chinese, Lin Wei Hi, lost, or was alleged to have lost, his life.[3] The situation had arisen which Sir George Robinson had visualized three years before.[4]

Elliot hurried to the scene on the 10th, and, besides offering

[1] *Chin. Rep.*, May 1839.   [2] Kowloon.
[3] *Corr. rel. China*, p. 432; *Chin. Rep.*, Aug. 1839, Oct. 1839.
[4] See *supra*, p. 47, 'a case of homicide'.

rewards of $200 and $100 for information leading to the apprehension of the offenders (if Englishmen), promptly, and no doubt indiscreetly, compensated the relatives of the deceased in the substantial sum of $1,500, with a further $400 as a protection against extortion by local officials, and $100 for the villagers who had suffered in the affair; and received, on his part, an acknowledgement that the death was accidental.[1]

It is not difficult to believe that Elliot would have been content had the incident not reached the ears of the High Commissioner. But, be that as it may, it is certain that Lin was promptly apprised of it, and no less promptly sent deputies to Macao to investigate.[2]

Elliot turned to face them; and on August 2nd invited the attendance of Chinese officials at an inquiry fixed for the 12th at Hong Kong. The overture was, however, not accepted; and Lin (seeing, perhaps, in the incident primarily a chance to inveigle the British shipping back to Whampoa and thereby renew his grip upon the opium situation) published on August 2nd[3] a manifesto—'to be pasted up on the Praya Grande, Macao, on a spot secure from wind and rain'—giving the result of his own investigations, and roundly accusing Elliot of paying 'hush-money' and concealing the murderers.

This was followed on August 15th by an ultimatum demanding the delivery of the murderer, and, on its expiry, by the moving of troops to the Macao barrier and the withdrawal of servants and supplies from British residences in the settlement.

In the hope of relieving the pressure—for it was clear that the attack was levelled at himself personally—Elliot, having

[1] *Corr. rel. China*, p. 432.   [2] Ibid., pp. 440, 441.   [3] *Chin. Rep.*, Aug. 1839.

already embarked his wife and child, took ship on August 23rd to Hong Kong.[1]

On August 26th he was joined by the entire British community, men, women, and children,[2] for whose safety, owing to the pressure of the Chinese authorities, the Governor of Macao could no longer be responsible.[3] On the 30th H.M.S. *Volage* (Captain Smith) made an opportune appearance on the scene. On the 31st Lin issued a manifesto[4] observing that 'the newly-arrived merchant vessels, neglecting to surrender what opium they have brought, have collected at Hong Kong', and calling upon the inhabitants of the coast not to provide food or water to the foreigners and forcibly to oppose any attempt to land.

On September 4th, failing in peaceable efforts to secure essential supplies, Elliot, 'greatly provoked', opened fire[5] from *Volage*'s pinnace on the Chinese war-junks anchored off Kowloon City for the express purpose of obliging the natives to take back food-stuffs already bought and paid for.

This, to quote Elliot's own words in reporting to Lord Palmerston, was 'a measure that I am sensible, under less trying circumstances, would be difficult indeed of vindication'.

In the result it ensured thenceforward a regular supply of food for the assembled shipping; and produced, on September 9th, a further manifesto from Lin addressed to the British merchants urging them, in effect, to take their ships to Whampoa and resume trade, and throw over their blundering Superintendent who had brought all their difficulties upon them.

---

[1] *Corr. rel. China*, p. 433.
[2] *Chin. Rep.*, Aug. 1839.
[3] *Corr. rel. China*, p. 438.
[4] *Chin. Rep.*, Sept. 1839.
[5] *Corr. rel. China*, p. 448.

On September 11th,[1] learning that a ship's boat with Englishmen on board was missing, and fearing they had fallen into the hands of the Chinese, Elliot invited Captain Smith of *Volage* to declare a blockade, which he at once withdrew on hearing later of the safety of the boat's crew.

The burning, on September 12th, by the High Commissioner's underlings, of the Spanish brig *Bilbaino* in Macao harbour, under the impression that she was an English opium-smuggler, and the persistence of Lin in declaring that the vessel was the English brig *Virginia*, gave Elliot—or so he thought—a handle to resume negotiations; for he conceived that, for all his protestations, the incident must have caused Lin some anxiety and that consequently a move towards the resumption of regular trade would be welcomed.

In thus opening negotiations for a resumption of trade Elliot would, at first sight, appear to have been guilty of serious inconsistency; for, so far, he had declared in the plainest terms his conviction that trade could not properly be resumed until due reparation had been made by the Chinese authorities for the restraints placed upon British subjects and the insults heaped upon Her Majesty's officer.

It would seem, however, upon closer examination, that Elliot stands acquitted of the charge. In June he expressed to the British merchants his view[2] that the entrance of British ships and goods within the Bocca Tigris would be 'intensely humiliating and mischievous, because it establishes the principle that British subjects entertain a confidence in the justice and moderation of this Government, notwithstanding all that has passed'; and in October, when these negotiations were on

[1] *Corr. rel. China*, pp. 454–8. [2] *Chin. Rep.*, July 1839.

the point of completion, it is expressly stated, in a memorandum of October 22nd,[1] by the Committee of the British merchants engaged in settling the commercial details, that 'the Committee further understood, from Her Majesty's chief superintendent, that on the arrangement for a recognized outside trade being completed, the injunctions against sending British property to Canton (*not ships*) will be withdrawn'.

In now arranging for the admission of goods he was indeed modifying his earlier declaration, but it was a purely technical modification in no sense affecting the essential principle. Elliot, in fact, whatever Lin's interpretation may have been, never for a moment in these negotiations intended that any single British ship or any single Englishman should be allowed within arm's length of the Cantonese authorities until insult and injustice had been punished.

If under these conditions the Chinese were willing to open an outside trade, well and good. Elliot could, with equanimity, await the arrival of further news from home.

Lin on his part insisted, as conditions preliminary to re-opening trade[2] and allowing British merchants to return to Macao to reside, that Elliot should collect and deliver all opium on board the British ships in Hong Kong Bay, should expel the British opium store-ships once and for all, and should send home sixteen named British merchants—the same sixteen that had been held as security for the original delivery of opium—alleged to have trafficked in the drug.

To all these requirements Elliot expressed himself as ready to accede, and took such steps as were open to him to give

---

[1] Ibid., Oct. 1839, and *Addl. Corr. rel. China*, Nov.–Dec.
[2] *Chin. Rep.*, Oct. 1839; *Addl. Corr. rel. China*, Oct.–Nov. 1839.

effect to them. On the matter of the bond (under which the ship's master was now to acknowledge, on behalf of himself, his officers and crew, liability to execution or strangulation at the hands of the Chinese if opium were found on board) Lin compromised and accepted as an alternative an arrangement by which the ship would proceed to Chuen Pei (outside the Bogue) and there discharge and submit to search. To his other demand—that an Englishman should be delivered over to answer for the death of Lin Wei Hi—Elliot returned a steady refusal.

Incidentally, during the course of protracted negotiations, a joint edict of High Commissioner and Viceroy, dated September 28th, enjoined upon Elliot, in plain allusion to earlier encounters with the Viceroy, to forward his reply in an open envelope and to cease carelessly using such expressions as 'mutual harmony'; a further reminder that he was dealing with a bitter enemy.

None the less a temporary agreement, strictly preserving Elliot's reservation, was on the point of being reached, indeed according to Elliot had specifically been concluded, when the English ship *Thomas Coutts*,[1] wholly disregarding the Superintendent and acting on legal advice from India, signed the objectionable bond and proceeded to Whampoa.

Here at last was that breach in the enemy's ranks which had proved so fatal to Napier's enterprise and for which Lin and Tang had so long worked in vain when pitted against Elliot!

Lin at once broke off negotiations—tore up the agreement, if you will—and issued manifestoes on October 25th, 26th, and 27th[2] threatening to surround and seize all English resi-

---

[1] *Addl. Corr. rel. China*, Oct.–Nov. 1839. [2] *Chin. Rep.*, Oct. 1839.

dents of Macao and to exterminate all the British ships at Hong Kong who did not, within three days, sign the bond.

'Regarding the murderer, Elliot must be required to send for trial the five men detained by him.[1] If he continue to oppose and delay, I must call upon the naval Commander-in-Chief to proceed at the head of the war vessels and fire ships, as also of the land soldiery encamped at all the various points of ingress that they may join in seizing the murderous foreigners.' (October 25th.)

'We have no course left but to send out war-vessels to proceed to Hong Kong, to surround and apprehend all the offenders, those connected with murders and those connected with opium, as well as the traitorous Chinese concealed on board the foreign vessels.' (October 27th.)[2]

Elliot's first reaction seems to have been one of anxiety lest the example of *Thomas Coutts* should be too much for some of the other British ships; and on October 26th he wrote to Captain Smith urging him to 'take immediate steps to prevent the future entrance of British shipping within the grasp of the Government—to the incalculably serious aggravation of all these dangers and difficulties'.[3]

But on learning of the High Commissioner's threats, and knowing that they were backed by a considerable array of force at the Bogue, he quickly changed his note and, in a letter of October 27th, invited Captain Smith to concert measures for the protection of the assembled merchant fleet against attack.

On October 28th *Volage*, with Elliot himself on board, and

---

[1] Elliot had, as the result of the findings of the court of inquiry of August 12th (*vide* p. 58, *supra*), found five British seamen guilty of brawling ashore on the critical date and confined them on shipboard pending their dispatch home.

[2] *Addl. Corr. rel. China*, Nov.–Dec. 1839.

[3] *Chin. Rep.*, Oct. 1839.

Hyacinth left Macao and proceeded to Chuen Pei, where, on arrival on November 2nd (through adverse winds), Captain Smith delivered a demand addressed to the High Commissioner for the withdrawal of his orders for the destruction of the merchant fleet; and for permission for the English merchants to reside without danger ashore.[1]

While they awaited the reply, the Chinese fleet was seen, on the morning of November 3rd, to 'break ground and stand out towards Her Majesty's ships', upon which Captain Smith delivered a peremptory order for their withdrawal. To this came the reply from the Chinese Admiral Kwan: 'For the moment I want one thing only—the murderer of Lin Wei Hi.' Whereupon Captain Smith, declaring that 'Elliot again and again solemnly repeats that he knows not the murderer of Lin Wei Hi', accepted the challenge and opened fire.

In the ensuing action the war-junks and fire-rafts, twenty-nine in all, suffered heavily[2] and retired in disorder.

This action, which came to be known as the first battle of Chuen Pei, was the opening act of the war.

Before the action Elliot had recommended that British merchant ships anchored in Hong Kong Bay should remove to Tong Kwu[3] (on the north-west of Castle Peak), and after its conclusion he insisted upon this course.

This evoked a protest by the ships' captains, supported by representatives of Lloyds, who urged that they should be allowed to remain in Hong Kong, pointing out that, besides having now a secure source of food-supply, Hong Kong provided better shelter in the south-west monsoon; moreover

[1] *Addl. Corr. rel. China*, Oct.–Nov. 1839.   [2] *Chin. Rep.*, Nov. 1839.
[3] *Addl. Corr. rel. China*, Nov.–Dec. 1839.

they claimed the move would be interpreted by the Chinese as a retreat.

Elliot, however, was adamant, remarking that he was not to be deterred by the chance of misinterpretation of his motives by the Chinese; and that questions of shelter from the south-west monsoon need not be considered till the wind began to blow from that quarter.

The reason which Elliot gave for the move was that Hong Kong was more exposed to attack by fire-craft than Tong Kwu; but on this point those who know the two places will no doubt agree with the shipmasters that Hong Kong Bay plainly had the advantage.

What then were his real motives? Writing on November 17th to Lord Palmerston he seems to suggest that he wished to remove the merchant fleet out of the way of temptation to attack the recently erected fort of Tseem Sha Chui.[1]

A contemporary writer, on the other hand, H. H. Lindsay (*Remarks on Occurrences in China*, p. 51), makes the suggestion that Elliot preferred Tong Kwu to Hong Kong because the former was much less convenient than Hong Kong for smuggling opium—a motive which Mr. Lindsay regarded as most unfair.

---

[1] In this connexion the following extract from the Imperial reply to the report of the Chuen Pei action perhaps throws some light upon this matter:
  'The foreign ship Smith, having seized upon a place called Kwan Chung as a stronghold and fastness, this is enough to show they harbour unfathomable designs in their hearts' (*Chin. Rep.*, vol. xi, p. 523 (Jan. 14));
which, being interpreted, means that H.M.S. *Volage* (Captain Smith) was in the habit of anchoring off Kwoon Ch'ung (Bowring Street), Kowloon Peninsula—thereby placing herself between the Chinese battery and the English merchantmen; a habit which, I conjecture, accounts for the present man-of-war anchorage at the spot and possibly the naval establishments on the foreshore adjoining.

For my own part I would suggest that his anxiety to prevent British ships entering the Bogue must have played a substantial part in deciding him in the first instance. To effect this it was plainly necessary that *Volage* and *Hyacinth*, at any rate, should take station in the Canton river estuary (and Tong Kwu was the natural anchorage); but if the rest of the shipping were to stay in Hong Kong Bay they would be unprotected. Hence his original notice, dated October 26th, to shipmasters.

Almost immediately afterwards other considerations supervened, and the role of *Volage* and *Hyacinth* changed; but, in the face of open hostilities with the Chinese fleet, the need for concentration under the eyes of Her Majesty's ships, now engaged in watching the Bogue, clearly lost none of its urgency.

It thus came about that Hong Kong Bay, which, for the last eight months, had sheltered upwards of sixty-six[1] British merchant ships, was once more deserted.

[1] *Chin. Rep.*, Sept. 1839.

CHAPTER VII

ELLIOT

1840 and 1841

On November 20th Elliot gave notice that he had requested the Senior Naval Officer to prevent the entrance of British ships to the Bogue; and on November 26th the High Commissioner, jointly with the Viceroy and Hoppo (Customs Commissioner), announced the Imperial will that trade with the English nation should cease for ever; allowing, however, until December 6th[1] for individuals to make up their minds.

It appears, none the less, that, despite an edict of December 18th forbidding the practice, the transference of British cargoes to other foreign bottoms continued.

On the 26th occurred the piquant case of the capture off Tong Kwu of Mr. Gribble, a member of the crew of *Royal Saxon*, the only British ship to follow the example of *Thomas Coutts* and enter the Bogue. On receiving the news *Volage* and *Hyacinth* hastened to the scene; but Mr. Gribble was, of course, released with unction as 'a good Englishman' on mentioning the name of his ship—clear proof that Elliot's apprehension for the safety of Englishmen in Chinese hands was mere hallucination!

On January 1st, 1840, with a view to saving demurrage and allowing ships to clear, Elliot applied to the Governor of Macao for leave to deposit cargoes there under pledge that they would not be put into the China trade. The Chinese

[1] *Chin. Rep.*, Jan. 1840.

authorities, naturally, not being disposed to relieve him of any of his difficulties, declined consent and retorted with a threat to seize Elliot and other Englishmen who had quietly resumed residence at Macao. Elliot thereupon asked the Portuguese Governor for a military guard, and, on its being declined in the name of strict neutrality, called *Hyacinth* into the harbour 'to show the flag'. A rapid exchange of notes ensued, and Captain Smith, bowing to the storm, withdrew; while Elliot once more took up his abode on ship-board.[1]

On March 24th H.M.S. *Druid* (44 guns) arrived at Tong Kwu. Six weeks later, June 3rd, her commander, Lord John Churchill, fourth son of the Duke of Marlborough, died, and was buried at Macao. With the change of the monsoon the merchant fleet removed to Kap Sing Mun, where in June it successfully survived an attack by ten fire-rafts.[2]

About the same time[3] as the arrival of *Druid* the first rumours reached Canton of an impending British expedition from India, and on 25th April, the American merchants having referred to the matter in a petition to the High Commissioner, Lin (who had, on Tang's transfer to Yunnan, been appointed Viceroy) scouted the idea as an egregious mistake, and bordering on falsehood.[4]

It was, however, no idle rumour, for in point of fact, on receipt of Elliot's 'SOS' of April 3rd, 1839, written in confinement at Canton, and of the petition of Dent and other British merchants of May 23rd (which, conveyed by *Ariel*,

---

[1] *Chin. Rep.*, Feb. 1840.

[2] The matter at one time looked unpleasant, but, in the words of an eyewitness—Commander Bingham, author of *The Expedition to China, 1840*—'the boats of the men-of-war quickly hooking on to these formidable looking fire-ships towed them ashore on The Brothers'. [3] *Chin. Rep.*, July 1840. [4] Ibid., May 1840.

specially chartered, had reached London in September), the British Government had taken prompt decisions, as a result of which a considerable fleet and expeditionary force was forthwith collected and equipped for service in China.

The supreme command was entrusted to Rear-Admiral the Hon. George Elliot, a cousin of the Chief Superintendent; with Commodore Sir James John Gordon Bremer and Lieutenant-General Sir Hugh Gough commanding the naval and military forces respectively. Admiral Elliot was, in addition, appointed Senior Plenipotentiary with Captain Elliot as his junior colleague.

The objects of the expedition—as expressed at length in a formal note dated February 20th, 1840,[1] addressed by Lord Palmerston to the minister of the Emperor—may be summarized as follows: first, the restoration of the valuable goods extorted in April 1839 by way of ransom for the lives of British subjects (or the monetary equivalent of those goods); second, satisfaction for the affront, 'during the last year', to Her Majesty's Superintendent—Elliot, be it observed—and a guarantee of treatment on terms of strict equality for the future; third, satisfaction for the violence offered to Her Majesty's subjects, and security for British traders for the future; and fourth, the payment of the 'Hong' debts to the British merchants.

The specific method by which the second and third demands were to be secured was, alternatively, the cession of an island or the granting of a detailed Treaty of Commerce providing, *inter alia*, under proper safeguards, for the establishment of factories on the mainland.

[1] Morse, *International Relations*, Appendix A.

In either of these alternatives, the cession of an island or the grant of a Treaty of Commerce, the opening of three or four ports on the east coast, so as to break the monopoly of Canton, was to be insisted on; except only that if, all other demands conceded, the Chinese stood out upon this one, then the cession of an island off the east coast, with full liberty to the Chinese to come thither to trade, might be accepted as a sufficient equivalent.[1]

The method to be adopted to serve these ends was to be neither simple war nor simple negotiation; but negotiation after the seizure of pledges. In plain words the ports along the coast were to be blockaded by the fleet, trading-junks were to be seized and detained, and, above all, the island of Chusan, lying off Ningpo, was to be occupied; simultaneously copies of Palmerston's note were to be proffered first at Canton, then at the mouth of the Yang Tze, and finally at the mouth of the Pei Ho.

In pursuance of these objects the fleet, consisting of three line-of-battle ships (seventy-two guns) and some fifteen frigates and sloops and four armed steamers of the Honourable Company, together with transports conveying the 18th regiment (Royal Irish), 26th (Cameronians) regiment of foot, 49th regiment, Bengal Volunteers, Madras Artillery, sappers, and miners, duly arrived off the Ladrones towards the latter end of June; and H.M.S. *Wellesley*, flying the broad pennant of Commodore Bremer, proceeded to Macao and thence to her old anchorage at Tong Kwu, whence a formal declaration of the blockade of the Canton river was issued on the 22nd.[2]

A conference then ensued between the two plenipotentia-

---

[1] Morse, *International Relations*, Appendix A.   [2] *Chin. Rep.*, June 1840.

ries at which the decision was, no doubt, reached not to proffer Palmerston's note at Canton (and so give Lin the first intimation of the business in hand): and accordingly, on 30th June, the main body of the fleet proceeded northwards taking Captain Elliot with them.

It was at this juncture[1] that Lin issued a proclamation, in strict accord with Chinese usage of the time, offering a scale of rewards for the capture or destruction of British ships of war or the seizure of Englishmen, combatant or non-combatant, dead or (preferably) alive.

On August 6th Mr. Staunton,[2] a divinity student of the mildest manners, was abducted while bathing at Macao, the firstfruits of Lin's manifesto; while six weeks later Lieutenant Douglas and Mrs. Noble, wrecked in the armed brig *Kite* off Chusan, and Captain Anstruther, surrounded and captured at Tinghai, fell into Chinese hands. China also had taken pledges.

On August 19th, unusual activity and the concentration of artillery and Chinese troops having been noted at the Barrier Fort at Macao, the senior naval officer, Captain Smith (now transferred to *Druid*), replied with a prompt and effective bombardment; the Governor of Macao preserving the most correct neutrality.

Meanwhile, in the north, Tinghai, the port of Chusan, was duly occupied on July 5th;[3] and Palmerston's note, rejected at Amoy and Ningpo, was delivered at the mouth of the Pei Ho on August 9th; where, on the 30th, an interview took place between Keshen, a Manchu, member of the Imperial Council and Viceroy of Chihli province, and Captain Elliot.

The reader may here pause to ask why, on an occasion so

[1] Ibid., July 1840.   [2] Ibid., Aug. 1840.   [3] Ibid., Feb. 1841.

clearly momentous, the junior plenipotentiary alone attended. The answer is perhaps to be found in Palmerston's instructions. Consistently with the theory that it was unsafe to allow British subjects or even officials to fall into Chinese hands and that the plenipotentiaries were there to demand redress and not to sue for favours, the Foreign Secretary had stipulated that the Chinese plenipotentiary should preferably be induced to attend on board[1] one of Her Majesty's ships; but if the Chinese utterly refused, then, under suitable conditions, a meeting on shore might legitimately be arranged.[2] The arrangement, therefore, by which the second plenipotentiary attended on shore was clearly a highly convenient compromise.

There is, however, the alternative possibility that Admiral Elliot, who, three months later, was compelled to resign by reason of severe ill health,[3] was already unfit to undertake the task.

The conference lasted six hours, 'during which period the loud voices of the plenipotentiaries, in high argument, had often struck upon the ears' of the British officers in immediate attendance.[4]

The upshot of the meeting was that, while Chusan was to be held in pledge, military action in Chekiang province (and presumably farther north) was to be stayed; and negotiations were to be resumed in Canton.[5]

---

[1] Morse, *International Relations*, Appendix A, p. 625.
[2] Ibid., Appendix B, p. 628.
[3] See note, p. 287 of Morse, *International Relations*. The sickness had been reported, for Palmerston replied in March 1841.
[4] Jocelyn, *Six Months with the Chinese Expedition*, p. 115.
[5] *Chin. Rep.*, Feb. 1841.

This arrangement was, on September 17th, ratified by the Emperor, and Keshen himself appointed plenipotentiary; Lin being ordered ten days later to hand over his seals and proceed forthwith in disgrace to Pekin.

Meantime, while the British plenipotentiaries were on their way back to Chusan, Captain Anstruther and the survivors of the *Kite* had fallen into Chinese hands; but the plenipotentiaries decided, on learning the news, that they could not properly break off their engagements just made, on that account.

Accordingly, on November 6th, after Captain Elliot had personally secured guarantees of fair treatment[1] for the hostages, the armistice was duly announced at Chusan and the plenipotentiaries proceeded to Macao, where they arrived on November 20th with the bulk of the force.

On the 25th the Honourable Company's iron steamer *Nemesis*[2] (Captain W. H. Hall), destined later to perform astonishing feats in the Canton estuary, reached Tong Kwu.

On the 29th it was announced that Admiral Elliot had resigned owing to sudden and serious ill health,[3] the announcement itself even being under the signature of Captain Elliot alone.

Captain Elliot thus was once more left to his own judgement; though he had now clear instructions and a considerable military force with which to compel compliance. In point of fact, in the month of December 1840, the following

---

[1] Ouchterlony, *The Chinese War*, p. 72. [2] Bernard, *Voyage of the Nemesis*.
[3] *Chin. Rep.*, Nov. 1840, &c. See also *Canton Press*, Aug. 18th. Rear-Admiral Elliot arrived in *Volage* at Portsmouth on May 6th 'in a rather improved though still very delicate state of health'.

British ships lay at anchor off the Bogue:[1] *Wellesley, Blenheim, Melville* (72), *Druid* (44), *Calliope, Samarang, Herald* (26), *Larne, Hyacinth, Modeste* (18), *Columbine* (16), *Sulphur* (8) (surveying-vessel), *Starling* (tender to *Sulphur*), *Jupiter, Louisa* (cutter), and the steamers *Queen, Enterprise, Madagascar*, and *Nemesis*.

Elliot's first act was to secure the release, on December 12th, of Mr. Staunton; a diplomatic gesture on the part of Keshen.[2] But thereafter negotiations lagged (as no doubt Keshen intended they should); and on January 6th Elliot, weary of the delay (and anxious, perhaps, for the health of the troops at Chusan), delivered an ultimatum; and, on the following day, January 7th, called upon the armed forces to assault the batteries of Tai Kok and Sha Kok comprising the outer defences of the Bogue.[3] This operation, known as the second battle of Chuen Pei, was promptly effected at negligible cost to the attackers, and enabled Elliot to announce from Macao on January 20th 'the completion of preliminary arrangements between the Imperial commissioner and himself' involving, *inter alia*, 'The cession of the island and harbour of Hong Kong to the British Crown. All just charges and duties to the Empire upon the commerce carried on there to be paid as if the trade was conducted at Whampoa.'[4] These arrangements provided also (in view of the fact that it would take time before commerce was actually practicable at Hong Kong) that trade should reopen within ten days of the New Year—that is to say by February 1st, being meanwhile conducted at Whampoa.

[1] *Chin. Rep.*, Jan. 1841, p. 57.
[2] Ibid., Feb. 1841, p. 118.
[3] Ibid., Dec. 1840.
[4] Ibid., Jan. 1841.

Hong Kong was, in effect, to be ceded in exchange for Chusan, and the forts and junks lately taken at the Bogue to be restored in return for the British prisoners at Ningpo.

Upon what date or dates these exchanges were to be effected does not precisely appear, but the reference to China New Year almost certainly provides the clue. China New Year's day was January 23rd; and we may be fairly sure that, the forts and junks having been given back, and a written undertaking to evacuate Chusan delivered into Keshen's hands, Elliot was to be free to take possession of Hong Kong on China New Year's day; a definitive treaty to be signed by the end of the moon—i.e. on February 21st—by which date the evacuation of Chusan would be completed and the hostages restored.

Elliot forthwith returned the forts on January 21st and, having handed to Keshen for transmission to Elepoo, Viceroy of Chekiang, a 'document by virtue of which he may receive back Tinghai',[1] and dispatched to Chusan, by H.M.S. *Columbine*, an officer to effect the evacuation, withdrew the fleet to Hong Kong harbour.[2]

The chronicler's task at this point becomes more complex, for now occurs that interesting event which forms the real starting-point of this narrative—the planting of a British Colony; and the reader will naturally expect to listen henceforward to a careful record of each stage in its vitally important early growth. But the beginning of a British colony in China does not synchronize with the end of relations with the Chinese; and while others plant the British flag on Hong Kong island and supervise the early beginnings of a British

[1] Ibid., April 1841, p. 236.   [2] Bernard, *Voyage of Nemesis*.

establishment, the founder concentrates his efforts upon securing from the Chinese authorities, by negotiation and if need be by force, an assurance for the Colony of a suitable status *vis-à-vis* the neighbouring continent.

The narrative therefore consists now of two main strands, the progress of the colony and the progress of the demand for recognition; but though they are closely interwoven, for example the 'Union' is run up on the island on the very day that Elliot is closeted with Keshen at the Second Bar, to attempt to handle the two simultaneously would merely mean constantly breaking the thread of both.

I adopt, therefore, the expedient of first following Captain Elliot through the tangled skein of conversations at the Bogue and inconclusive assaults at Canton, before inviting the reader to turn back and attend the simpler function—the birthday of Hong Kong.

Having dispatched the fleet, Elliot proceeded without a day's delay to press on with negotiations for a definitive treaty; but before we attempt to follow him, it is as well to point out that, unlike the period leading up to hostilities, which is fully covered by British official documents, we rely in the main, for the period of negotiation, on Chinese sources —dispatches, that is to say, submitted by Keshen (or Keshen's successors or judges) to the Emperor, and the Imperial replies—with incidental guidance from English sources, notably Bernard's *Voyage of the Nemesis*, the vessel which Elliot regularly employed to convey him at this time.

The story therefore tends occasionally to become obscure, and the truth is only to be arrived at by the somewhat technical process of calculating 'windage', or, in other words, assessing the allowance to be made for the language of Oriental officials addressing their Imperial master.

On January 26th, 27th, Keshen, who since reaching Canton had thus far declined all personal interviews with Elliot, met him, with considerable ceremony, at the Second Bar Pagoda[1] on the Canton river; when a rough draft of the treaty, chiefly concerning the ' "minutiae" of commerce', was presented, in which, incidentally, the English plenipotentiary expressly agreed to the confiscation of both ship and cargo in the event of opium being found on board a British vessel.

According to the official report of Keshen's impeachment a second interview took place, on February 6th,[2] at the Bogue; and it is certain that the two met again at the Bogue on February 11th;[3] when Elliot 'earnestly besought that the whole of Hong Kong should be given to him', but Keshen (playing desperately for time) 'withheld consent'[4] and gained a respite of an odd ten days while the final treaty was drafted.

On the 14th—Bernard is here our informant—*Nemesis* proceeded to the Bogue with the final draft for delivery to Keshen,[5] and, having waited for a reply the stipulated four days, returned empty-handed. Accordingly on the 19th orders to the fleet to move up to the Bogue were issued; and on February 22nd Elliot 'once more proceeded to the Bogue where he remained about an hour as if in anxious expectation of some communication' from Keshen;[6] failing which he finally left the situation in the hands of the navy.

[1] Bernard, *Nemesis*, vol. i, p. 294; *Chin. Rep.*, April 1841.
[2] Ibid., Oct. 1841, p. 591.   [3] Ibid.; Bernard, *Nemesis*, vol. i, p. 307.
[4] *Chin. Rep.*, Oct. 1841.   [5] Bernard, *Nemesis*, vol. i, p. 312.   [6] Ibid., p. 326.

The Chinese account—I refer again to the official report of Keshen's trial[1]—here fills an interesting gap, for we are told that

'on the 19th being anxious for the safety of the Bogue, [Keshen] sent Paou Chung—[interpreter and ex-comprador]—to present a document in which it was stated to them that they could proceed to Hong Kong to remain there for the time being ... and ordering them to keep quiet, as the negotiations would be determined after an answer had arrived in reply to the clear memorial which had been made to the Court. Paou Chung was also ordered that if the barbarians did not manifest obedient tempers then to take the document and bring it back. Paou Chung, having seen the barbarians and finding their designs to be murderous and wicked, withheld the document.'[2]

It may conveniently be added here that the charge which Keshen had to face on impeachment was that he 'became willing, in behalf of the English, to memorialize the Emperor to give them the region of Hong Kong as a place at which to dwell: [whereby] The said barbarians, intently scheming to have the rule of the place, immediately issued their false proclamations there and spread out their tents'.[3] The inquiry showed that 'he, without delay, fully delivered Hong Kong over to the English, for the time, not daring to deceive them' —(a serious act of omission)—'nor persevering to receive the things they had to offer' (i.e. Chusan);[4] and the final conclusion and sentence was that 'He incoherently presented them a place to dwell at, and for the time being gave Hong Kong to them, which is the excuse they give for taking possession of it. ... We sentence him to be beheaded, but to be imprisoned until after autumn and then to be executed.'[5]

[1] *Chin. Rep.*, Oct. 1841, p. 591. [2] Ibid. [3] Ibid.
[4] Ibid. [5] Ibid.

ELLIOT, 1840 AND 1841   79

Keshen (who, of course, was not beheaded) was between the devil and the deep sea, as the dates of the various Imperial edicts clearly show. Thus on January 20th,[1] the very day of the announcement of the preliminary agreement, and on the 26th,[2] the very day of the formal meeting to settle the outstanding details, he received decrees from Pekin announcing the decision to make 'a most dreadful example of severity' and 'an awful display of celestial vengeance'. On or about February 6th, in reply to his dispatch reporting the engagement of January 7th,[3] he received the Emperor's rebuke and the announcement of the approach of reinforcements 'within the second month'[4] (starting on February 21st); and on February 11th,[5] the day of the final interview with Elliot, he received the Imperial decree of January 20th announcing the appointment of Yik Shan as 'General pacificator of the rebellious' and his two colleagues, Yang Fang and Lung Wan. On March 12th, no doubt on receipt of a reply to his main dispatch[6] (of which the exact date is not known) recounting the result of negotiations up to January 26th, and urgently requesting ratification, Keshen retired in disgrace, indeed in chains, from Canton.[7]

But if Keshen's arrangements were thus sweepingly rejected by the Emperor, Elliot's were no less indignantly repudiated by Palmerston.[8] His dispatch of January 21st announcing the

---

[1] Ibid., April 1841.   [2] Ibid.   [3] Ibid., Feb. 1841.
[4] Ibid.   [5] Ibid., p. 119.   [6] Ibid., April 1841.
[7] Ibid., March 1841.
[8] Queen Victoria was very angry too, but finally decided, at any rate *vis-à-vis* the world, to pass it off as a joke, and she writes to the King of the Belgians:
'I think, dear uncle, that you would find the East not only as "absurd" as the West, but very barbarous, cruel and dangerous into the bargain. . . . Albert is so

cession of the island was in fact the last which the Foreign Secretary received before deciding to supersede him.[1] That decision was conveyed in a dispatch of April 21st, the very day on which a deputation of the East India and China Association, including Mr. W. Jardine (who explained at length the difficulties of transferring the seat of trade from Canton to Hong Kong),[2] waited upon the Foreign Secretary to inform him that not only traders resident in China but the merchants of Calcutta, Bombay, and London had entirely lost their confidence in Captain Elliot.

Palmerston, in his dispatch, faithfully pointed out to Elliot that he had failed to secure full compensation for the opium which he had taken upon himself to deliver over, had got nothing in respect either of the debts due by the Hong merchants or of the expenses of the expedition, had secured no additional openings for trade farther north, and had sealed his failure, contrary to express orders, by prematurely restoring Chusan.

In return he had 'obtained the cession of Hong Kong, a barren island with hardly a house upon it', and incidentally a cession clogged with conditions which left it doubtful whether the sovereignty had really been yielded.

'It seems obvious', he concludes (though carefully allowing the possibility of being mistaken), 'that Hong Kong will not be the mart of trade any more than Macao is so. . . . Our commercial transactions will be carried on, as heretofore, at Canton, where our mer-

---

much amused at my having got the Island of Hong Kong, and we think Victoria ought to be called Princess of Hong Kong in addition to Princess Royal. She drives out every day in a close carriage with the window open, &c. . . .'
(*The Letters of Queen Victoria*, vol. i, p. 329.)

[1] Morse, *International Relations*, Appendix G.   [2] *Canton Press*, July 31st.

chants will be, as hitherto, at the mercy of the Chinese; but they will be able to go and build houses to retire to in the desert island of Hong Kong instead of passing the non-trading months at Macao.'

This dispatch could not, of course, reach its destination for some three months, and while it is being conveyed across the world we must resume the story of the operations at Canton.

On February 23rd, 'the Imperial minister having failed to conclude the treaty of peace lately agreed upon by H.M.'s plenipotentiary, within the allotted period'[1]—I quote Elliot's official announcement of February 24th—hostilities were resumed; and on February 26th Elliot was able to announce to Her Majesty's subjects the complete capture of the batteries of the Bogue.[2]

Simultaneously (the date, February 20th, given in the *Chinese Repository* being a palpable misprint) Bremer announced that permission would be given to British and foreign ships to return to the Bogue and, in due course, to proceed higher up the river.[3]

The Chinese responded with a manifesto, in the traditional manner, dated February 27th,[4] under the hand of the Lieutenant-Governor, offering a scale of rewards—including $50,000 for Elliot, Bremer, or Morrison[5] (a curious indication of the value of interpreters) if taken alive and $30,000 for the head only. The manifesto, incidentally, drew a distinction between Englishmen and foreigners of all other nations, but did not explain how unfortunate mistakes were to be avoided.

Meanwhile the British naval light division, including *Cal-*

[1] *Chin. Rep.*, Feb. 1841, p. 116. [2] Ibid. [3] Ibid.
[4] Ibid., March, p. 174. [5] J. R. Morrison, son of the Rev. Robert Morrison.

liope with Elliot himself on board, pressed on up river, and at 9 p.m. on the 27th Elliot announced by circular to Her Majesty's subjects the capture, in face of obstinate resistance, of one hundred pieces of artillery off the Brunswick Rock in the Whampoa Reach.[1]

In the course of this engagement the late British ship *Cambridge*, re-named *Chesapeake*,[2] anchored to protect the rafts stretched across the river at this point, was blown up. This vessel had a curious career. She first appeared in Hong Kong Bay on August 27th, 1839, having been armed with twenty-two eighteen-pounder guns in Singapore by her master, Captain Douglas,[3] apparently on the off-chance of being able to render assistance. As it turned out her arrival was opportune, and she got the thanks of Elliot for services rendered at the affair at Kowloon on September 4th. She was subsequently sold to an American firm, Russell & Co., and in June 1840, immediately before the blockade was established, she was loaded[4] 'her deck full to the rail with English goods valued at £150,000 and sent to Whampoa'; and in due course sold again to Lin to form part of his elaborate improvisation for the defence of Canton against the English.

The road to Canton was now wide open; but Elliot, having on March 3rd allowed an armistice[5] of three days, checked further action against the city itself and issued a general invitation to resume trade[6]—a gesture to which the city authorities responded, not without certain grounds of logic, by giving pilot-passes exclusively[7] to foreign merchants other

---

[1] *Chin. Rep.*, March, p. 179. [2] *Corr. rel. China*; *Chin. Rep.*, Sept. 1842.
[3] Ibid.   [4] Hunter's *Fan Kwai in Canton*, p. 147.
[5] *Chin. Rep.*, March 1841, p. 180. [6] Ibid. [7] Ibid., March 1841.

than English. Elliot then returned to Macao, to reappear a few days later, as if by magic, having safely negotiated the Broadway in *Nemesis*,[1] a considerable feat considering the length of the ship and the narrow and tortuous character of the channel.

On March 19th the light naval division closed in upon the town,[2] carrying, in the course of two hours, 'all the works in immediate advance and before the city' (the Dutch Folly inclusive),[3] and Canton was at their mercy.

On March 20th Elliot, established in the hall of the British factory (where he had been detained with the British merchants almost exactly two years before), announced by circular once more the suspension of hostilities, having effected (with Yang, the only one of the three special Commissioners thus far to have arrived) an *ad hoc* agreement designed exclusively to ensure the resumption of trade; the British naval forces to remain meantime *in situ*.[4]

This was immediately followed by a Public Notice by Bremer, dated March 21st,[5] to British and foreign merchants giving effect indeed to Elliot's arrangement but warning them, significantly, that if they resumed trade they did so at the risk of sudden resumption of hostilities.

Two days later Bremer left *en route* for Calcutta, leaving Sir Humphrey Le Fleming Senhouse as Senior Naval Officer, to return in mid-June armed with a commission as joint Plenipotentiary.

Whence the commission emanated is not clear, but the most likely guess is that on receipt, presumably about February 1st, of the news of Admiral Elliot's collapse, the Home Govern-

---

[1] Bernard, *Nemesis*, vol. i, p. 367. [2] *Chin. Rep.*, March 1841. [3] Ibid., p. 181.
[4] Ibid., p. 182. [5] Ibid.

ment forthwith endorsed Captain Elliot's automatic elevation to the post of Senior Envoy and appointed Bremer, the Senior Naval Officer, to the vacancy, a decision which would reach India in mid-April. Indeed the fact that Bremer signed the manifesto posted in Hong Kong on February 1st jointly with Elliot (see Chap. VIII, p. 94, *infra*) lends colour to the suggestion that Elliot of his own initiative informed the Home Government of his intention to regard Bremer as his colleague pending further orders. But, if this is so, it is certain that the arrangement was still-born; for (as we shall see) after an interval of barely six months a further dispatch, announcing the appointment of Pottinger and Parker in succession to Elliot and Bremer, followed hot-foot across the world.

Elliot's declaration of March 20th was followed by the return of British merchants to their old residences in Canton and of the shipping, so long detained outside the Bogue, to the familiar anchorage at Whampoa—'so that at the beginning of the month, the river was again crowded with passers to and fro and the foreign factories showed signs of becoming again what they formerly were'.[1]

During April Yik Shan,[2] the 'general pacificator', and Lung Wan joined their colleague Yang Fang at Canton, and Chinese reinforcements from external provinces, long ago set in motion by the Emperor, began to pour in. Elliot, however, was able to announce from the factories on April 16th: 'a satisfactory communication has this day been received from Yang declaring the faithful intention of his colleagues',[3] and the following day returned to Macao. But on May 10th, learning

[1] *Chin. Rep.*, April 1841, p. 233.
[2] *Vide supra*, p. 79.
[3] *Chin. Rep.*, April 1841, p. 234.

of many palpable signs of hostile military activity at Canton,[1] he hastened back there, indicating, however, his reluctance to attribute ill faith to the Chinese authorities by taking his wife with him.[2] The visit apparently decided him;[3] and on the 17th the British military expedition under Sir Hugh Gough which was in readiness to proceed to Amoy, presumably with the idea of imposing further terms, perhaps the opening of alternative ports, was diverted to Canton.

On the 21st, despite a proclamation of the day before by the prefect[4] informing the foreign merchants that they could remain without fear at the factories, Elliot issued a brief circular recommending them to retire from Canton before sunset.[5]

It was a timely precaution. At 11 p.m. fire-rafts, of which there were over two hundred, were floated off against the naval ships. Next day first Chinese troops and then the rabble successively looted the factories; and on the 24th Sir Hugh Gough and Sir Le Fleming Senhouse (acting Commodore in the absence of Bremer) moved up their forces for an attack on the city; and a general action ensued.

It would be out of place to describe the action in detail here, but the following two extracts from contemporary accounts, the first taken from the official report of Yik Shan to the Emperor, the second from an English eyewitness, are perhaps worthy of record:

'A number of native traitors, dressed like sailors, in the confusion got into our ships which were filled with paddy-straw and set fire to them right and left and burned the greater part of the fuel in the rear of our troops.'[6]

---

[1] See *Chin. Rep.*, May 1841, p. 293. [2] Ibid. [3] Ibid., July 1841, p. 402.
[4] Ibid., p. 294. [5] Ibid. [6] Ibid., p. 402.

'The guns were loaded and primed. The port fires were lit, and the general and the commodore were taking a last look, previous to giving the signal to commence firing. . . . A few minutes more and the work would have commenced had not an unlooked-for message arrived with dispatches from the plenipotentiary.'[1]

Yet once more Elliot had intervened to save the city. Having received overtures on May 27th he demanded the retirement within six days to a distance of sixty *li* (twenty miles) of all extra-provincial troops, and the payment within one week of $6,000,000; and was able on June 3rd to announce substantial compliance with the demands.

Captain Elliot's exact object in demanding a fine and in fixing the amount at this particular figure was the subject of much speculation at the time. Was it merely the sort of figure which the city was considered capable of putting up by way of ransom in the recognized Oriental manner? Or was it a levy-in-aid of the cost of the expeditionary force? Or was it, as others alleged (stressing particularly the similarity of the amount exacted with the assumed value of the confiscated opium), compensation to private merchants for losses sustained?

n. 4   For these exertions he was honoured by the appearance, on May 29th at Casa Branca, Macao, of a Notice, ostensibly under the hand of Yik Shan and his colleagues, amending general orders relating to rewards; the new scale promising $100,000 instead of $50,000 for Elliot (in addition to official rank and a peacock's feather) while Dent and Thom (an interpreter) were added to the select list valued at $50,000.

[1] *Chin. Rep.*, July 1841, p. 395.

Two further extracts from the report of Yik Shan are of some interest for our particular purpose:

'Inquiring of them regarding Hong Kong, if they would give it back, they answered that it had been given to them by the minister Keshen, and that of its being so given to them they possessed documentary evidence'; and 'your minister, in turning the matter over and over again, ... deemed it was his undoubted duty to draw the enemy forth without the Bocca Tigris; and then to renew all fortifications, and seek another occasion for attacking and destroying them at Hong Kong and thus to restore the ancient territory.'[1]

The British troops withdrew from their position (behind the north and north-east gates) on June 1st,[2] and on the 5th left the river and returned to Hong Kong.

Elliot himself returned forthwith to Macao, whence, on the 7th, he advertised the forthcoming sale of land at Hong Kong and broadcast his invitation to merchants to resort there freely to trade.

n. 5

On the 17th Sir Humphrey Le Fleming Senhouse, Senior Naval Officer, having died four days before in Hong Kong as a result of his strenuous efforts[3] in the heat at Canton, was buried at Macao. And the very next day Bremer returned from Calcutta[4] armed with his appointment as joint plenipotentiary.

Five days later the appointment of Mr. A. R. Johnston, deputy Superintendent, to act as Governor of Hong Kong[5] on behalf of the Chief Superintendent, was announced; Elliot, with the office and archives of the Superintendency, remaining at Macao.

[1] Ibid., June, p. 347.
[2] Ibid., p. 350.
[3] Ibid., 1841, p. 352.
[4] Ibid., p. 352.
[5] Ibid., p. 351.

On July 20th, together with Bremer, who was on his way to rejoin his flagship *Wellesley*,[1] Elliot embarked on the cutter *Louisa*, bound, in company with *Young Hebe*, for Hong Kong. The wind gradually freshened 'to about a double-reefed topsail breeze . . .', and on July 21st

'At about 12.30 o'clock we weighed again and endeavoured to weather the island of Ichow but could not; and the cutter being close to the shore, and having missed stays twice, we were compelled to go to leeward of it. Wind north, a little westerly: course to Hong Kong, north east. Attempted to work to windward, but could do nothing; cutter again missed stays, and in wearing when the mainsail was jibed, the main-boom snapped in halves. We double-reefed the sail, got a sheet aft, and tried her under that sail, with the mizzen, fore-stay sail, and jib, but she was lagging away to leeward so fast that we were forced to anchor between Ichow and Chichow with a reef of rocks astern of us; as we anchored the mizzen bumkin went. . . .'

n. 6

Louisa had, in less nautical language, met a typhoon (*Young Hebe* having returned dismasted to Macao after narrowly escaping shipwreck near Dumbbell Island), and ultimately ran ashore on one of the Ladrones and broke up. Elliot, we may be sure, lent a hand:

' "Hard a port" and "hard a starboard" were shouted in quick succession by Captain Elliot, who was standing forward holding on by the fore rigging; . . . and we passed within a few yards of a smooth granite precipice. . . . We were within 30 yards of the rocks, and embayed . . . we slowly drifted towards the shore, Captain Elliot conning her. . . .'

Barely saved from the sea, the plenipotentiaries now fell into the hands of the Chinese inhabitants of the island; but

[1] *Chin. Rep.*, p. 406, July 1841.

contrived, after some bargaining (with $100,000 and $50,000 respectively on their heads), to secure a passage to Macao for $3,000. There Elliot appeared in 'a Manila hat, a jacket, no shirt and a pair of striped trousers and shoes' on the evening of July 23rd.

The next day he read in the local press[1] the news, to be confirmed on the arrival on the 29th[2] of the steamer *Phlegethon* with official dispatches, of his supersession.

On August 10th his successor, Sir Henry Pottinger, Bart., Her Majesty's sole plenipotentiary in China, arrived in company with Sir William Parker, K.C.B., Rear-Admiral and Commander-in-Chief of the East India station; and on August 24th Captain Elliot with his lady and family[3] embarked on board the Honourable Company's steamer *Atalanta*, which proceeded to sea the same evening.

[1] *Canton Press*, July 24th.
[2] Ibid., July 31st, and *Nemesis*, vol. ii, p. 114.   [3] *Chin. Rep.*, Aug. 1841, p. 479.

CHAPTER VIII

THE BIRTH OF VICTORIA
1841

Having taken farewell of Elliot we must now concentrate on our primary objective, the island of Hong Kong.

And here is a convenient opportunity to touch briefly on the subject of the island's name. The origin of the name Hong Kong has been suggested in an earlier chapter. To Englishmen plain Hong Kong (or at least Hongkong) has always sufficed, whether for the Colony as a whole, for the island, or for the city (formally designated Victoria) on its northern slopes. Not so, however, for the Chinese, amongst whom, or at any rate among that section which dwells on the shores of the harbour, the place is familiarly known as Kwan Tai Lo. Besides verbal tradition the name Kwan Tai Lo has documentary support. Thus when Keshen, the plenipotentiary, consulted Tang, the Viceroy of Canton, on the subject of offering the island to Elliot, the latter, according to *The Chinese Account of the Opium War*,[1] argued that 'it occupied a prominent and central position in Canton waters, sheltered from bad weather by the two islands of Tsim Sha Choü and Kwan Tai Lo'. The name appears also in the earliest list of place-names on the island published in the *Government Gazette* of May 15th, 1841, where it is described as a 'fishing village of 50 souls';[2] and it appears also (in a slightly altered form) in a later list dated August 1843. It was cut, too, on

[1] E. H. Parker, 1888.   [2] See Appendix II; *Chin. Rep.*, vol. xii.

the tall granite pillars which marked the miles along the military bridle-path from town to Chekchu (Stanley) and also along the road from town to Aberdeen.

This evidence, taken together, should leave us in no doubt as to the situation of the place; for the 1843 list, in other respects, is a list of familiar place-names along the sea-shore given in their proper order from West to East, and we may therefore surely conclude that Kwan Tai Lo, which appears in the list between Ha Wan and Wong Nei Chung, was in fact situated somewhere between these two places.

Moreover, given our milestones (and the third and fourth starting from town towards Stanley and the second, third, fourth, and fifth along the road to Aberdeen are still *in situ*), n. 1 ought we not to be able, at the expenditure of very little energy, to trace back the routes to their source, the presumptive site of Kwan Tai Lo?

But in point of fact tradition has invested the name with at least one curious meaning—the 'petticoat-girdle road', and this has evoked endless speculation. Dr. Eitel, in particular, has indulged in some wild flights, postulating, in the face of all probability, the existence of a tow-path high above the beach, along which, before the coming of the English, junks used to be tracked against adverse winds; a solution which blissfully ignores the fact that it still remains to be explained why, in that case, the name should have attached not to the path but to the village which he himself identifies with East Point.

An alternative interpretation, equally legitimate, is 'Kwan shows the way', Kwan, I conjecture, being the admiral who joined issue at the first battle of Chuen Pei and, in the second, died fighting gallantly for a lost cause.

But the third theory is more intriguing. It is that the word Kwan is a mere transliteration (if the expression is legitimate) to represent the sound 'Queen', and that (Tai Lo meaning 'the big road', as it plainly might) Kwan Tai Lo means nothing more nor less than the Queen's Road, which, running round the foot-hills for four miles or so, might fairly be compared to the girdle of a petticoat.

This hypothesis assumes not merely that the name did not exist before the English came to cut the road but also that it was invented almost before the road took shape (for on May 15th, 1841, the date of the first list of place-names, it must still have been in its very early stages). It assumes too, of course, that the road had immediately been named after the Queen. None the less it is undeniably attractive, for the verbal juggling in the title accords well with the Chinese genius in such matters, and if it is not the true solution it is a very curious coincidence; while if it is objected that we have still the 'fishing village of fifty souls' to account for, the ready answer is that that difficulty is rendered less acute by the fact that no trace of the village (apart from the name) ever seems to have been discovered.

And now at last I must invite the reader to observe with me the remarkable spectacle of a barren island in the throes of giving birth to a British Colony; and for the purpose it is necessary to turn back to January 26th, 1841, the date on which the commander-in-chief first took peaceful possession in the name of Her Majesty.

The date has indeed the authority of the *Chinese Repository*, but as the occupation receives only the most cursory notice in the February issue as an 'occurrence' of the previous month, it being left to a retrospect made in November 1842 to record the actual day of the month for the first time, the critical will perhaps emphasize rather the lack of attention taken of this interesting occasion in the appropriate issue.

The date, however, is well authenticated, our authority being Captain Belcher commanding H.M. survey ship *Sulphur*, a prominent actor in the events described, and incidentally one destined to leave both his own name and that of his ship on the charts and plans of the colony. The following is extracted from his *Voyage round the World*, published 1843, vol. ii, p. 147:

'The only important point to which we became officially partners was the cession of the island of Hong Kong, situated off the peninsula of Cow Loon within the island of Lama. . . .

'On the return of the commodore on the 24th we were directed to proceed to Hong Kong and commence its survey. We landed on Monday, the 26th January at fifteen minutes past eight, and being "bona fide" first possessors, her majesty's health was drank with three cheers on Possession Mount.

'On the 26th the squadron arrived and the marines were landed, the union hoisted on our post, and formal possession taken of the island by Commodore Sir J. G. Bremer, accompanied by the other officers of the squadron, under a *feu de joie* from the marines, and a royal salute from the ships of war.'

An historical event of the first importance marred in the telling by a printer's error! But a justification, I suggest, of the gallant author's precision; for though we hesitate to amend the text, we may surely infer that the healths were 'drank' on January 25th, which fell on a Monday in the year in question, and the more serious formalities took place on Tuesday, January 26th.

94 THE BIRTH OF VICTORIA

The spot on which the post was established is still named Possession Point; but, having been preserved as an open space for the benefit of the Chinese residents of the locality, is more familiarly known as the 'Chinese Recreation Ground' or, in the vernacular, 'Tai Tat Tei' (the big plot of ground).

n. 2

On January 29th Elliot himself, coming straight from his negotiations with Keshen within the Bogue, joined Bremer at Hong Kong and 'took the opportunity of steaming all round it on board the *Nemesis* and seemed to be more than ever proud of its possession'.[1] On February 1st a manifesto in Chinese addressed to the inhabitants of the island appeared over the joint names of Elliot and Bremer—a curious document in that it not merely joined the commander-in-chief with the plenipotentiary but actually gave the former precedence.

n. 3

The following day a proclamation in English under Elliot's sole name and title formally declaring the cession of the island to the British Crown was given out from H.M.S. *Wellesley*. (See Appendix I.)

Having established itself upon the island the Navy forthwith turned its attention to the mainland, and Captain Belcher thus continues his narrative, still dealing, one presumes, with January 26th or possibly 27th or with the immediately ensuing days:

'On the Cowloon peninsula were situated two batteries which might have commanded the anchorage but which appeared at present to be but thinly manned: these received due notice to withdraw their men and guns as part of the late treaty.'

Apparently the notice was disregarded: and we must pursue the matter somewhat further under the guidance of

[1] Bernard, *Nemesis*, vol. i, p. 304.

Commander Bingham, first Lieutenant of *Modeste* and author of *The Expedition to China, 1840*, published in 1842: 'It was further agreed', he tells us, referring to Elliot's interview with Keshen on January 26th–27th, 'that the batteries of Cowloon should be dismantled'; but somehow *Modeste* appears to have been no more successful than *Sulphur*, and 'the Mandarin, being called on some days afterwards to comply—replies that he had no order'.

Accordingly, 'On February 7th'—interesting corroboration of the statement in the official report of Keshen's trial that an intermediate interview between Keshen and Elliot took place —'in consequence of a representation to Keshen of their refusal, he [Keshen] requested permission to move the guns from Cowloon by water as they could not, he asserted, be removed by land'. This, Commander Bingham tells us, was in fact carried out, the guns being removed to the First Bar Battery, where they were found by the British when the Bogue was captured later in the month.[1]

Dismantlement of the forts, however, was apparently not enough; for at some subsequent date they were occupied by the British forces in circumstances which Commander Bingham thus describes: 'The peninsula of Cowloon was, by the terms of the treaty, to be neutral ground: on the breach of faith of the Chinese it was seized by right of conquest—a garrison being kept in Fort Victoria where many commissariat and other stores were deposited.'

[1] We are left to speculate whether Keshen's request was merely a *ruse de guerre*, enabling him to turn upon the enemy the guns which had fallen into their power, or a deft move of an old diplomat designed to lend colour to the suggestion that the concession of the harbour of Hong Kong to England implied the admission of the right of China to exclude the British from Canton.

That a fort on the peninsula was so seized at some period during 1841 and actually received the Sovereign's name is not open to serious doubt; for it is confirmed by contemporary prints.[1] It is confirmed also, and indeed underlined, by Lieutenant Ouchterlony, who tells us that 'Two batteries of heavy pieces were erected at either extremity of the southern coast, and two masonry forts which had been built by the Chinese in 1839 close to the water's edge to command the anchorage, were destroyed, and the promontory entirely evacuated.'[2] But we could have wished that our authority had been rather more explicit both on the date and on the objects and reasons of this exploit.

What in fact was the breach of faith which led to it? Was it the rearming, by the local Chinese authorities, of the forts dismantled by Keshen's orders? Or is the reference to Keshen's own failure to implement his agreement with Elliot, by signing, sealing, and delivering, by February 21st, a definitive treaty? Or was this a mere act of reprisal for the rearming, contrary to the express provisions of the convention of May 27th, of the forts within the Bogue?

n. 4 These things are left to speculation; and so also are the actual 'terms of the Treaty'. It is not necessary to remind the reader that in his public announcement of January 20th Elliot made no reference at all to Kowloon. But the point for consideration is perhaps the true import of the express cession, in addition to the island, of the 'harbour of Hong Kong'. Herein perhaps lies the seed out of which sprang the notion of the neutrality of the Kowloon Peninsula. And in this connexion it is worthy of note that Lord Palmerston, in his dis-

---

[1] e.g. Allom's *China Illustrated*.   [2] *The Chinese War* [1844].

patch of June 5th, 1841,[1] to Sir Henry Pottinger, in intimating the view of the Government that Hong Kong should be retained, directs his particular attention to this point:

'It seems that some portion of the opposite Coast commands one of the principal anchorages of the Island and it will therefore be necessary to stipulate that the Chinese shall not erect any fortification or work, or plant any cannon, or station any military force within a certain distance of those points from which the anchorage of Hong Kong is commanded.'

Palmerston writes, no doubt, after receiving Elliot's account of his negotiations with Keshen: and we may perhaps have in this instruction to his successor an echo of a stipulation actually made by Elliot and accepted by Keshen in their verbal discussions of January.

As to the date of the seizure of the forts I append two extracts from the *Canton Press*. The first, dated September 19th, 1841, invites us to share an open secret:

'The forts of Kowloon will, we are informed, be the next object of attack and will probably be destroyed on Monday or Tuesday next. This we consider an act of sound policy since the position of Kowloon enables the Mandarins there to interfere with the Chinese population of Hong Kong';

but the second, dated a week later, curtly tells us 'that the intention, if it ever existed, of destroying the Chinese forts at Cowloon seems to have been abandoned'—and all is peace. n. 5

With this statement of the case I must leave the subject to the reader's solution; but before withdrawing from the Peninsula altogether I take the opportunity to add one or two more references to it which indicate that, besides the British Navy,

---

[1] Morse, *International Relations*, Appendix L.

other influential parties found Kowloon Point worthy of attention even in those early days.

The following is from *The Chinese Account of the Opium War*:

'The Co-Hong merchants were unwilling to go to Hong Kong on account of the perils of the sea: and it was proposed to exchange Hong Kong for Tsim Sha Choü point and Kowloon.'

And the following is taken from the *Canton Press* of July 19th, 1841:

'As regards the contemplated site of the town and the line of commercial buildings stretching along the shore, we have been told that on the island itself there are more eligible situations but that particularly Kowloon opposite to Hong Kong offers great advantages for the building of a town';

a sentiment repeated in May of the following year:

'We do believe that spots better qualified for a town than the present site of Hong Kong could have been found. The opposite shore, for instance, at Kowloon, so memorable for the poultry fight in September 1839, offers a fine level space.'[1]

We now return to Hong Kong—Hong Kong in the early days of February 1841, and though I grant I may be a few weeks out in my chronology, I fancy we shall find a certain limited progress has already been made by both naval and military authorities in establishing themselves on the island. The Navy has, I think, already laid claim to 'Navy Bay', lying due east (not west) of the bluff now known as Belcher's Battery, and is already running up store-houses, later to develop into a regular commissariat depot, on the sloping fore-

[1] *Canton Press*, May 7th, 1842.

shore afterwards to be occupied by St. Peter's Church and the Sailors' Home. The Navy also is comparing the merits of Navy Bay, and in particular the present gas-works site, with the rival charms of Causeway Bay and Aberdeen as a permanent dockyard.¹ The Army meantime has selected two camps, one on Cantonment Hill (later known as the 'Artillery' and later still 'Victoria' Barracks, and Seven-and-sixpenny Hill) running through the present military section and meeting the sea just opposite the present Wellington Barracks, and the other on the long slope which now carries on its shoulders the Hong Kong University and at its foot the old Reformatory Building. The latter is known for obvious reasons as 'West Point' and is destined to provide the name 'Sai Ying Pun', the Western Encampment, to a large district of the town; and also to acquire a terrible reputation for unhealthiness. On the site (in Battery Street) where the Reformatory now stands a small battery, West Point Battery, not to be confused with Belcher's Battery, a later and more pretentious erection, has, I surmise, already been mounted. And a similar battery, 'East' (subsequently 'Pottinger's') Battery, is about to be mounted on the site of Wellington Barracks.

That, I surmise, is the utmost extent of the military occupation in these early weeks. But commerce too has also taken certain steps. Messrs. Jardine, Matheson, representing big business, have already, I fancy, selected for themselves a spacious area at East Point; indeed, if we can accept the evidence of Mr. Alexander Matheson given in May 1847 before the Select Committee on Commercial Relations with

¹ Bernard, *Nemesis*, vol. ii, pp. 77 and 79.

China,¹ they have beaten the pistol and already started building. As for retail trade Bingham again supplies us with authentic evidence: 'The native bazaar had been removed from Tong Kwu and was established on the north side of Hong Kong, where a military police was constituted from the *Modeste*,² who had charge of the bazaar to prevent the sale of Shamshu to soldiers and sailors.'

Here we see in embryo either 'the Bazaar', subsequently to blossom out into the Central Market, or the 'Canton Bazaar' which settled itself on the narrow recesses between Cantonment Hill, Scandal Point, and the hillock on which Flagstaff House now stands.

n. 14

n. 15

Such was the situation in Hong Kong when, on February 20th, the assault upon the Bogue was ordered; and on February 20th (I quote Commander Bingham once more) it was 'found requisite to haul the flag down at Hong Kong as it was impossible to spare a sufficient number of troops to garrison it. The town, therefore, flitted to Saw Chau'—an island lying midway between Tong Kwu and Lantao.

n. 16

This incident has, I think, not been hitherto noticed in Hong Kong chronicles, but I see no reason to reject it: and it is certainly difficult, while accepting Bingham's account of the transference of the bazaar to Hong Kong, to reject his account of its removal back to Saw Chau; and hardly easier, while admitting Captain Belcher's account of the hoisting of the flag, to decline to accept Commander Bingham's of its hauling down.

¹ *Comm. Rel.*, p. 174, q. 2260. Question: 'The first sale was in 1841?' Answer: 'We commenced building before the first sale even, to a certain extent.'
² His own ship.

Commander Bingham, however, though disconcerting, is at least thorough, and enables us to report, under date of March 6th, 1841, that 'the Commodore [returned] to his own ship, and the troops to Hong Kong, where the flag was again re-hoisted'.

The month of March secures the preference also of the merchants, who in a petition to Lord Stanley, Secretary of State for the Colonies, speak of 'the time which intervened between the occupation of the island by H.M. Government, in March 1841, and the Treaty of Nankin in June 1843'.[1] n. 17

The camps at Cantonment Hill and West Point were again filled with Indian troops, the 37th Madras Native Infantry and the Bengal Volunteers respectively; the two small batteries east and west were again mounted; detachments, under canvas I presume, were now posted also at Aberdeen, Stanley, and Sai Wan on the south, south-east, and eastern extremities of the island; and military head-quarters were now, I fancy, established somewhere within the boundaries of the present Botanical Gardens—a conclusion which I draw partly from the early prints (notably the frontispiece of Ouchterlony's narrative) and partly from the following extract from a lecture (which I quote extensively later) delivered by Dr. James Legge in 1872 on Hong Kong as he knew it in 1843: n. 18

'Far up'—he is speaking of 'Government Hill' on which the Colonial Secretariat, Government House, &c., are situated—'if I recollect aright, might be seen a range of barracks out of which have been fashioned the present Albany residences. . . .'[2] n. 19

[1] *Commercial rel. with China*, p. 384.
[2] And this perhaps accounts for that curious name 'horse-grass garden' (Ma Ts'o Un) by which Queen's Gardens, a little higher still, is familiarly known to the Chinese.

During March the navy and Captain Elliot himself were, as we have seen, preoccupied at Canton, but having patched up an arrangement for the reopening of trade Elliot flung himself, without a moment's delay, into the business of creating a trading settlement at Hong Kong.

This the *Chinese Repository*, breaking silence for the first time since it had published Elliot's proclamation of February 2nd, laconically records in the 'Occurrences' for the month of April 1841: 'A British settlement in Hong Kong is about being commenced.'

From that day the city of Victoria dates its birth, and from that day to this the town proceeded to grow almost without a halt.

It is the duty of the historian to record this growth, a task of considerable difficulty, for he is entirely dependent for his facts on unconsidered trifles, odds and ends of maps and plans, old pictures and prints, old buildings, scraps from the contemporary press, occasional extracts from memoirs dealing with the China wars, and so forth; and he has (with a strict curb upon his imagination) to piece the bits together into a coherent whole. Nor is his task ended there; for the fourth dimension, the dimension of time, is of the essence of the figure which he has to produce. Is he, then, to watch constantly at the bedside and issue daily bulletins, in other words to attempt to keep pace with the growth? Or is he to stand aside, and at intervals make an exploratory examination—and, if so, at what intervals?

Moreover there is the added difficulty that even as he writes his subject swells, and the familiar landmark by which he seeks to fix for all time some forgotten feature of the past is itself swept away, perhaps before the ink is dry on the page.

In April a Court was in session[1] (no doubt on one of Her Majesty's ships) in Hong Kong to inquire into the mortality among the troops at Tinghai (Chusan). And on the 30th of the month Elliot, styling himself 'Her Majesty's plenipotentiary etc. charged with the Government of the island of Hong Kong', announced, by Public Notice in the first issue of the *Hong Kong Gazette*, the appointment of Captain William Caine, of Her Majesty's 26th (or Cameronian) regiment of infantry, to be Chief Magistrate of the island pending Her Majesty's further pleasure.

In his warrant to the Chief Magistrate Elliot required him to

'exercise authority according to the laws, customs and usages of China as near as may be (every description of torture excepted) . . . over all the native inhabitants in the said island and the harbour thereof', and 'where the crime according to Chinese law shall involve penalties exceeding in severity capital punishment, corporal punishment of 100 lashes, or 3 months' imprisonment, or a $400 fine, he was to remit the case for the judgment of the head of the Government for the time being'.

n. 20

This may appear to have imposed a fairly severe responsibility on the gallant captain, but lest the reader should be wondering what penalty could be more severe than death, it may be explained that, according to Chinese usage at the time, death was a matter of degree. Execution, entailing the severance of head from body, was more severe than strangulation; and neither was comparable with the death by a thousand cuts reserved for serious offences such as parricide.

As regards persons other than natives of the island or

---

[1] *Chin. Rep.*, April 1841, p. 240.

persons 'subject to the mutiny act' (i.e. soldiers) or 'to the General Law for the Government of the fleet' (i.e. sailors)—Captain Caine was to apply British police law.

But any one whatsoever, be he native of the island or Chinese immigrant, soldier, sailor, civil servant, or merchant, found committing a felony (according to the law of England) was to be detained, and the matter reported to the head of the Government.

In the first issue of the *Gazette* there appeared also a Public Notice and Declaration of great importance announcing that arrangements had been made for the permanent occupation of the island, and explaining the principles and conditions on which grants of land there would be made.

n. 21

The issue of these *Gazettes* heralded 'more active measures for the colonization of the island', and we learn that 'a number of coolies', as many as six hundred, we are told, 'have been paid at $10 a month to cut roads, and level the ground of the site of the intended fort and town'; while 'some provisional buildings have already been erected'.

A fortnight later the first Gazetteer and Census of the island appeared, and will be found reproduced (excepting the Chinese characters) in Appendix II.[1]

---

[1] Some doubt has been thrown on the reliability of this list by Dr. Eitel, who, writing fifty years later, somewhat vaguely claims that Stanley never housed more than 'a few hundred inhabitants'; and (encouraged possibly by Bingham, who may well have seen the place and allows 1,000 only) proceeds to cut the total to a figure more in accord with his own ideas.

In so doing, however, he seems entirely to miss the really striking point that, if Stanley's population was exaggerated, Aberdeen (Shek Pae) is credited with none at all; though Captain Cunynghame, writing in 1843 (*An A.D.C.'s Recollections*, p. 78), speaks of 'Chuk-pi-waan' as 'having a very respectable appearance' and 'containing about 200 houses'.

These activities met with a mixed reception in Macao, and besides local property-owners and house-agents, whose interest in the matter was obvious, some of the British merchants felt excusably hesitant to abandon the comfort of those pleasant old residences on the Praya Grande for the cheerless northern slopes of Hong Kong island.

The *Canton Press* of Macao played upon their doubts, and besides recording (not without an occasional smack of the lips) each piracy, robbery, typhoon, and fire which beset the island in those early days, reminded intending settlers to beware lest 'as has been done before, it be abandoned for a while or perhaps for an indefinite period'.[1]

The weapon of ridicule was also employed, and I am indebted to the *Canton Press* for the following:

'THE WANG TUNG ARGUS'—(*Canton Press*, May 15th, 1841)   n. 22

[Through secret influence at Government House we are enabled to present our readers with the first number of the Wang Tung Argus, which appears to contain some entertaining matters. We need not say that the paper shews internal evidence of its being an authentic document.]

. . . .

'We are happy to announce to our readers that the new settlement "progresses" in a most surprising manner. The site of the principal town has been selected with the judgment which is characteristic of the English authorities in China: and we may mention in proof of this that every street will be perfectly sheltered from the south wind, which will be an immense comfort during the approaching hot season. There are abundant supplies of granite and cold water, and we need not point out the facility with which provisions can be

---

[1] *Canton Press*, May 8th, 1841.

obtained from Canton and Macao. A street on a gigantic scale is already far advanced, leading from an intended public office to a contemplated public thoroughfare; and we now only require houses, inhabitants, and commerce to make this settlement one of the most valuable of our possessions.

. . . .

'We understand that several offices will soon be erected, without reference to expense. Those decided proofs of the march of civilization, a Gibbet of the largest size, and a range of stocks, are already designed; and we understand that a Bedlam, after the model of the Company's Hall in Canton, is contemplated. It is intended to reserve the principal room, commanding a view of a particular part of Cowloon Bay for a certain "eminent person". We are further informed it is intended to build a Cathedral and that the Superintendent of Trade for the time being will exercise the functions of Archbishop. We recommend our Musulman friends to petition for the erection of a Mosque; and we doubt not that "our Proteus" will considerately agree to officiate as a Mullah!

. . . .

'As it has naturally been deemed impracticable to establish the foundation of a large Commercial Entrepot at the foot of a hill in a small island, H.M. Plenipotentiary has determined, after the most anxious consideration, to reduce the trade with China to a size commensurate with the actual extent of the settlement; and it is confidently expected that another year will enable him to achieve this object.

. . . .

'It is rumoured that a statue of H.M. Plenipotentiary in the character of Janus Bifrons will be erected opposite the Hospital of the Incurables; and with the view of its proving as durable as the works of that eminent person, it is proposed that the materials should be selected from the salt of the captured junks; and the whole structure to rest on a foundation of solid sand.

. . . .

'We hear the well-known and active officer Captain Bludgeon, has been appointed Bowstreet Magistrate of the settlement and its dependencies; and in order that the natives of the island may appreciate the blessings of civil Government, care has been taken to establish beforehand that state of general disorder and disorganization which renders such an office specially necessary. n. 23

. . . .

'We are gratified to announce to our readers that H.M. Plenipotentiary has presented to the public library of Hong Kong a splendid edition of the Blue Book; a copy of his letter to Lord Palmerston of November 1839, printed in characters of fire; and a complete edition of his Hong Kong "General Orders" bound in Calf.

> 'Advertisement.—The steamer *Nemesis* will make half weekly trips to Canton to enable family parties to see the town. Ladies and children half price.
>
> 'Hong Kong Theatre. On the 1st proximo:
>
> '"She stoops to conquer" or "The Plenipo's last shift".
>
> 'To conclude with
> Harlequin and Mother Goose.
> Harlequin by "our Proteus"
> Mother Goose by "a certain distinguished character".'

'THE WANG TUNG ARGUS NO. 2' (*Canton Press*, May 29th, 1841)

'The sale of the Crown Lands advertised in our last is postponed *sine die*. Various rumours are afloat as to the cause. It is said by some that the title deeds, though satisfactory to the sellers, are not quite so to the intending purchasers,—but there exists a general feeling of doubt that there will ever be either a settlement or a sale. The swamps and marshy grounds will not be put up to sale at all; being reserved for the cantonment of the army.

· · · · · · ·

'A census of the population of the island and its dependencies has been taken, and the result will be made known so soon as it can be correctly ascertained, the operation being materially retarded by the Chinese authorities, who daily drive away numbers of the inhabitants.

'The latest estimate gave a grand total of 222 souls; and should no further diminution take place the island will be divided into districts and townships. A magistrate and collector of revenue will be appointed for every district numbering 10 inhabitants, and a collector of revenue only for the deserted fishing hamlets.

'There will be a great saving effected by the collection of all duties being performed by the Chinese.

· · · · · · ·

'There will be no law of arrest, action or imprisonment for debt in the new settlement—a certain eminent person having declared it inexpedient and likely to prove very inconvenient.

· · · · · · ·

'A Government notification has been issued, warning Her Majesty's subjects that all purchases of land made under whatever authority, all permanent fixations or landing of property, made under whatever guarantee of protection, will still be made (as far as the private interests of Her Majesty's subjects are concerned) on their own responsibility.

· · · · · · ·

'A premium of one thousand dollars will be paid to any person who shall devise means for feeding Cattle on granite rock, or raising crops from the sands of the sea shore; as both materials are to be found in good abundance on the new settlement.

· · · · · · ·

'Appointment. Mr. C. Froth is appointed Vice-Supernumerary-deputy-assistant-turnpike-gate-keeper to this settlement. His appointment to date from the formal surrender of the island by the Chinese.'

n. 24

In Canton the 'pacificator of the rebellious' became, as we have seen, feverishly active at this time; and we can well believe that it was not mere coincidence that the fever reached its climax immediately after the announcement of Elliot's intention to remain in Hong Kong and the cutting of the first road-line on the island. There ensued, as we know, that swift assault upon the city which in the last ten days of May brought it to its knees.

Thereafter Elliot returned with renewed vigour to the business of launching a Colony. His first act was calmly to implement his preliminary declaration of May by announcing, on June 7th, in his capacity of Chief Superintendent charged with the Government of Hong Kong, his intention of disposing, after a delay of five days, by Public Auction at Hong Kong of a hundred lots having sea-frontage and a hundred town or suburban lots.

The same day he declared Hong Kong a free port, issuing a general invitation to merchants to resort there to trade, coupled with a warning that obstruction to the freedom of Hong Kong would result in a blockade of Canton; and a proffer of rewards for the detection of pirates.

On June 10th, by Public Notice to His Majesty's subjects, he warned British shipping of the dangers of entering the river, and recommended them to proceed to Hong Kong.

The first land sale, postponed for two days, took place on June 14th, but even so, so short was the notice that it had

110 THE BIRTH OF VICTORIA

only been possible to peg out fifty marine lots, while no town or suburban lots were offered at all.

The reader will not fail to note the specifications of these earliest lots, 100 feet frontage on the road, 100 feet on the sea, and a depth varying according as the road approached or departed from the sea. But the supreme virtue of these lots lay in the fact, to be discovered later, that their rights to sea frontage were admitted, with the result that they have reaped n. 25 the benefit of every subsequent reclamation sea-ward.

Of the fifty lots marked out thirty-four were duly knocked down, the remainder being either reserved for Government or, one presumes, withdrawn at the eleventh hour. The authentic list of the results of the auction will be found in n. 26 Appendix III.

To be fully understood the list should be read with the aid of a plan of the city bearing lot numbers; but the following short notes of some of its features may be of interest to the local reader. Lot 1 lay approximately in Ice House Street and Nos. 1–19 ran westward to just beyond the Central Market.

n. 27 Lot 1 disappeared, and lots 6, 7, and 8 were thrown up and reverted to Government; but 2, 3, 4, and 5 provided the sites for those two conspicuous mercantile houses 'Dent's' and 'Lindsay's'; Dent subsequently securing a town lot on the opposite side of the Queen's Road on which he built a sumptuous private residence 'Green Bank'.

Lot 9 had been reserved, probably for a pier, but lot 6 was destined to fill this role and became Pedder Street.

Nothing was sold westward of the Central Market, and there was a gap eastward between Ice House Street and Head-

THE BIRTH OF VICTORIA

quarter House; but here a block of six lots, Nos. 20–25, running west from the Wellington Barracks, constituted the 'Canton Bazaar'.

n. 28

On lots 21 and 22 substantial mercantile offices were built, but 23 and 25 were reserved, perhaps for piers, and 24 was abandoned; the whole ultimately being resumed for Ordnance stores.

Lots 26 (adjoining lot 20) to 47 (under the lea of the Naval Hospital, Wantsai) presented a continuous front; while an outlying member, lot 51, was knocked down to Captain Morgan, ship's captain of Messrs. Jardine, Matheson & Co., and became 51 and 52 East Point. Like 20–25, lots 26–30 stretching to Arsenal Street were 'offered for repurchasement' and resumed, to become the 'Commissariat'. This involved, *inter alia*, compensating Messrs. Jardine, who had acquired 26–28 (the site of Wellington Barracks); and this was effected by giving them in exchange lots 72 and 73 at West Point—the site, in fact, of the original naval stores—on which subsequently (largely thanks to the firm's munificence) the Sailors' Home was erected.

n. 29

East of Arsenal Street all the lots up to 39 (Ship Street), excepting No. 36, were thrown up; but thereafter came 'Spring Gardens', a group of high-class residences (Nos. 41–43). The next two, Nos. 44 and 45, were reserved, perhaps for a retail food market: and 46 became the Albany Godowns stretching along Stone Nullah Lane.

n. 30

n. 31

n. 32

The financial result of the sale was surprising, and caused so much dissatisfaction on the ground that prices had been forced up by the competition of 'men of straw' and by the limitation of the number of lots offered that Elliot, on the 17th, wrote to

Messrs. Dent and Jardine, representing the purchasers at large, assuring them that his object was not to secure high prices but simply to provide for the reasonable needs of the merchants.

On June 22nd, as we have seen, Mr. A. R. Johnston, Deputy Superintendent of Trade, was appointed to take charge of the government of Hong Kong; a step which gives rise to speculation as to the motives actuating Captain Elliot. Did he wish to await the pleasure of the Crown before transferring the office of the Superintendency to Hong Kong? Or was he preparing, in collaboration with Bremer, who had lately returned, to strike another blow farther north? Or was Macao more convenient for the conduct of the outstanding business with Canton? Or is it possible that he had already wind of his own supersession?

Whatever the reason, the result was that while Elliot remained at Macao Johnston joined Caine in Hong Kong; and in this decision, at any rate, Elliot may perhaps be accounted fortunate, for, though he was shipwrecked and nearly drowned, he did at least avoid having his residence blown about his ears by the typhoon of July 21st, a fate which overtook both Deputy Governor and Chief Magistrate.

From Macao, however, Elliot continued to act as recruiting agent for Hong Kong; and on June 28th we find him encouraging the waverers by announcing his intention of urging Her Majesty's Government to grant a rebate on tea certified as shipped in Hong Kong, thereby adding something to the connotation of the expression 'free port' used in his announcement of the 7th.

n. 33 On July 31st Lieutenant William Pedder, First Lieutenant

Pedder's Hill and Harbour Master's House, Hong Kong

[*By permission of "Illustrated London News"*]

of *Nemesis*, was gazetted Harbour Master and Marine Magistrate. It will be recalled that it was in the capacity of Master Attendant to the original Commission that Elliot himself had first come to China, and it is perhaps worthy of note that this appointment was his last official act before leaving.

The name of Hong Kong's first Harbour Master is, of course, preserved in Pedder Street;[1] but lest the connexion pass out of memory I take the opportunity to record it here. Pedder chose for his residence a small bluff immediately behind the site, at the junction of Queen's Road and Wyndham Street, now occupied by the Asiatic Petroleum Company building. At the foot of the bluff, immediately across the Queen's Road, a short flight of granite steps led to the water, where Pedder's gig no doubt lay. In process of time Pedder's Hill was pared away almost out of existence and successive reclamations thrust Pedder's Wharf farther and farther northward, leaving Pedder Street to maintain the connexion with the Queen's Road.

The construction of the Queen's Road, and other public works, was pressed on with, the labour force rising from 600 to 1,500; a state of affairs which the *Canton Press*, hesitating whether to attribute the delay in private construction to the unwillingness of the merchants to buy a 'pig in a poke' or to the action of the Government in monopolizing the labour, in July thus grudgingly records: 'At Hong Kong only Government work proceeds.'

---

[1] As 'Pedder Street' it is universally known to Europeans, at any rate, but among Chinese residents of Hong Kong it remains 'Tai Chung Lau' (the Great Clock Tower) —in persistent reference to a clock-tower erected by public subscription on the site of Pedder's Wharf in 1862, and demolished, on the arrival of the motor-car, in 1913. n. 34

No doubt there was some hesitation by purchasers of lots to implement their 'building covenants'; and no doubt there was a scramble for labour; but one private trader, at any rate, got well off the mark, and I venture to record here the case of Mr. C. V. Gillespie as an excellent example of confidence in the future of Hong Kong.

n. 35   Of Mr. C. V. Gillespie's antecedents I know nothing beyond the fact that he was a general merchant in Macao; but I find that on July 15th, 1841, barely a month after the sale of land, he was advertising a godown 'with double-mat roof' at '46 Victoria Avenue Hong Kong'—thus correctly anticipating the name of the city. On August 7th (two typhoons having intervened) it is '46 Victoria Avenue Honwan' and then '46 Victoria Avenue Houwan'—gallant attempts to render into terms of the English alphabet the Chinese word for 'the lower harbour'. In September it is '46 Queen's Road'; and the following March it is no longer 'a double mat-roof' but a granite godown—none other, in fact, than the Albany Godowns, on marine lot 46, the first solid mercantile building
n. 36   completed in Hong Kong.

Alas for the uncertainty of human affairs! On July 21st a typhoon, the same that had nearly drowned Elliot, struck Hong Kong—Hong Kong the 'safe and commodious', Hong Kong the chosen anchorage in the south-west monsoon—and flattened the upstart town. Tents, mat-sheds, bazaars, godowns, hospitals, and even the brand-new residences of Deputy Governor and Chief Magistrate—all were blown down; and the fleet was scattered over the face of the waters.

This was duly reported to the throne with unction by the 'pacificator of the rebellious' and the report duly acknowledged with grave satisfaction by the Emperor, a situation to which a gleam of humour is lent by the picture of Elliot landing from a sampan at Macao, with $100,000 on his head, unshaven, bedraggled, shirtless, but full of resource and full of fight.

It was a severe blow, and it was followed by another, somewhat less severe, five days later; and then, after just sufficient interval to allow the mat-sheds to be rebuilt, the entire bazaar was burnt to the ground on August 12th and again early in September.

In September, too, fever flared up among the troops;[1] and so serious was the situation that the commanding officer ordered all on board the transports.

n. 37

It needed, however, more than two typhoons, two fires in quick succession, and virulent malaria to quench the spirit of the embryonic Victoria.

[1] *Canton Press*, Oct. 2nd, 1841.

CHAPTER IX

POTTINGER
1841–1844

Sir Henry Pottinger, who, as we have seen, reached Macao on August 10th, announced on the 12th his general endorsement (until Her Majesty's pleasure was known) of Elliot's arrangements in respect to Hong Kong,[1] and, in particular, of his notice of June 10th recommending British shipping to proceed thither in preference to Canton.

Pressed by Dent and others as to his intentions regarding the island, and the extent of the protection they would receive if they remained at Macao, he declined to be drawn.[2] But in point of fact he came possessed of the deliberate view of Her Majesty's Government that 'the island of Hong Kong ought to be retained'.[3]

On August 21st–22nd, when *en route* to join the expedition proceeding to the north, he stopped to visit the island[4] and to note personally the progress thus far made in its settlement by Englishmen.

He found construction work on the Queen's Road being actively carried on; the jail and magistracy, on their present site, within two months of completion; a land office (near the cathedral site) already functioning; and a post office (adjoining the land office) on the point of opening its doors.

He found also a retail food market, complete with price-list

---

[1] *Canton Press*, Aug. 14th.   [2] Ibid., Oct. 12th.
[3] Morse, *International Relations*, Appendix I, p. 661.
[4] *Chin. Rep.*, vol. x, p. 523.

under the hand of the Chief Magistrate,[1] in full swing;[2] and a cemetery on the site of St. Francis Square, Wantsai, conveniently situated to Cantonment Hill, set aside for the accommodation of European and 'other' troops.

No permanent mercantile buildings were yet built and no regular barracks;[3] and it still needed a month before Caine's

n. 1

---

[1] *Canton Press*, Oct 1841.

[2] Whether Caine's list fixed prices in advance or recorded them in arrears I cannot say, but I conceive it has an historical value; and I extract the following from a more comprehensive list headed 'Half monthly prices of provisions at Hong Kong':

Beef 12 cents a catty.	Fowl 15 cents a catty.
Pork 16 cents a catty.	Rice (best quality) $3\frac{1}{2}$ cents.
	(inferior) $2\frac{1}{2}$,,
Oysters (without shell) 16 cents.	

I append also (1) the Land Officer's notice respecting the cemetery above referred to; and (2) a Post Office notice, possibly the first issued by the Hong Kong Post Office; both curious examples of improvisation by the budding executive before the establishment of a legislature.

1. *Notice.*

A piece of land to the eastward of Cantonment Hill having by Government been allotted as the ground for the burial of the dead of Europeans and others, Notice is hereby given that persons burying their dead in any other unauthorised place will be treated as trespassers.

Jno. F. Mylius, Land Officer,
Hong Kong 30th August 1841.

2. *Public Notice.*

'All ship-masters and Commanders or others intrusted with mail packets to the address of the Postmaster at Hong Kong are required to deliver the same to the Harbour Master, or clerk in charge of the Post Office immediately on their arrival at that Port; or at the office of the Superintendent at Macao, on their arrival at Macao roads. All persons acting otherwise will render themselves liable to the fines and penalties by Act of Parliament established.

By order of the Deputy Superintendent,
T. G. FitzGibbon
Clerk-in-charge of the Post Office, Hong Kong.

Hong Kong August 25th 1841.

[3] *Canton Press*, Nov. 1841.

original house, the first foreign house on the island, a bungalow in a semi-Chinese style in the region of Lan Kwai Fong, west of Wyndham Street, would be ready for occupation.¹

Pottinger himself, on this occasion, occupied a pitched tent, the Deputy Governor, Mr. Johnston, not yet having succeeded in providing a roof for himself.²

In the first rush there had been difficulty in engaging mechanics and obtaining material to build houses; and in September, to meet the latter want, 'several vessels brought from Singapore wooden houses in frame intended for the new settlement'.³ By that time, however, both local labour and local materials were cheap and abundant and an enterprising importer seems to have missed his due reward.

Next month another gentleman—Mr. Matheson, I suspect —not to be outdone, proceeded to introduce from Manilla a carriage and pair 'to shew off on the new road'.⁴

In September the infant post office began to be vocal; and we find Mr. Johnston (who had assumed the additional title of Postmaster) blandly expounding to British merchants in Macao the pure orthodoxy of postal methods which quite precluded him from allowing a mail consigned to himself in China to be opened in Macao or elsewhere than at the post office at Hong Kong.⁵

In October the upstart jail threw open its gates, apparently to a considerable queue, and, as the *Canton Press* unkindly remarks, 'is already filled with pirates awaiting trial'.⁶

---

¹ Bernard, *Nemesis*, vol. ii, p. 83: *Contemp. Prints.*
² Loch, *Events in China*, p. 19.   ³ *Canton Press*, Sept. 11th.
⁴ *Chin. Rep.*, Oct. 1841.
⁵ *Canton Press*, Sept. 25th, 1841.   ⁶ Ibid., Oct. 16th.

Under October 'Occurrences' the *Chinese Repository*, laconic as ever, announces its estimate of the population—fifteen thousand.[1]

The tide was now definitely flowing in favour of Hong Kong, and the *Canton Press* was able to report in December

'that the commercial community now generally begins to give more attention to Hong Kong than hitherto, and great activity in building godowns and private houses has of late been observed there; while many merchants have, during the week, gone over, with a view, we believe, of commencing building. The public buildings are several of them completed and the construction of others is urged on with spirit so that we suppose the island which was, eight or nine months back, inhabited by none but poor Chinese fishermen, will soon boast of a stately town. A practicable bridle road has been cut across the island to Tytam Bay and a road fit for carriages is already several miles long, whilst a great number of workmen are employed to complete it. . . .'

In January 1842 the same newspaper makes a considered survey of progress in Hong Kong during the preceding twelve months. It is a valuable contemporary account, too valuable to be allowed to fade; and with all due acknowledgements I venture to reproduce it here—or the bulk of it—annotating as I go:

'In January 1841 Hong Kong was ceded to the British Crown and the island was taken possession of on the 26th; but nothing was done for its improvement until May, when a Chief Magistrate was first appointed and shortly after a Road was commenced under the superintendence of the corps of engineers belonging to the Chinese expedition. From May to August the population increased most rapidly, and an extensive bazaar shortly followed this congregation of people—though it received several severe checks from tyfoons

[1] *Chin. Rep.*, vol. x, p. 592.

and fires. After the departure of the Chinese expedition to Amoy and Chusan in August permanent public buildings were commenced on the side of the island facing the present anchorage which is called by the natives "Kwun-Tai-Loo".

'Commencing from the westernmost part of the present settlement there are at this date, independent of the temporary barracks[1] which afford quarters for the Bengal Volunteers, one of a permanent nature for about 60 men nearly completed—a stone store-house of considerable dimensions ready for use—and another smaller one in a state of forwardness. A road runs from these buildings to the bazaar[2] a distance of about one mile and a half, on the side of which some private buildings have been commenced, while in and about the bazaar itself some 20 permanent shops are in different states of completion.

n. 4

'From this latter point to the residence of Mr. Gillespie[3] a distance of about 2 miles, is the present scene of greatest activity; and on both sides of the road permanent buildings of some importance, both as to size and number, have been and are in progress of construction; while a little higher up Magistracy Hill we see 3 or 4 permanent houses already finished and inhabited, overlooked by the Magistracy and Prison itself,[4] and on about the same elevation but more to the east on Government Hill[5] a public office to serve as a temporary residence for the head of the Government is just finished; having a guard house at no great distance from it,[6] where at present are quartered an officer and more than 60 men of the 55th foot. Near to this is the residence of the land officer and a small public building at present used as a post office. Pursuing the road to the east, one arrives at Cantonment Hill[7] on which a barrack is nearly finished for the Madras Native Infantry, with a powder magazine[8] a little way behind it. At the foot of this hill a small battery[9] is about to be commenced.

n. 5

n. 6

n. 7

n. 8

n. 9

[1] West Point Barracks. [2] Central Market. [3] Naval Hospital.
[4] Present site. [5] Site of Cathedral, &c.
[6] Murray Battery near P.W.D. offices. [7] Seven-and-sixpenny Hill.
[8] The existing Magazine in Bowen Road. [9] East Battery.

'Arrived at Mr. Gillespie's, the road crosses a granite bridge and ascends rather suddenly to a gap[1] cut through a hill which commands a view of the whole valley and village of "Wong-nei-chung" and the road to "Tai Tam" winding up it until lost to sight among the hills in the centre of the island. If instead, however, of pursuing this road, the branch which crosses the valley and goes on east is followed, one at length arrives at the villages of "Soo-kon-poo" at present a sequestered, well wooded, and very pretty part of the island. It is from the western end of this village that a point[2] runs out into the sea whereon an European building has already been commenced and off which lies Kellet's island, where the Government are constructing a battery. The road to the east terminates at the village of "Soo-kon-poo": but about three miles farther is the fishing village of "Soo-ke-wan"—a place with a large migratory population having in its neighbourhood some vast stone-quarries. From "Soo-ke-wan" a native footpath, sufficiently good to ride on, leads to "Tai-Tam" which is at present a place of little note—though situated at the head of an extensive and deep bay of that name.

n. 10

'On the west side of the little southernmost point of "Tai Tam" bay there is a little cove called "Chek Chu"[3] the resort of large fleets of fishing-boats, and the site of a considerable town with a population of about 2,000 souls,—having a very good bazaar, an extensive rope-walk, and shops well stocked to supply the wants of Chinese seafaring people.

'It is at this place the Government have determined on erecting a barrack of two or three hundred men[4] and where one capable of holding a hundred is now in an advanced state towards completion. A branch of the "Tai Tam" road will lead to this town.

'Tracing one's steps westward as if continuing round the island, one at length comes to "Heong Kong" proper, a small agricultural village situated in a remarkably pretty and the most extensive valley on the island. "Shek-pae-wan",[5] often called by the Chinese "Heong

---

[1] Gap Road.   [2] East Point: Messrs. Jardine, Matheson & Co.
[3] Stanley.   [4] Now site of St. Stephen's College.   [5] Aberdeen.

Kong, Shek-pai-wan", would seem to be the seaport of Hong Kong proper, and to have once been a more flourishing place than it now is. There is too on an isolated spot the largest Chinese temple to be found on any part of the island. The port of "Shek-pae-wan" though small, is nearly landlocked; and having both a northern and a southwestern entrance, it is pretty easy of ingress and egress. An island of about two miles in circumference, called "Tap-Le-Chow",[1] protects it from southwest to north and the island of Hong Kong completes the circle.

'There is abundance of water for a line-of-battle ship, and its only fault is in being too small as an anchorage for many European vessels; yet there may be nearly as much anchoring ground in it as in the Inner Harbour of Macao.

'There is at present a small detachment of the Madras native infantry with two officers and one doctor stationed at the place: and the road has been projected and partially finished from "Kwun-tai-loo" to it across the hill, a distance of 3 to 4 miles. . . .

'. . . The first who set the example of a stone and brick House was Mr. Matheson; Government soon after commenced the magistracy and prison, others followed in their train, and now few Europeans think of a palm leaf house, except with certain forebodings of fever and ague. Some wooden houses have been imported from Singapore, and are at present being erected upon a lower story of stone. . . . Hawkers of every description abound, as well as the various sorts of fortune-tellers, jugglers, quacks, and actors, that are seen in all well-populated Chinese towns.

'. . . The population has often been estimated at about 15,000 souls: and it is probable this number is by no means an over-estimate. . . . There are not more than a dozen horses on the island, and one carriage; a few small flocks of sheep and some goats—Cattle for the consumption of Europeans are easily obtained, and some of the cows have been found to afford rather a good supply of rich milk, when taken care of and fed with grain.

[1] Ap-Li-Chau.

'Many of the complaints about excessive heat, and excessive cold and dreadful unhealthiness, are being forgotten, except among those who have little else to occupy their attention—amidst the general bustle and activity of Hong Kong.'

While the town of Hong Kong thus grew, the expeditionary force proceeded north to repeat with emphasis its performance of the previous year. For some five months Sir Henry Pottinger followed its fortunes in person, sending *communiqués* periodically to the south. But on February 1st, 1842, he returned to Hong Kong.

His first act was to reverse[1] the policy of the local British naval authorities of seizing Chinese trading junks—a policy which, though in strict accordance with Lord Palmerston's instructions, was hardly calculated to encourage the beginnings of trade at Hong Kong; and one, moreover, which the Cantonese might well regard as a breach of Elliot's arrangements of May 27th, 1841, and, as such, a colourable excuse for their own disregard of that convention in rearming the forts and repairing the defences on the Canton river.

A fortnight later (February 16th) he issued a proclamation[2] announcing that both Hong Kong and Tinghai (the port of Chusan) were free ports—thereby mystifying friend and foe alike as to his ultimate intentions in regard to both these places. But on February 27th he took the significant step of transferring the seat of the Superintendency of Trade from Macao to Hong Kong.[3]

Almost immediately afterwards Mr. James Matheson, a familiar Canton figure, retired from the stage, leaving in the

[1] *Canton Press*, Feb. 12th.
[2] *Chin. Rep.*, vol. xi, p. 119.
[3] *Canton Press*, Feb. 26th.

hands of the Governor of Macao a sum of $5,000 for purposes of public benevolence. Mr. Matheson, besides being a member of Messrs. Jardine, Matheson, had the distinction of being the founder of the British press in China; and having, both in the *Canton Register* which he had himself launched in 1827 and elsewhere, consistently advocated the creation of a British settlement at Hong Kong, he may well have read in this step of Pottinger's a welcome signal enabling him to depart in peace from the China coast.

It was no doubt this step, too, which decided the editor of the *Canton Press* to make the trip to Hong Kong and see for himself 'the promised land'. His impressions duly appeared in the issue of February 26th, and as the close student of Hong Kong's early beginnings will doubtless find embedded several interesting gems, I have provided a niche for them in the Appendixes.[1]

The growth of the town during his absence at once attracted Pottinger's attention, and his first official act was to announce[2] on March 22nd[3] his intention of appointing a Committee to investigate claims regarding 'allotted locations of ground and finally to define the locations already sold or otherwise granted, to fix the direction, breadth, &c., of the Queen's Road and all other existing roads; to remove encroachments, to prevent reclamations in infringement of Her

---

[1] Appendix IV.   [2] *Canton Press*, March 26th.

[3] This announcement was issued from 'Government House' and was the first official reference to the place; and the reader, recollecting that the familiar building below the Botanical Gardens was not erected till ten years later (1852), may speculate where the Government House of the period was. Once more, lest I interrupt the story, I exclude the subject from the text, but the student of local history will find it discussed at length in Appendix V.

n. 11

Majesty's royalties', and so forth: an announcement which, to those who can penetrate beyond the façade of official phraseology, calls up a vivid picture of the early struggles to save Victoria's main artery from strangulation by private encroachment.

A week later the personnel of the committee was announced—Major Malcolm, Captain Meik, H.M. 49th foot; Ensign Sargent; W. Woosnam, Esq.; Mr. J. Pascoe, 2nd Master of H.M.S. *Blenheim*. But in the interval Pottinger, impressed no doubt by the indiscriminate way in which naval, military, and civil buildings had sprung up, and perhaps foreseeing an increasing conflict between the claims of commerce and defence in future, had decided to give the Committee much wider powers—town-planning powers, in fact; and it was called upon, besides reporting on any case where compensation should be paid to native Chinese on account of the British occupation of land on the island, to 'select places for public landing places; to define limits of Cantonments: to fix the extent of ground to be reserved for a naval depot and for a dockyard and to select a watering place with a running stream of good water for shipping'. n. 12

The step seems to have been a timely one, for the Committee soon found itself under the necessity of prohibiting all further sales of land.[1] The erection of buildings, however, proceeded rapidly; and by May 'a market for the accommodation of Chinese in disposing of provisions had been opened'.[2] Erected by the Committee, it became known first as 'Malcolm's' and subsequently as the 'Canton Bazaar' and occupied 'a central position fronting upon the Queen's Road n. 13

[1] *Canton Press*, May 14th.   [2] *Chin. Rep.*, May 1841.

and facing also in a long line on the water'—a description culled from the contemporary press, from which the reader may not readily identify the actual site—a recess below the bluff on which Flagstaff House now stands.[1] But the description of the interior—'a judicious arrangement with separate and well constructed departments 1st. for all kinds of meat, 2nd. fruit and vegetables, 3rd. poultry, 4th. salt fish, 5th. fresh fish, 6th. weighing room, 7th. money-changer houses etc., etc.'—leaves the Hong Kong resident in no doubt that it was the veritable prototype on which all the Colony's later markets were modelled.

Simultaneously with the provision of marketing-facilities the currency was dealt with; Spanish, Mexican and other republican dollars, Company's rupees and their component parts, and Chinese cash being accepted; and a ratio of one to two and a quarter fixed between dollars and rupees.[2]

The following month, under instructions from H.M. Government, the axe of retrenchment fell, and the appointments of Land Officer, Surveyor, Acting Colonial Surgeon, and Superintendent of Roads were abolished.

On June 13th[3] Pottinger, feeling perhaps that with the establishment of the Land Committee he had done all that immediately required his personal presence on the island, or perhaps having received word that the time was at last ripe for treating with the Chinese, left Hong Kong and rejoined the expeditionary force.

[1] The sea-front of the period is also indicated in the Prison Report of September 1843. 'The prisons stand . . . directly below the Chief Magistrate's own house . . . 50 or 60 rods from the sea and about 300 feet above sea-level.'
[2] *Chin. Rep.*, vol. xi, p. 296.
[3] Ibid., p. 397; *Canton Press*, June 18th.

Once more Mr. Johnston was left in charge in Hong Kong; but, thanks to the assistance of the Land Committee, it was possible to report 'slow improvement'[1] in July; while in August 'the progress of public and private works had been somewhat accelerated'.

Among the 'private works' two may be singled out as worthy of notice—a Baptist chapel[2] in the Queen's Road, of which the Rev. J. L. Shuck, an American, was the first minister, 'a very neat and commodious building costing less than $1,000', which was dedicated[3] on July 17th; and the Morrison Education Society's house,[4] on Morrison Hill, which in September was 'begun and would soon be ready for the reception of the pupils'.

The faith of these pioneers was duly justified, for on September 9th news reached Hong Kong that Pottinger had on August 29th concluded a treaty[5]—to be known as the Treaty of Nanking—by which, *inter alia*, 'the island of Hong Kong was to be ceded in perpetuity to Her Majesty her heirs and successors'.[6]

Hong Kong island had thus, by a stroke of the pen, become a British possession; but its peaceful occupation and settlement continued to be vigorously disputed by a persistent and ubiquitous third party. In August the *Canton Press* regrets 'to learn that the climate or too liberal potations of samshoo are causing the death of many of the soldiers of whom no less than 47 were buried last month'.[7] In September the *Friend*

---

[1] *Chin. Rep.*, vol. xi, p. 400. [2] Ibid., p. 677.
[3] *Canton Press*, Aug. 6th. [4] *Chin. Rep.*, vol. xi, p. 520.
[5] Ibid., p. 519.
[6] Art. III of the Treaty will be found in Appendix VI.
[7] *Canton Press*, Aug. 20th.

128   POTTINGER

n. 14

of China records 'much sickness among the troops stationed at Chek Chu'.[1] At the end of October the 26th Cameronians arrived in Hong Kong from the north, 'where instead of finding a body of well drilled recruits (439 having landed here in the previous June) they found a mass of emaciated dying lads: 127 had already died'.[2] In November the troops lately returned to Hong Kong from the north were themselves suffering very severely from illness; the 98th regiment (which had arrived—with the 26th—from England the previous June) having not more than 36 men fit for duty.[3]

On December 2nd Pottinger returned to Hong Kong, and on the 20th 'transports and ships of war to the number of 50 and upwards sailed for India',[4] leaving only a small garrison.[5]

The 'captains and the kings' departed, but there still remained work for the plenipotentiary to do. Besides the cession of Hong Kong the Treaty had abolished the Hong monopoly in Canton and, by opening four new ports to foreign trade, had abolished the monopoly of Canton itself. In these five ports—Canton, Amoy, Fuchow, Ningpo, and Shanghai (to become familiarly known as 'Treaty ports')—all comers were to be free to trade subject only to a tariff on imports and exports at fixed and reasonable rates. Pottinger lost no time in taking the British merchants into consultation at Macao on the subject of the rates,[6] and in due course, though he found them strangely apathetic, an agreed tariff was announced. With the announcement Pottinger took the

---

[1] *Friend of China*, Sept. 1st.
[2] *China Rep.*, March 1843.   [3] *Canton Press*, Nov. 5th, 1842.
[4] Ibid., Dec. 10th, 1842.
[5] Ibid., Oct. 8th, 1842: the whole of the 98th, one wing of the 55th, one wing of the 41st Madras Infantry.   [6] Ibid., Jan 21st, 1843.

opportunity to urge the merchants to eschew all temptation to smuggle; and it is plain that the opening of fresh ports and the settling of a fixed and reasonable tariff was the obvious remedy for any tendency to do so, if by smuggling is meant evasion of legal duties. But it is equally plain that smuggling in the sense of the introduction of contraband remained unaffected no matter how many new ports were opened, or how fixed and reasonable the tariff; except, of course, in so far as the increased opportunities for legal trade might induce traders to abandon the illicit.

And, in the absence of all reference to it in the Treaty, opium, which had still continued during the war to be introduced from India, still remained in the category of contraband.

The opium situation, in fact, stood exactly where it had stood before the war and the Treaty; except for this one important difference, that England now had in Hong Kong (or was shortly to get) a place in the immediate proximity of China over which she was to exercise full sovereignty, and upon which she could accordingly store opium, or any other article she pleased, to her heart's content, by virtue of a right at least as incontestable as the right of China to prohibit its introduction to the mainland. I speak here in terms of what may be described as legality, though in actual fact international law is at best a shadowy region and, as touching the relations between Europe and China at this time, was non-existent.

As to the morality of the situation I forbear to pronounce. Many no doubt will indignantly deny that in such circumstances England had any excuse for permitting the storage of opium at Hong Kong: many will with equal indignation deny that China had any moral ground for prohibiting its importation while she grew the poppy within her own borders. Many will sympathize with China's weakness, and many unsympathetically diagnose the weakness as simple venality. Some will maintain that, in prohibiting opium, China acted from the noblest of motives—the love of humanity; and others, observing the actual relationship between Imperial officers ('mandarins') and the mass of the people, will allege that the motive was not love for their own people but hatred of the foreigner. Some will contrast the peaceful character of China with England's display of military force. But others will recollect the three strangulations staged at the Macao Barrier and the Canton factories by Commissioner Lin in 1839 and contrast them with Captain Elliot's solicitude for the welfare of two humble Chinese coolies caught carrying for Innes[1] in December 1838.

Of Pottinger's hopes to persuade the Chinese authorities to remove opium from the category of contraband; of the fading of those hopes; of his offers to them, and his threats to his own countrymen, to deny the protection of Hong Kong waters to opium-smugglers, some account is given in the succeeding chapter. Here the bald statement must suffice that, in point of historical fact, opium was at this time openly introduced into Hong Kong harbour, and openly stored in Hong Kong warehouses and store-ships; and that, for reasons which require little tax on the imagination to guess, these warehouses and store-ships constantly required replenishment.

With the new orientation of relations with China two

[1] *Vide supra*, Chap. VII, p. 53.

important Orders in Council, made under the provisions of the 'Act to regulate the Trade to China and India' (which provided the Superintendent with his power and authority), appeared at this time. The first prohibited, under pain of a fine of £100, the resort of British ships to any port in China excepting the agreed five, and the second transferred from Canton to Hong Kong the seat of the Court of Criminal and Admiralty Jurisdiction.

The announcement of its cession in perpetuity naturally gave heart to those who had thus far hesitated as to the wisdom of settling on the island; and in February we learn that 'buildings are progressing rapidly':[1] while in April a series of aquatints from sketches made by Mr. J. Prendergast,[2] draughtsman in the Land Office, recorded the early beginnings of Hong Kong's urbanization. But the taking out of titles did not keep pace, and in April, also, all and sundry were called upon to establish their claims to the land.[3] These signs of civilization were, however, counterbalanced by an epidemic of house-breaking—an indirect consequence, perhaps, of the withdrawal of the fleet—which reached such dimensions that Major Caine, in May, decided to impose a curfew requiring Chinese residents to carry a lantern if abroad between sundown and 10 p.m. and forbidding them to be abroad after that hour.[4]

The time for Treaty ratification now approached. Colonel Malcolm, who had taken the document home, had returned with it ratified in March.[5] In April Keying, another Manchu (in succession to Elepoo, who had died), received the

n. 15

[1] *Chin. Rep.*, vol. xii, Feb.   [2] *Canton Press*, April 29th.
[3] Ibid., April 15th.   [4] Ibid., Feb. 4th, 1843.   [5] Ibid., March 25th.

132 POTTINGER

appointment of High Commissioner for the exchange of ratifications.[1] On June 23rd the High Commissioner was duly escorted[2] by a British naval vessel from Canton to Hong Kong; and

'on Monday June 26th 1843 at 5 o'clock p.m. the ceremony of the exchange of the ratification of the Treaty of Nanking took place.[3] ... Her Majesty's proclamation declaring Hong Kong to be a possession of the Crown was read by Lieutenant Colonel Malcolm and, when this was finished, and Keying had retired, the Royal Warrant was read, appointing Sir Henry Pottinger Governor of the Colony of Hong Kong and its dependencies.'

The Royal Charter and Commission are heavy fare for this narrative, but the briefer public announcement[4] by the first Governor will be found in the Appendix.[5]

'In the evening of the same day a large dinner party was given at Government House in honor of the Chinese Commissioner';[6] an affair in which even the phlegmatic Sir Henry Pottinger unbent sufficiently to indulge in song, to the apparent pleasure of the ever polite Keying.

Almost simultaneously with the exchange of ratifications—on June 11th, to be precise—the first Roman Catholic Chapel in Hong Kong, the chapel of the Conception, was consecrated.[7] This chapel was situated at the junction of Wellington and Pottinger Streets, and, as we know, was destined to be the forerunner of many important Roman Catholic establishments in the Colony.

As for the general appearance of the town at this date we

---

[1] *Canton Press*, May 6th.
[2] *Chin. Rep.*, vol. xii, p. 335.
[3] Ibid.
[4] *Canton Press*, July 8th, 1843.
[5] See Appendix VII.
[6] *Chin. Rep.*, vol. xii, p. 335.
[7] Ibid., p. 336.

are again fortunate in having the considered account of an eyewitness, the Rev. James Legge.[1] His description, it is true, was made at an interval of nearly thirty years, and to that extent must no doubt be discounted. None the less it is the account of a highly reliable witness describing his first impressions on arrival, and is therefore, I think, worthy of credence.

n. 16

After pointing out that 'the waters of the bay came up to the Queen's Road for the greater part of its extent between East and West Points' he proceeds:

'Hollywood Road and the streets running down from it to the Queen's Road were also indicated in a rudimentary fashion. A little beyond the present Sailors' Home were the Naval Stores, and south of them, all the indentations of the Hill where the reformatory now stands were occupied with the tents and huts peopled by the 55th Regiment.

'From that eastward all was blank to the bluff where the Civil Hospital rises, and on which was a bungalow built by Jameson, How and Co. . . . The next European buildings were Gibb, Livingston and Company's premises, enclosed within a ring fence.[2]

'Turning to the West where Wellington Street runs into Queen's Road you could see a few Chinese houses on either side of the latter, and Jervois Street was in course of formation, the houses on the north side of it having the waters of the bay washing about among them. Eastwards from the same point on to Pottinger Street Queen's Road was pretty well lined with Chinese houses; the Central Market was formed. . . . Looking up Aberdeen Street you saw a few indications of building, and a house on the South of Gage Street forming the headquarters of the Madras Regiment, and looking up Pottinger Street you could see the Magistracy and Gaol of the day, where the

---

[1] See *China Review*, Nov. 5th, 1872.
[2] At foot of Aberdeen Street—Gough Street on site of Kau U Fong.

n. 17

dreaded Major Caine presided, and below them were 2 or 3 other buildings. On from Pottinger Street a few English merchants had established themselves. On the West of D'Aguilar Street (not then so named) building was going on and just opposite to it was a small house called the Bird Cage out of which was hatched the Hong Kong dispensary. All the space between Wyndham Street and Wellington Street was garden ground with an imposing flat-roofed house in it built by Mr. Brain of the firm of Dent and Co.[1] That great firm had its quarters where the Hong Kong hotel is now, and further on was Lindsay and Company's house. . . . All else on the North side of the street was blank on to the Artillery Barracks which were building.

n. 18

'On the South of the street was the Harbour Master's establishment on Pedder's Hill—and as conspicuous as are now Messrs. Heard and Company's offices which were manufactured from it, rose the house of Mr. Johnston who had been administrator of the island on its first occupancy.

'On the parade ground was a small mat building, which was the Colonial Church, and above it, about where the Cathedral and Government offices now stand, were the unpretending Government offices of that early time, and the Post Office. Far up, if I recollect aright, might be seen a range of barracks out of which have been fashioned the present Albany residences; and beyond the site of the present Government House was a small bungalow where Sir Henry Pottinger and Sir John Davis after him held their court. . . .'

The new Governor proceeded without delay to establish a Civil Service, or rather to adopt, with some modifications, the existing establishment. Mr. A. R. Johnston became, with the abolition of the post of Deputy Superintendent, 'Assistant and Registrar to the Superintendent'; the Lieutenant-Governorship devolved on the General Officer Commanding the

n. 19

[1] The reference appears to be to 'Green Bank', which stood between Zetland and Wyndham Streets.

troops; Lieutenant-Colonel Malcolm, Secretary of Legation, was appointed officiating Colonial Secretary; Mr. Charles Stewart became Treasurer; Major Caine, Lieutenant Pedder, and Mr. J. R. Morrison were confirmed each in his office of Chief Magistrate, Harbour Master, and Chinese Secretary.

At the same time forty-three J.P.s, a number which comprised practically all the leading British residents of the Colony, were appointed,[1] with responsibilities (as the original oath clearly shows)[2] not only vis-à-vis their fellow residents in the Colony but also vis-à-vis 'all British subjects resorting to the Dominions of the Emperor of China'; an experiment in administration which was revoked a year later on the appointment of stipendiaries in the persons of consuls and vice-consuls at the Treaty ports.

n. 20

A month later[3] as required by the Royal Charter the first Legislative and Executive Council was created, Messrs. Johnston, Morrison, and Caine—a merchant, a missionary, and a soldier—being nominated.

n. 21

Meantime negotiations for a tariff had been concluded and in July Pottinger formally published it,[4] taking the opportunity, as noted above, strongly to adjure the merchants to abstain from smuggling and duty-evasion.

The military authorities had by now also decided on their requirements in the matter of land at the centre of the town; and I append, as showing the origin of the military lands at Hong Kong, a letter addressed by Government to certain land-holders.[5]

---

[1] *Canton Press*, July.
[2] Norton Kyshe, vol. i, p. 25.
[3] *Canton Press*, Aug. 26th.
[4] Ibid., July 22nd.
[5] Ibid., July 29th.

> Government House, Victoria,
> Hong Kong, July 22nd, 1843.
>
> Gentlemen,
>
> I am directed by His Excellency the Governor to acquaint you, that a plan has been proposed by Major Aldrich of the Royal Engineers for laying out and fortifying the centre part of this city by which plan the locations at present in your respective possession, lying between the ravine separating Government Hill from the adjoining one to the Eastward, and the Protestant Burial Ground will be included within what will be termed 'Ordnance Ground', and that it is therefore possible that you will hereafter be called on to restore these locations to Government, being paid for the buildings you have erected, and the expenses you have incurred on them, and being granted other locations in lieu of them.
>
> Major Aldrich's plan will be referred to England by the mail that leaves this Colony by the 'Akbar' steamer on the 1st of next month, and the early decision of H.M.'s Government will be solicited regarding it.
>
> H.E. the Governor further directs me to acquaint you, that he has not himself, after full consideration, seen cause to recommend Major Aldrich's plan to the authorities at home, but as its adoption or otherwise rests entirely on the pleasure of H.M.'s Government, His Excellency thinks it right to give you this timely notice of the question that has arisen. In the meantime, under the uncertainty that exists, you will, of course, be exempted from the payment of any ground rent, until the point shall be decided.
>
> I have, etc.,
> RICHARD WOOSNAM.

The first executive act of the new Governor was to appoint two Committees,[1] one a Committee of Public Health to enforce 'a rigid system of attention to Sanatary Rules'; and the other a special Land Committee to determine the equitable

---

[1] *Canton Press*, Aug. 19th.

claims of land-holders in view of the refusal of Her Majesty's Government to recognize grants made prior to the exchange of ratifications 'upon which event the Island of Hong Kong' (I quote Pottinger's proclamation) 'became a "bona fide" Possession of the British Crown'.[1]

n. 22

The appointment of the Public Health Committee was, no doubt, largely determined by a recrudescence of sickness. The 55th regiment (which had followed the Bengal Volunteers to West Point) suffered particularly, losing a hundred men between June and the middle of August.[2] Civilians suffered too, the most prominent victim being Mr. J. R. Morrison, who, at the very moment of the announcement of his appointment, as acting Colonial Secretary in the absence of Colonel Malcolm, to the Councils, was being transferred, sick with 'Hong Kong fever', to Macao, where he died a week later.[3]

n. 23

'An irreparable national calamity' was the epitaph of Sir Henry Pottinger—another striking tribute to the value of Anglo-Chinese interpreters.

The attack on this occasion was a severe one, and the stoutest hearts quailed. Pottinger himself transferred temporarily to Macao.[4] The *Friend of China and Hong Kong Gazette*—Hong Kong's keenest partisan—voiced its doubts:

'What with the insecurity of life and property from the numerous robberies and piracies—the prevailing sickness—the low tariff at Canton ... and more than all the contingent interference with our privileges as a Free Port it is in no way surprising that some of the earliest friends of the colony have now abandoned it in disgust ...

[1] Ibid., Aug. 26.
[2] Bernard, *Nemesis*, vol. ii, p. 75.
[3] *Canton Press*, Sept. 2nd.
[4] Ibid., Aug. 26th.

there is hardly an individual who has invested funds in Hong Kong who would not, if reimbursed his outlay, be but too glad to depart never to return—so drear and black are our present prospects.'[1]

The same sentiment was repeated from the same quarter three weeks later:

'Compared with what it could and should have been, all must admit Hong Kong as now is but a notable failure, the death-birth of the most promising settlement ever founded by British enterprise.'[2]

The news appears even to have reached the ears of the Queen, who, on January 10th, 1844, thus addresses her Secretary of State:

'The Queen understands . . . that there is a notion of exchanging Hong Kong for a more healthy colony.

'The Queen, taking a deep interest in all these matters, and feeling it her duty to do so, begs Lord Aberdeen to keep her always well informed of what is on the tapis in his Department.'[3]

The press would seem to have had advance intelligence of what was afoot. On October 8th Pottinger and Keying concluded at the Bogue a Supplementary Treaty embodying the agreed tariff;[4] laying down the conditions of conducting trade at the five ports, and making a number of important provisions for its conduct as between China and Hong Kong.

The ninth article provided for the reciprocal extradition of criminals; the fifteenth for the reciprocal recovery of debts incurred on the one hand by British merchants at the five ports and on the other by Chinese merchants at Hong Kong. The thirteenth required all persons, whether natives of China or otherwise, conveying goods to Hong Kong, to provide

[1] *Friend of China*, Sept. 7th. [2] Ibid., Sept. 28th.
[3] *Queen Victoria's Letters*, vol. ii, p. 4. [4] *China Rep.*, vol. xiii, p. 440.

themselves first with a pass from one of the five ports; and further for all natives of China desiring to import goods from Hong Kong in a Chinese vessel to secure first from the Customs of one of the five ports a pass for the vessel. The fourteenth article provided for the examination of such passes by a British officer at Hong Kong; the sixteenth for a monthly return of passes to be exchanged between the British officer and the Hoppo (Customs Commissioner) at Canton; while the seventeenth (or additional) article caught in its mesh the lorchas and cutters and such-like smaller craft plying between Hong Kong and Canton.

Lord Palmerston, it will be recalled, had demanded, with a view to opening up trade with the more northerly ports, either an island off the east coast or a limited number of ports where British traders could reside with their families and trade. He had no doubt assumed that, given an island, Chinese trading-vessels from every port in China would resort there freely for trade. But I surmise he had not realized that, given Hong Kong and a limited number of ports, the logical result would be to limit to those ports the trade with Hong Kong.

Pottinger could claim to have secured both an island and four additional residential ports; but the price paid was the unavoidable one of confining the trade to the 'tram-lines' so carefully and clearly marked out by the Supplementary Treaty.

Whether he himself foresaw the result is an open question. It is by no means impossible that he accepted it with his eyes open, as the method best calculated in the long run to thwart the smuggler and build up a law-abiding trade between England and China.

Except for particular extracts the Treaty was not made

public until the following July. The delay is accounted for by the necessity once more of securing ratification from home; but it may well be that Pottinger was not altogether unwilling to leave to his successor the task of breaking unpalatable news.

At the very end of December two figures of some interest took the stage: Staunton,[1] who four years before had been taken prisoner by the Chinese at Macao, and who now came to Hong Kong to become the first Colonial Chaplain; and Major-General D'Aguilar,[2] General Officer Commanding and the first Lieutenant-Governor.

n. 24   The year 1844 opened with a second land sale,[3] 101 lots, averaging 105 feet square, being put up to auction on a 75-year lease and fetching a yearly rental of just over £2,500. During the early months of the year the newly created Legislative Council also gave proof of considerable vigour, passing a series of ordinances[4] for the government of the Colony and also (by virtue of an Imperial Act vesting legislative power in the Superintendent, so long as he be also Governor of Hong Kong, with the advice of the Legislative Council of Hong Kong)[5] a parallel series for the control of British subjects elsewhere in China.

With the latter we are not concerned here. But the early Colonial ordinances are documents of much value as indicating the Colony's early problems. I single out the first of all,
n. 25   which (gratuitously, as it proved) proscribed slavery; the third, providing for the registration of deeds affecting land, which
n. 26   still survives as Ordinance 1 of 1844; the fifth, providing for 'good order and cleanliness', the forerunner of Ordinance 1

---

[1] *Chin. Rep.*, vol. xiii, p. 46.   [2] Ibid.   [3] Ibid., p. 51.
[4] Ibid., p. 165.   [5] Ibid., pp. 48, 49.

of 1845 (Summary Offences); and the twelfth, establishing a Police Force.

Ordinance No. 5 of 1844 is, I conceive, the classical example of the 'omnibus' ordinance, covering, as it does, not only every conceivable crime, misdemeanour, peccadillo, or foible to which European soldiers and sailors of the middle nineteenth century were susceptible, but also that remarkable parallel range more favoured by the Chinese.

It was an offence, without obvious necessity, to drive upon the footpath; and equally, being a pedestrian, to fail, as much as possible, to keep to it. The highly improbable event of one horse and carriage meeting another is fully provided for. All good citizens must affix to their houses and keep alight during the night 'such lamp or lantern' as the superintendent of police required. It was an offence 'to be seen drunk in any public road or passage or to insult a female in public'. One could not with impunity either challenge another to a fight or expose one's sores to excite compassion and obtain alms. It was an offence to be abroad at night and fail for a satisfactory reason; and equally an offence to exercise the magic arts and impose upon the credulity of any for the sake of gain. And, finally, one could not leave one's employer's service without affording him sufficient time to engage a successor.

Sir Henry Pottinger had completed to the letter the task for which he had been sent out, and now awaited his relief.[1] He arrived on May 7th in the person of Mr. J. F. Davis.

On the following day the new plenipotentiary, Superintendent, and Governor was duly sworn; Pottinger remaining until June 21st, when he embarked for Bombay.

[1] Ibid., p. 266.

CHAPTER X

JOHN F. DAVIS
1844–1848

MR. DAVIS was no stranger to China. As a young man, aged 22, he had, in 1816, accompanied Lord Amherst on his embassy to Pekin, in the role of secretary. He had afterwards risen in the service of the East India Company until he reached the dignity of member of the Company's Select Committee in Canton. When serving in that capacity he had been selected as third member of the original superintendency of trade of which Lord Napier was the Chief; and on Napier's death in October 1834 he had succeeded for a brief period as Chief Superintendent.

In January 1835 he had resigned and returned home, where he had spent his spare time publishing three or four volumes in which, with great industry and no little insight, he had touched upon almost every aspect of Chinese manners and customs.

And now, after an absence of nearly ten years, he was renewing his old association with the Far East.

Neither his connexions with the East India Company nor, perhaps, his interest in things Chinese would tend to make him *persona grata* with the British 'free traders'. But we need not conclude that the Foreign Secretary, in choosing him now, had overlooked his past. No doubt he regarded him, after making due allowance for the mellowing effect of increased years, as a suitable instrument for toning down any excessive crudities of free-trade notions.

Sir Henry Pottinger had attained all his objectives precisely according to programme. The island of Hong Kong had been ceded unconditionally and in perpetuity. The monopoly of the Hong merchants at Canton had been abolished. Four new ports had been thrown open to foreign trade. The indemnity, in so far as it was not already paid, was amply secured by the retention of Chusan.

Nevertheless, the task which fell to Mr. Davis, of consolidating these gains, though more prosaic, was scarcely less difficult. It required of him in his capacity of Governor to rear the young Victoria, a lively but sometimes fractious infant; and simultaneously, as Superintendent, to bring to birth a new trade at each of the four new ports; and, more exacting still, to supervise the re-birth, according to modern principles, of the old-established commerce at Canton.

Nor was this all: for the mantle of plenipotentiary also fell upon his shoulders, giving him authority to settle any outstanding points, in connexion with the treaties, left undetermined by Pottinger.

With the new Governor came the first Chief Justice—Mr. J. W. Hulme,[1] automatically relieving him of the judicial functions which hitherto had resided in the Superintendency. In his judicial capacity Sir Henry Pottinger had, on the top of his other duties, been called upon to preside at the Supreme Court in criminal sessions to try a charge of murder; and at the opening session he had expressed the fervent wish—with which no doubt Major-General D'Aguilar, the G.O.C., who was co-opted to the bench, heartily concurred—that he were well out of it. But, as it turned out, his successor found the

[1] Norton Kyshe, vol. i, p. 37.

division of authority inconvenient—at any rate in regard to affairs at the Treaty ports. Nor is this to be wondered at, for the relations of foreigners to Chinese at the Treaty ports were still largely a matter of improvisation. And though the Chief Justice was doubtless legally correct in quashing the sentence passed by the Canton Consul (and confirmed by Mr. Davis) fining an English merchant, Mr. Compton, $200 for his share in an assault in July 1846 which had led to a riot and loss of life, the practical result was deplorable. The arrangement was, however, at least in accordance with the pure orthodoxy of English administrative machinery; but, unhappily for consistency, it was forthwith stultified by the appointment of the Chief Justice to be a member of the Legislative Council. This was probably unavoidable, for a lawyer was a rarity on the China coast; but it is tolerably clear that it afforded frequent opportunities to Davis and Hulme to cross swords; and it may be shrewdly guessed that it was to fortify frayed nerves after some particularly exasperating encounter with the imperturbable and keen-witted Governor that Hulme yielded himself too easily to the solace of the cup. In due course retribution, in the form of an inquiry before the Executive Council, ensued; and Mr. Hulme, found guilty of insobriety, was suspended and sent home; ultimately to be reinstated, after Davis's departure, by the Secretary of State.

n. 1

Another fellow passenger of Mr. Davis, the new Treasurer, Mr. R. Montgomery Martin, soon fell foul of his Chief; and the reader who has personal acquaintance with a humdrum P. & O. sea voyage of four or five weeks' duration will perhaps doubt the wisdom of packing into the same cockleshell for a journey of as many months gentlemen destined on arrival at their destination to bandy official business for the ensuing five or six years.

Mr. Davis, having reached Hong Kong on May 7th, 1844, proceeded forthwith to assume his triple functions; although Sir Henry Pottinger did not leave for a further six weeks. Whether this delay in Pottinger's departure had any special significance or was caused merely by lack of transport is not revealed; but it is certain that the occasion of the overlap was taken to arrange a meeting with Keying at the Bogue, at which the departing envoy introduced his successor to the High Commissioner.

It is probable that on this occasion the ratifications of the Supplementary Treaty of the Bogue of October 8th were formally exchanged; for a month later, in July 1844, that treaty was published in full for the first time by Davis.

It may perhaps also be surmised that Sir Henry Pottinger made a final effort to induce Keying to grasp the nettle of opium legalization, and so rid his successor of a *damnosa hereditas*. But, if so, he was, as we shall see, unsuccessful.

On Pottinger's departure Mr. Davis applied himself at once to the business of legislation both for the government of Hong Kong and for the government of British residents in China. The latter part of his work is, as I have already pointed out, beyond my last; but it is well to bear in mind that all the time there were such parallel activities, and that not only was the Governor himself doubling the part of Superintendent, but the Legislative Council of Hong Kong, besides making laws for the residents of the Colony, made laws also for British subjects resorting to the Treaty ports or the China Seas; while the Supreme Court of Hong Kong exercised a like double jurisdiction.

Mr. Davis's first piece of legislation, which was doubtless already on the stocks before he arrived, created native Chinese Peace Officers. This Ordinance—No. 13 of 1844—in return for a little brief authority seems to have imposed on the selected gentlemen liabilities to heavy penalties for dereliction of their honorary task, and was repealed in 1857.

Ordinance 14 of 1844 prohibited public gaming, a principle persistently supported by the Chinese people; Ordinance 15 established the Supreme Court of judicature; and Ordinance 16, requiring all inhabitants of Hong Kong to be registered, provoked the first general strike.

The British mercantile community apparently regarded the measure as appropriate if applied to the Chinese 'riff-raff', but as an intolerable affront as applied to themselves: while the Chinese community, though perhaps arguing from somewhat different premisses, very readily made common cause against the Government. In the result the obnoxious features of the Bill were softened by exempting all of whatever nationality who could produce $500.

But a serious rift between the Government, then purely official, and the British merchants had been created; and the Colony had its first taste of the power of corporate action on the part of the Chinese populace.

Mr. Davis's next Ordinance—No. 17 of 1844, 'for the better securing the peace and quiet of the town of Victoria'—embodied and amplified Pottinger's No. 5 'for the preservation of good order and cleanliness' and was destined to be incorporated in No. 14 of 1845, better known as the Summary Offences Ordinance 1 of 1845.

Ordinance 1 of 1845 survived with few amendments until

1932; indeed it remains to this day virtually unchanged (except in title) as one of the main pieces of police legislation in the Colony. Mr. Davis can therefore, like his predecessor, claim, by the test of long survival, to have placed something of considerable importance upon the statute-book of Hong Kong.

It fell to Mr. Davis's lot, too, to strike the first blow against the habit, to which the Chinese immigrants were in particular incorrigibly addicted, of encroaching beyond the legal limits of their lots by the erection of verandas or even of establishing themselves—in the true tradition of Heath Robinson—in mat-sheds and other improvised dwellings without the formality of acquiring any title whatever to the land. A peremptory proclamation against 'mat-houses' was issued in October 1844 and followed next month by another against verandas. But in the following January a compromise had been reached; and verandas, an obvious convenience to the pedestrian in a tropical country, were treated as a legitimate easement, and have so remained to this day.

So too, it must be confessed, has the squatter and the mat-house, though the prohibition still holds good.

It was, however, by a series of revenue bills, Ordinances 2, 3, 4, and 5 of 1845, that Davis achieved immediate notoriety and evoked fierce opposition by the British merchants.

Ordinance 2 raised a mild rate for the maintenance of a very necessary police force; Ordinances 3 and 4 required licences for the sale of liquor and tobacco; and Ordinance 5, among other things, farmed out the monopoly of the retail trade in opium in the Colony.

Hinc illae lacrimae. The British community—or at least

the early pioneers who had taken up land under Captain Elliot or Mr. Johnston in 1841—conceived themselves aggrieved when, in 1843, on the formal cession of the island, the Crown, instead of granting them the fee simple or at least a perpetual lease, for which they claimed they had been encouraged by Elliot to hope, approved a lease of seventy-five years only, non-renewable.[1] They had made this a subject of protest to Sir Henry Pottinger in 1844, but the Secretary of State, though making some concession on the question of renewal, had substantially maintained his original conclusion. This decision reached Hong Kong very shortly after Mr. Davis's arrival;[2] but—we have Mr. Davis's own word for it—had been accepted philosophically by the parties concerned. Two months later, however, they presented a heavily signed petition, complaining comprehensively of the exactions imposed on them, for immediate transmission to the Secretary of State.

The straw which had broken the camel's back was the police-rate, calculated on the assessed value of tenements and chargeable on Crown lessees, imposed by Ordinance 2 of 1845. So much is clear from the letter covering the memorial demanding the immediate suspension of the Ordinance. But the memorial itself, having opened with a full and detailed account of the early land sales, concluded, with remarkable inconsequence, with an 'urgent entreaty for the abolition of the opium farm', a proposition to which Mr. Davis, bland as ever, retorted: 'The opium and smaller licensed farms have been strictly adopted in their details from Singapore—a place generally quoted as a model of free trade prosperity.'[3]

---

[1] *Comm. Rel.*, pp. 414, 415.   [2] Ibid., p. 422.   [3] Ibid., p. 417.

The petition, like an earlier one which passed through Mr. Davis's hands ten years before, was perhaps somewhat 'crude and ill-digested'; but it produced, in 1847, a full-blown parliamentary committee to inquire at large into commercial relations with China; before which the whole of the grievances of the pioneers—not to mention the jeremiad of Mr. Montgomery Martin[1]—were brought out into the cold light of day.

In the event the view of those who defined a free port as one at which opium could be freely bought and sold by the local merchants while the expenses of the civil and military establishments were paid by the Home Government was not accepted. But, while opium for local consumption continued to be taxed and ground-rents continued to be charged, the tenure of the land was extended, in the case of 'pre-cession' lot-holders, to nine hundred and ninety-nine years.

The balance-sheet for the Colony for the year 1845, too long to reproduce here, shows that Sir John Davis can claim, besides his achievement in police legislation, to have laid the foundation of the Colony's fiscal system. Indeed it may be surmised that it was largely for this service that he became Sir John.

The year 1844 had produced a general strike by the civil community of Hong Kong; 1845 an appeal to the Secretary of State by the British residents. In 1846 and 1847 it was Canton that provided the more stirring events.

Unlike the native inhabitants of the newly opened ports the Cantonese people remained irreconcilably hostile to the English. Various motives have been suggested for this—the contempt bred of familiarity, the more mercurial temperament of the Cantonese, and so forth—but the elimination of vested

[1] *Vide infra*, pp. 160–1.

interests and, in particular, the loss by the linguists of that highly valuable monopoly, the monopoly of interpretation, unquestionably accounted for much.

Spasmodic incidents occurred. In 1842[1] and again in 1844 serious rioting took place at the factories. In 1843 Pottinger had agreed that, despite the express terms of the Treaty, the time was not opportune to insist on the right of entry to the City of Canton. In 1846 Davis reopened the matter, and, under pressure, Keying endeavoured to force the pace; but with fatal results: for the Cantonese mob attacked the prefect in the city in January, and in April Davis, while securing an admission of the principle from the Emperor, consented to an indefinite postponement of its exercise. In July, by one of those strange coincidences which are known to occur on the China coast, on the very eve of the due date for the return of Chusan to China a grave clash occurred between the Cantonese mob and the residents of the British factories, resulting in the death of several Chinese;[2] while in 1847, in conjunction with Major-General D'Aguilar at the head of a handful of troops drawn from the Hong Kong garrison, Davis carried out a successful *coup de main* against Canton, in the course of which several hundred guns mounted in the Bogue forts were spiked without the loss of a man.

This remarkable demonstration was undertaken to enforce the demand for redress against violence offered to British residents in Canton; and its immediate effect was salutary. But if Davis had hoped, at the same time, to obtain immediate admission to the city he was disappointed. The most he got was a definite date, but that date involved a delay of two years

---

[1] *Chin. Rep.*, Dec.; *Insults*, 1857.   [2] The 'Compton' case, *vide* p. 144.

—until April 1849, in fact—with the result that both Keying and Davis had vacated their posts before the time came round.

But it was left for the closing weeks of the year to provide the most serious outrage hitherto perpetrated by Chinese on foreigners—the murder of six English merchants, young and perhaps foolhardy, in a village two or three miles from Canton.

Davis promptly and unremittingly demanded the punishment of the guilty, and ultimately secured it. But no change of heart was evinced by the Canton populace, which to the last remained hostile and defiant.

All this time Victoria continued to grow. In July 1844 another sale of land took place. By November the civil officers' quarters at the Albany were already[1] built and occupied. In October the *Chinese Repository*, which, it may be noted, had itself just removed to Hong Kong, reports that 'the number of houses now building in Victoria—is 100'.

In February 1845 the same periodical describes the place as 'improving and rising rapidly . . . but the fear is it will outgrow itself'.

A month or so later it provides us with a detailed description of the centre of the town, which I reproduce in full:[2]

'The ruins of a market with an old military hospital and a magazine come first in the centre division of the town. Next on high ground are the badly-contrived, half built, and half-demolished death-generating buildings once known as the Artillery Barracks.

'In front of them three buildings are being erected, which will be an ornament of the settlement. One is a military hospital;[3] the others are for the engineer and ordnance departments.

n. 2
n. 3

n. 4

n. 5

[1] *Chin. Rep.*, vol. xiii, Nov.   [2] Ibid., vol. xiv, p. 294.   [3] Now Wellington Barracks.

'Between these are three large commercial houses, and behind the latter are some twenty or thirty Chinese shops. A line of commissariate buildings partly occupied by the Ordnance and engineer departments fill up the space to the streamlet, descending from the east side of Government House. Behind these commissariate buildings is the Canton Bazaar: and above it westwards some new buildings designated the "General's Quarters" are in progress, the old ones occupied by Lord Saltoun having been justly condemned and demolished.

n. 6

'Passing the streamlet the ground instead of being only a few rods in breadth, stretches off up a gentle acclivity for a full half mile. Close by the mouth of the streamlet are some barracks, with naval stores on the beach. South of them three buildings are being erected for officers and soldiers. Beyond these southward are lines of mat-houses in which are Indian troops.

'The parade ground comes next as you go westward. Between it and the Queen's Road is the Colonial Church, a building without prototype, but worthy to be sketched and preserved among the annals of the Colony. The post office is on the South and the Governor's private residence on the West of the parade ground. Further westward and higher up the hill is Government House. . . .

n. 7

'Westward still and on the beach are three commercial houses among the best in the Colony; above them on the south of Queen's Road is the Harbour-master's house. Here terminates the central district of Victoria. . . .'

At this time the Surveyor-General had already elaborated schemes for extensive reclamation; the construction of a continuous praya in front of the marine lots; and the construction of a canal to enable goods to be water-borne into the town.

n. 8

In October 1845 an ice-house was advertised—the same, no doubt, as that referred to in the Governor's dispatch of October 10th, 1846:

'A square of 80 feet by 60 was required for the erection of a public ice-house by subscription; and as ice has been found of

View on the Queen's Road looking East from the Canton Bazaar
20th August, 1846

Facing page 153]

important efficacy as a remedy in fevers I was induced to grant that small space free of rent.'

In January 1846 the formation of a cricket-ground and race-course at 'Wiang La Chung' was mooted in the *Friend of China*. In May the Hong Kong Club was opened. In July Mr. M. Bruce, surveyor of roads, advertises his prints 'delineating Architecture of Victoria, the villages, temples, and picturesque scenery of the Island with descriptive letter Press: the whole intended to convey to the eye and the mind a complete Picture of Hong Kong.' In March a list of houses appearing in the *China Mail* shows the grand total for the entire island to be 1,874. In August tenders were called for to prepare the site of the Colonial Chapel and Government offices, i.e. the Cathedral and the Colonial Secretariat; and the approaching advent of a bishop was hailed as proof that the 'Hong Kong Government believes that Hong Kong should be something more than a mere garrison town or a sanatorium for residents of Canton during the summer months';[1] while at various dates during the year Mr. W. H. Franklyn advertises a lorcha running to Canton, Macao, and Kum-sing-mun with opium, a typical merchant's house 'with Treasury and stable below', and the approaching departure for England of 'the fine 500 ton ship "Augusta Jessel" boasting a splendid, airy poop accommodation for passengers'.

n. 9
n. 10

On March 11th, 1847, the first stone of the Cathedral was laid by Sir John Davis, whose coat of arms—a bloody hand—appears over the *porte-cochère*.[2]

[1] *Friend of China*, Aug. 1st, 1846, p. 1284.
[2] *Comm. Rel.*, p. 432. The date will be found at the west end of the Cathedral. The date—November 16th, 1869—at the east end is the date of the chancel only, a

n. 11

In October a further sale of Crown land, the third since the cession, took place, including 'the lots in the valley where the ice-house is situated',[1] as a result of which Mr. George Duddell, among others, secured accommodation.

With the expansion of the town the British civilian population increased, having risen from 158 in 1837, 230 in 1841, and 259 in 1842 to 618 (of which 167 were females) in 1847.[2]

The state of health was also decidedly improving, but still left something to be desired, for 'though there was no fatal fever between Pedder's House and Shuck's Baptist Chapel'—i.e. between Wyndham Street and Kau U Fong—'the Artillery Barracks and the Government residence of Pottinger [sic] remained pestilential'. For civilians the suggestion was made that 'a hospital on the Peak would be the means of saving many lives'.[3] Service men had more tangible consolation in the shape of 'the magnificent construction of barracks and hospital'—Murray and Wellington Barracks—'monuments to the ability of D'Aguilar'.

Major-General D'Aguilar had also seen to it that the G.O.C. was provided with a substantial and pleasant residence—Head-quarters or Flagstaff House. He appears to have been of a convivial temperament, and during his tenancy sounds of revelry by night not infrequently floated down from Head-quarters House to the Canton Bazaar below.

n. 12

The place was undoubtedly growing, and growing quickly; but, nevertheless, no one appeared to be quite clear what all the activity was about.

subsequent addition, of which (as the tablet indicates) the foundation-stone was laid by the Duke of Edinburgh.

[1] *Comm. Rel.*, p. 430.   [2] Ibid., p. 433.   [3] *Chin. Rep.*, vol. xv, p. 126.

The *Friend of China*, at any rate, was vague. In January of 1846 Hong Kong is 'a possible naval depot'; in May 'it is not valuable as a commercial entrepot'. In October 'as a market Hong Kong is valueless. ... As a port of trans-shipment it is of importance!' In November (quoting *The Times*) 'the prospect of Hong Kong as a Commercial Colony are not good. ... It is a supplementary establishment to the five ports and it appears to have been looked upon as a most important opium station —a depot for the Indian market and a place of security whence the whole coast might be conveniently supplied with the drug.'

It was, indeed, opium which still loomed large and darkened the relations between Britain and China at this time. The situation was a strange one and, despite the anachronism, may justly be described as Gilbertian. Indeed it is probable that it actually suggested to Mr. W. S. Gilbert many of his most whimsical conceits.

True to his instructions Sir Henry Pottinger had studiously avoided reference to opium in his negotiations for the Treaty, but, also by instructions, he had, immediately after the Treaty had been signed, informally raised the subject, urging the Chinese plenipotentiaries to face the facts and legalize the trade. He had pointed out, as instructed, that Great Britain had not the power to prevent the importation of the drug; though they might control their own people they could not control those of other nations; though the great bulk of what was then imported was raised within her territory there was no assurance that that would always be the case and therefore not even suppression of the present source of supply was the complete answer.

As for China, owing to the venality of her officials and the insistent demand for the drug by her people she could clearly not exclude it.

The drug was bound to find its way in. Why not then recognize it and divert to Imperial coffers at least some part of the illicit gains which now poured into the pockets of disloyal officials?

There was this added advantage that, the trade become legal, the outflow of silver which China had regarded as such a deplorable feature would tend to cease. The existing situation, moreover, held this objection: that in the midst of evasion and connivance some zealous official might (as in the past) arise and come into violent conflict with the smuggling vessels, to the hazard of all those friendly relations recently sealed by the Treaty.

The obligation to prevent importation, it must be distinctly understood, could not be accepted by Great Britain, any more than Great Britain could expect, say, France to prevent the importation into England of some article, produced in France and eagerly desired by the English people, which England chose to declare contraband.

England would give no countenance or protection to opium-smugglers, if their offence was specifically brought home to them individually (though their lives must not be forfeit); and if cases were noticed by the Consuls they would inform the Chinese officials; but the duty of search and prevention they would not undertake. It must be for China herself to enforce the rule which she elected to make.

To all these arguments the Chinese plenipotentiaries turned a deaf ear; explaining that it was impossible, at the very moment that a treaty of perpetual amity and friendship had been signed leaving *in statu quo* the opium situation (at the very moment when, in the American Treaty, it had been expressly declared to be contraband), to reopen the matter with the Emperor.

The result was that the opium trade, for which Hong Kong had been the distributing centre during the war, continued to flourish and expand. At Whampoa it was carried on so openly and on such a large scale that in April 1843 Pottinger called the attention of the Chinese High Commissioner Keying to it, giving the desire to dissociate himself from the business as his excuse. To this Keying had replied that, while not for a moment suspecting the plenipotentiary's complicity, he supposed a certain amount of such evasion was unavoidable.

A similar situation arose on a subsequent occasion at Shanghai, when the British Consul venturing to draw the attention of the local Chinese official to a flagrant case of opium-smuggling received no thanks whatever for his pains.

The British merchants, on their part, endeavoured to force the issue by openly entering the Treaty ports with opium, claiming that it was one of the unspecified articles in the tariff admissible at a flat rate. And this had evoked a proclamation from Pottinger expressly warning them that it was not so, and that they must not look to him for protection if they were caught by the Chinese officials.

The resort of ships anywhere off the coast of China north of 32° latitude—the latitude of Shanghai, the most northerly of the Treaty ports—or south of that line, to any port other than the five opened by treaty, was prohibited by Order in Council, and the naval Commander-in-Chief—Sir Thomas Cochran—was entrusted with the task of giving

n. 13

effect to it by seizing British trading-vessels found off the beaten track. When, however, Keying had drawn Pottinger's attention to the appearance of two foreign ships in northern latitudes, the latter had at once pointed out that, after all, the most effective remedy was an absolute refusal of supplies and a heavy fine—$1,000—on the indispensable Chinese linguists accompanying the enterprise.

The net result was that opium-receiving ships came to anchor, and remained at anchor, at each of the Treaty ports, just outside the limits of the port, where, on delivery orders signed by British merchants (as in the old Lin Tin days), opium was openly transferred to Chinese craft and imported openly and without restriction so long as the necessary commission was forthcoming.

Such was the situation at the Treaty ports which had developed, or was developing, at the time that Davis arrived.

As for Hong Kong, Pottinger had, also in April 1843, expressed his readiness, on the authority of the Earl of Aberdeen, to refuse the protection of the island or its waters to smugglers, and, while warning the Chinese High Commissioner that the result would probably be merely to drive the opium trade to its old haunts at Namoa, Lin Tin, Kap Sing Mun and elsewhere, where he could exercise little or no control, he had in fact issued such a proclamation.

How far he actually intended to go must be guesswork, for at the time of his proclamation the island had not yet been regularly ceded and the threat could, therefore, not be legally substantiated. But even so it was sufficient to make the opium-ships sheer off and, in preference to Hong Kong, where their reception seemed uncertain, to turn to Namoa, where 'they had constructed several buildings, a bridge and a road'[1] and were sure of a very warm welcome indeed.

The following April (1844) the Chinese High Commissioner drew attention to this; and Pottinger replied indicating that these people had neither his countenance nor his support, but, with much tact, suggesting that having been allowed to remain for so long undisturbed they should be given a certain time to remove their chattels. Six months was duly accorded and an announcement, under Pottinger's hand, duly appeared in Hong Kong warning any interested parties not to look for protection after the lapse of six months.

The period had still some time to run when Davis arrived to relieve Pottinger; and the situation having, in due course, been pointed out (as in duty bound) to the new-comer, Davis at once blandly suggested as appropriate a short extension of the period of grace—a suggestion readily accepted by Keying. So the settlement continued undisturbed; and in 1846, having occasion to reproach the High Commissioner for the mobbing of the Canton factories in July (to which reference has already been made), he was able effectively to contrast the insecurity of merchants established legally at a Treaty port with the complete immunity of smugglers at Namoa.

Davis contrived also to create a second Namoa at Kumsingmun (Ki O, near Macao) by inviting attention once more to the open and unabashed way in which the opium-ships were carrying on their illicit traffic at Whampoa; and, when the High Commissioner complained of Kumsingmun, at once turned the tables and with considerable force urged that, in the face of such notorious facts, legalization was the only solution.

[1] *Chin. Rep.*, vol. xiii, June, p. 333.

An interchange of notes ensued, the discussion at one time reducing itself to the question of how much revenue the British Government would guarantee if legalization were introduced. But, in the end, nothing came of it.

There remained the case of the internal consumption of opium within Hong Kong itself; for it must be remembered that the Chinese population of Hong Kong was growing and the number of opium-smokers was growing in proportion. The British Government had consequently fairly to face the question: What was to be done about opium-smoking in the Colony? Was it to be made a crime and declared illegal as it was in China? Or was it to be treated as a luxury, like tobacco, and subjected to some form of restriction? Or was it simply to be disregarded?

Mr. Davis answered the question with his customary realism. The British Government had urged China to legalize. Hong Kong could hardly, in the same breath, prohibit its use in its own borders. The Chinese Government had indicated plainly its dislike of the habit; one could hardly permit its unchecked indulgence in a British Colony just over the frontier. Moreover, funds were much needed to finance the Colony. Accordingly, Mr. Davis decided upon a luxury tax, and he effected it by selling to the highest bidder the sole right to retail opium, in quantities of less than a complete chest, within the Colony.

This evoked, as we have seen, strong protest from the British merchants. It evoked also an equally violent protest from a less expected quarter—namely Mr. Davis's own Treasurer, brought out by him in his own entourage, Mr. R. Montgomery Martin.

Mr. R. Montgomery Martin adopted the moral ground that private vice must not be made a source of public revenue, and having failed to move the Governor resigned and returned home, after scarcely two months' residence in Hong Kong, and there 'with pen dipped in gall' denounced the Colony and all its works.[1]

Mr. Davis was thus attacked on his opium policy simultaneously from two widely divergent standpoints. He contrived, however, to defend himself successfully, and, having a robust constitution, survived to die in the year 1890 quietly in his bed at the age of ninety-six.

[1] See *China, Political, Commercial, and Social,* by R. Montgomery Martin (1847).

CHAPTER XI

SAMUEL GEORGE BONHAM
1848–1854

Sir John Davis's successor, Mr. Samuel George Bonham, was the son of a captain in the maritime service of the East India Company[1] and had himself served in that Company prior to 1837, in which year he was appointed Governor of the Straits Settlements at the early age of thirty-four.

This post he had held ever since; and accordingly brought with him to Hong Kong ten years' practical experience of administration in an Eastern colony. It was, no doubt, a valuable asset, for, however widely the native communities of the two colonies differed, the reaction of the British residents could be depended upon to be broadly the same in similar circumstances. And there is no doubt that one of Mr. Bonham's chief tasks was to smooth the ruffled feathers of Hong Kong's British merchants and to lubricate the machinery of Government which in his predecessor's term of office had generated considerable friction.

In this he achieved a large measure of success; and, although he started with the initial advantage of following a thoroughly unpopular Governor, there is no need to grudge a tribute to his shrewdness and the human touch with which he conducted affairs.

But besides the Governorship Mr. Bonham, like his predecessors, was appointed Trade Superintendent and Envoy-in-ordinary to China, and it is convenient, before considering

[1] D.N.B.

domestic affairs, to sketch his career in these other capacities. It is convenient, but the reader must, of course, not suppose that Mr. Bonham, any more than his predecessors, was actually able to dictate the sequence of events or to divest himself at will of one of his roles in order to devote his attention exclusively to the other. The contrary is the case, and it frequently happened, in this administration no less than in the preceding ones, that colonial affairs became particularly urgent at the very moment that diplomatic and commercial relations were most acute; and that the personal presence in China of the Superintendent and Envoy was particularly needed precisely when, as Governor, he could least afford the time to leave Hong Kong. Thus Sir John Davis was searching the pockets of the residents of the Colony for his essential revenues at the same time that he was spiking the guns of the Bogue forts; and Mr. Bonham was treating with the High Commissioner on the delicate subject of entry to the city of Canton and simultaneously treating with the British residents of Hong Kong on the scarcely less delicate subject of municipal autonomy in the Colony.

Mr. Bonham's instructions from the Foreign Secretary were, in one respect at least, quite explicit. Lord Palmerston, perhaps with recollections of the Compton case[1] still in mind, warned him of the need to restrain British residents in China from actions likely to embroil themselves with the Chinese; and he lost no time in making clear his general attitude on the subject to officials and unofficials alike. He had brought an olive-branch with him; and neither official nor merchant who employed high-handed or overbearing methods need

[1] *Vide supra*, p. 144.

look to him for support. In March, immediately on arrival, he administered a mild rebuke to Mr. Rutherford Alcock, Consul at Shanghai, for having held up the entire Chinese grain-fleet[1] in order to exact redress for an assault by certain of the Chinese crews upon British nationals. In May, the British Consul at Canton having threatened to withhold duties payable on British goods to the Chinese authorities pending the settlement of a complaint,[2] he caused the withdrawal of the threat. And again, in May, he referred in a circular to 'acts of doubtful legality' committed by foreign ships[3] in the course of convoying Chinese junks engaged in the coastal trade, and warned British shipmasters of the risks of engaging in such employment.

The convoy system, it may be interpolated, was a countermove to the activities of the local pirates, to whom the growing trade at the Treaty ports, and at Hong Kong in particular, constituted an irresistible attraction—like sugar to a swarm of flies, and who, in the last year or two, had so grown, both in number and audacity, as to constitute a positive menace to the trade. Convoy was not undertaken by Her Majesty's ships, but by privateers which were already defensively armed, and which guaranteed safe conduct in return for a fee. No doubt many earned the fee; but it was a short step from a guarantee of safe conduct in payment of a fee to a hint of trouble if the fee were not forthcoming; and when it is realized that the pirates themselves—or at any rate some of them—probably aimed at nothing more than a regular toll on shipping, the rights and wrongs of the proceeding become difficult of assessment.

But Mr. Bonham approached the matter with typical direct-

[1] *Insults*, pp. 92–123.   [2] *Chin. Rep.*, May, June 1848.   [3] Ibid.

ness and proffered his own solution, namely a direct attack by Her Majesty's ships on the piratical craft, with the collaboration, or at least the countenance, of the Chinese authorities.

Almost simultaneously with Bonham's arrival in Hong Kong, Hsu Kwong Tsin had assumed duty in Canton as Viceroy of the two Kwang provinces and acting High Commissioner in place of Keying, who, while retaining the substantive post, had been ordered to Pekin in the preceding month.[1]

It was the substitution of a Chinese for a Manchu, and it is hardly to be supposed that the change of personnel, coming so pat at the same time as the substitution of Bonham for Davis, was fortuitous. And, although it is not easy to guess the precise purpose of the acting appointment, it seems clear that it was no less deliberate, and calculated to afford some diplomatic advantage in the discussions, which doubtless were clearly foreseen, in respect of the right of entry by foreigners to Canton.

With Hsu there came also to Canton, in the capacity of Governor, a figure destined eight years later to achieve considerable notoriety, Yeh.

Bonham lost no time in seeking a personal interview, and obtained it on April 29th,[2] the venue being Hoo-Mun-Chai (the Little Tiger's Mouth), where Davis and Pottinger had previously met the representative of China.

It was a sufficiently uninviting spot, and at a subsequent interview Mr. Bonham did not fail to draw attention to the point; but it was significant—and intended to be significant—of the lack of enthusiasm which the Cantonese people felt for more intimate relations with foreigners; and Viceroy Hsu took the occasion to issue for the benefit of the Canton public

[1] Ibid., Feb. 1848.   [2] *Insults*, p. 171.

(who were, of course, exactly acquainted with the actual situation) a typical proclamation suggesting that his visit to this out-of-the-way spot was for the purpose of visiting the fortifications and, by implication, seeing that any hostile advance was nipped in the bud.

The interview, which was of a purely formal character, passed off without incident, and Mr. Bonham waited a further six weeks before raising in a formal dispatch the question of entry into Canton.

It will be recalled that, after the ratifications of the Treaty of Nanking had been exchanged, Sir H. Pottinger had, in 1843, originally expected to be received in the High Commissioner's Yamen within the City of Canton, but had yielded to the representations of Keying that a little delay was desirable. In 1846 Davis had flirted with the idea of connecting the enforcement of the treaty-right with the return of Chusan island; but ultimately, so far from pressing it, had accepted a convention deferring its exercise *sine die*. The following year, having spiked the guns of the Bogue and disposed his ships in a position to command the city, he had again raised the subject, but, though he secured the promise of the Chinese representative that entry would be given on a fixed day, that day was to be after a delay of two more years; and, before its expiry, both negotiators had removed to other spheres of activity.

The sands were now running out, the due date being April 6th, 1849; and something must clearly be done about it.

A desultory and fruitless correspondence ensued; and in February 1849, nothing having been effected meantime, a second interview took place at the Bogue: at which Bonham, seeking, on the suggestion of Palmerston, a compromise which would save the face of all concerned, proposed that he should assert the right of entry by paying a personal visit to the Commissioner at his Yamen within the city on the first day on which the convention gave him liberty to do so. Hsu, however, though non-committal, hinted at the dislocation of trade which might ensue; and these hints were followed, as the days passed, by manifestoes of unknown origin posted in the Canton streets, and by intimations by Hsu himself to the British Consul warning him of his inability to control the angered populace. Finally a cryptic message arrived from Pekin which was interpreted as supporting Hsu in his objections; and Bonham, deeming discretion the better part of valour—indeed having no practical alternative—allowed the crucial day to pass, with the city still intact.

In due course—that is to say in August, after reference had been made to Lord Palmerston—a formal protest was sent to the High Commissioner (now apparently confirmed in his post); and, in diplomatic language, freedom of action in the future was reserved.[1] But Chinese officials and the populace of Canton surrendered themselves immediately to celebrate their success, and Hsu and Yeh received respectively the double- and single-eyed peacock's feather for 'tranquillizing the people and managing the barbarians'.[2]

It proved, however, to be a case of *Victrix causa deis placuit, sed victa Catoni*; and, his refusal to make this empty right a *casus belli* finding favour with the Foreign Secretary, Mr. Bonham in turn received the honour of knighthood the following November.

[1] *Naval Forces*, p. 205.   [2] Ibid., p. 200.

Meantime conditions in the Canton delta went from bad to worse, and in the latter part of 1849 and the early months of 1850 the waters surrounding Hong Kong were infested with pirates.[1] In 1850, too, a rising of peasants professing a garbled form of Christianity occurred in Kwong Sai; and spread rapidly southward to Canton and north-eastward to the Yang Tze and Shanghai. This was, of course, the famous Tai Ping rebellion which, raging with increasing fury during the next three years, established a *de facto* government at Nanking, and maintained itself there for several years more.

A man with a less level head than Sir Samuel might well have seen in this rebellion an opportunity to secure concessions under pressure from the Imperial authorities; and there were not lacking advocates of a policy of succouring the rebels and thereby securing a christian China overnight. But Sir Samuel saw safety only in strict neutrality; and, his policy once more finding favour, on proceeding to England on leave in 1852 he had the satisfaction of exchanging his knighthood for a baronetcy.

The fact that home leave was granted should not be passed over as a matter of course. This it certainly was not; for though it can hardly be described as unprecedented (the history of the Colony being far too short), the contrary practice, by which the Governors and Governors-General remained at their posts for their full terms of office, was well established in India, and India would naturally provide the model for Hong Kong; as indeed it subsequently did. We are therefore led to speculate as to the reasons for the trip. Was the ostensible ground—Sir Samuel's ill health—the real one? Or was leave

[1] *Chin. Rep.*, Nov., March.

of absence granted to enable the home authorities to note how Dr. Bowring—the Consul-General of Canton—shaped in the role of Chief Superintendent, in which he deputized in Bonham's absence? It may well have been so; for there can be little doubt that he had from the first been earmarked as a possible successor to the post. Or was the object to enable these authorities to experiment with a system by which the roles of Superintendent and Governor were not doubled? If so, it would seem that the experiment was not successful: for in the event (as we shall see) Dr. Bowring succeeded to the double role. A definite answer to this question can, no doubt, be found in the official dispatches; and it is therefore idle to speculate. But we may be sure that the occasion of Bonham's presence at home was taken by the Foreign Secretary and the Colonial Secretary to confer with him on the matter. And the China Order in Council of August 11th, 1853, was assuredly a result of such conference. This Order abolished the Consular Ordinances, that is to say the Ordinances made by the Legislative Council of Hong Kong for the British residents at the Treaty ports, and substituted a code empowering the Chief Superintendent (and the Consuls with his approval) 'to make and enforce rules and regulations for the observance of treaties and the good government of Her Majesty's subjects in China'.

The net conclusion was, therefore, that while the two roles of Superintendent and Governor should continue to be exercised by one person, they should cease to be fused; in other words, as Superintendent Bowring became answerable solely to the Foreign Secretary and as Governor solely to the Colonial Office; and Hong Kong ceased to be the seat of 'extraterritorial' government.

On Sir Samuel's return in February 1853 Dr. Bowring in turn took leave and in turn received the honour of knighthood and in succession to Sir Samuel the appointment, dated December, to the Superintendency and Governorship. It seems therefore fairly clear that the subject of a successor was itself discussed also with Sir Samuel while at home; but whether or no it was a reason for his proceeding home in the first instance remains undetermined.

After his return from furlough, Nanking having fallen to the Tai Pings, Sir Samuel himself paid a visit to that city and to the rebel head-quarters; and came away confirmed in his policy of neutrality.

I turn now to domestic affairs at Hong Kong. Here Bonham's task was plainly to implement (so far as need be) the findings of the parliamentary Commission of 1847. Dealing with the question of municipal autonomy he deftly converted the slogan 'Taxation implies representation' into 'Representation implies taxation' and offered to entrust to the residents both police and sanitary affairs provided they put up the necessary funds; tactfully adding that he conceived that busy merchants like themselves would probably not have the leisure to bother themselves with the petty affairs of municipal administration. This argument appears to have had its effect, and in the event, after discussions lasting for nearly two years, a compromise was reached by which two unofficials were added to the three officials constituting the Legislative Council. These unofficials were to be the Governor's appointees. But Mr. Bonham waived his rights, and, either from genuine desire to deal handsomely with the British unofficials or a reluctance to undertake the invidious task of selection, invited them to nominate their representatives themselves. This task they accepted, and a meeting being held at the Club on December 6th, 1849, chose David Jardine and Joseph Frost Edger,[1] who were in due course appointed and took their seats the following June (1850).

No legislation of importance stands to Mr. Bonham's credit, though Ordinance 3 of 1853 designed to extend the jurisdiction of 'Tei Po' (or Chinese peace officer)—the fruit, perhaps, of Bowring's brain—is not without interest, for it marks the climax of the attempt to allow the Chinese of Hong Kong to have control of their own affairs. A number of public works, however, were either started or completed during his tenure. A road was cut along the face of the cliff from the Albany godowns to the Wong Nei Chung valley, now known as Wantsai road. And a reclamation, destined to form the very heart of the Chinese business section of the town, was formed, the two main streets, Bonham Strand and Jervois Street, being named after Governor and General Officer Commanding. Caine Road, too, was extended westward and the extension given the Governor's name.

The Supreme Court, on the site now occupied by the Queen's Cinema theatre, was opened three days before Bonham's arrival, and its basement floor used temporarily as a church, pending the completion of the new Cathedral of St. John.[2] Previous to this the Court had occupied premises in Wellington Street.[3] The Government offices known as the Colonial Secretariat near St. John's Cathedral were opened

n. 1

n. 2

n. 3

n. 4

---

[1] Norton Kyshe, vol. i, p. 261. [2] Idem, vol. i, p. 237.
[3] Apparently a warehouse at the junction of Wellington and D'Aguilar Streets. Idem, vol. i, p. 266.

in 1848, and the cathedral itself in March 1849. Government House, which Sir John Davis had 'left to the last', was begun in 1852.

The establishment of the Cricket Club in June 1851 on 'the Plazza' below Murray parade-ground completed the epitome of typical English life.

Sir Samuel Bonham, so far as concerns his career in China, may perhaps be compared to the Gilbertian House of Lords which 'throughout the war did nothing in particular and did it very well'.

Perhaps his supreme achievement in this respect is to be found in his handling of the opium question. His predecessor had left it burning, or at least smouldering, and under his successor it quickly flared up again. But somehow or other Bonham contrived quietly and unostentatiously to relegate it to the background. In April 1854 he was succeeded by Dr. John Bowring, being then only fifty-one, and died nine years later.

CHAPTER XII

DR. JOHN BOWRING
1854–1859

SIR JOHN BOWRING had, as Dr. Bowring, gained a European reputation, indeed (if we adopt the European connotation of the word) a 'world-wide' reputation, as a linguist, and was the author of many erudite publications.

Latterly he had taken considerable interest in Far Eastern affairs. Thus in February 1845 we find him moving the House of Commons for a copy of the correspondence relating to the abortive Registration Ordinance of Sir John Davis; an unsuccessful application affording Sir George Staunton an opportunity to defend an absent ex-colleague on the Committee of the East India Company. Again in August 1846 he is found calling the attention of parliament to the flogging of fifty-four Chinese in Hong Kong on a single day, and lastly in 1847, as member for Blackburn, he had been put on the Parliamentary Commission to inquire into Commercial Relations with China, and had taken a prominent part. Indeed, so interested had he shown himself in the Far East that when a vacancy occurred in the consulship at Canton he had been offered the post; and, his private fortunes at the time being at rather a low ebb, had accepted it, assuming his duties in March 1849.

We may perhaps guess that the chance of succeeding to the dignity of Superintendent and Plenipotentiary was dangled before his eyes; and in point of fact, as we know, during Sir Samuel Bonham's absence on leave in 1852 he had acted for him.

On that occasion it is noteworthy that he did not assume the function of Governor of Hong Kong, which naturally devolved upon the Lieutenant-Governor—Major-General Jervois. But, notwithstanding this, he took up residence at 'Government House'; with the curious result that while the Officer Administering the Government of Hong Kong resided elsewhere—presumably at Head-quarters House—'Government House' (possibly still at 'Spring Gardens') housed the Superintendent of Trade for China.

n. 1
n. 2

Dr. Bowring, though of studious and literary propensities, was by no means a mere dreamer. Indeed he possessed his full share of those robust qualities which pre-eminently mark out the Victorians, and while on the one hand he was able to produce the highly popular hymn 'In the Cross of Christ I glory' he was at the same time able very effectively to rebut many of the arguments appearing in the famous anti-opium memorial to which, in 1856, Lord Shaftesbury lent his name. Nor did his heart quail when it came to giving practical effect to robust notions. Indeed this mild-mannered and bespectacled scholar was a regular fire-eater; and, even as a mere 'locum tenens', Dr. Bowring exhibited his restiveness against the conciliatory policy adopted by his principal, Sir Samuel, *vis-à-vis* the Canton authorities. At that time his views got little support at home and he was quietly told not to force the pace. But later, as we shall see, he authorized the bombardment of that city to secure the right of entry. He was, however, destined to meet his match in the person of a scholar equally mild-mannered as himself and at least equally inflexible of will—the High Commissioner Yeh.

Yeh, a Chinese, had been appointed Governor of Canton in

View of Spring Gardens
20th August, 1846

February 1848 when the Manchu High Commissioner Keying was transferred; and in August 1852, almost simultaneously with Bowring's appointment to act as Superintendent, he had been promoted to the post of High Commissioner. He had thus already crossed swords with Bowring (and had, in fact, come off best) before the latter returned to the scene to take up the substantive post of representative of his country in 1854.

Bowring came armed with a specific mandate from the Foreign Minister, Lord Clarendon, to press for revision of the Treaty of Nanking; such revision becoming due, by virtue of the 'most-favoured-nation' clause of the French Treaty of 1844 (and possibly also of the American Treaty of the same year), on August 29th, 1854—twelve years from the signing of the Treaty of Nanking.

He reached Hong Kong on April 13th and, time being short, proceeded without delay to approach the High Commissioner Yeh in Canton; but, finding him obdurate, turned his face northward in October. Here, too, he met with procrastination, and ultimately, the Crimean War having meantime broken out, he was compelled to drop the matter of treaty revision for the time being.[1] He declined, however, to be reduced to inactivity.

---

[1] It is perhaps worth recording here that during Bowring's absence on this excursion the government of Hong Kong was administered for the first time by a civil servant, in the person of Colonel Caine. Colonel Caine was, in fact, sworn in as Lieutenant-Governor at the same time that Sir John Bowring took the oath as Governor, relinquishing the post of Colonial Secretary into the hands of Mr. Mercer.

The result was curious; for whereas the position of Colonial Secretary was a 'key-position', that of Lieutenant-Governor was (except in the absence of the Governor) a sinecure; and though, as such, it might suit some it certainly would not suit Caine, who, both as Magistrate and Colonial Secretary, had established a considerable personal position.

To meet this difficulty an attempt was made to give the Lieutenant-Governor special

Ever since 1850 the Tai Ping rebellion had continued to rage; and it was no doubt out of the dislocation to trade thereby caused that the notion was evolved of giving the protection of foreign flags to the ships of Chinese merchants engaged in the foreign trade.

Bowring decided to apply the notion to Hong Kong. It was fully intelligible to the Chinese and, provided the implications of neutrality were admitted, would probably be readily accepted by them. And it had already been applied, with far less justification, by other foreign nations who did not possess a Hong Kong. Hong Kong after all was a sovereign state and it was quite within its rights in giving the protection of its flag to the ships of its inhabitants; and if it were objected 'But who are the inhabitants of Hong Kong?' the answer would be, 'We give this privilege only to our Crown Lessees.'

Ordinance No. 5 of 1854 was accordingly passed by the Legislative Council and was, in due course, fully approved at home as legally unimpeachable by the high law officers of the Crown.

Nevertheless, the likelihood of awkward points of jurisdiction arising must surely have been foreseen; and it is safe to say that had their relations been less strained and frigid Bowring would not merely have passed his Ordinance and left Commissioner Yeh to swallow it as best he might.

powers, the official *Gazette* notification of April 15th, 1854, requiring that 'all communications to the Government were for the future to be addressed to the Colonial Secretary for submission to the Lieutenant-Governor'. He was, in fact, to be a sort of deputy. But the result was necessarily to reduce the importance of the post of Colonial Secretary, and the Secretary of State, on hearing of the notification, promptly cancelled it.

Caine was, however, specially created 'Senior Member' of the Legislative Council (presumably after the Governor), thereby taking precedence in the Council of the Chief Justice.

It is equally clear, on looking back, that the step was a highly tempting one from another point of view. The Supplementary Treaty of the Bogue in 1843 required, as we know, passes from all Chinese vessels, as distinct from foreign vessels, desiring to trade with Hong Kong—a provision strenuously objected to by the British merchants, who characterized it as throttling the freedom of the port. If then this obnoxious provision could be overcome by the simple process of transferring Chinese vessels to the foreign register what could be more attractive?

So much is clear as we look back; but, in the absence of all evidence, it would be wholly improper to suggest that Bowring had looked so far ahead, or was actuated by any motive except the immediate (and sufficiently pressing) one of affording protection to those who formed a vital link in the foreign trade against the opposing forces engaged in the domestic struggle in China.

It is easy, too, to believe that an opportunity to get the better of Commissioner Yeh would not have come amiss to Bowring; but to suggest, therefore, that Bowring was influenced by motives of personal animosity is equally illegitimate; and it may be observed that, if such were the case, he was 'hoist with his own petard'; for one of the first consequences of the train of events starting with the Registration Ordinance—'For the proper control of Colonial ships'—was the appointment of Elgin as plenipotentiary extraordinary and the consequent relegation of Bowring to second place.

The *Arrow* incident (to be briefly described below) was directly traceable to this Ordinance; and the *Arrow* incident directly led to war. It is, however, probably true—perhaps more than usually so—that the incident was not the cause but the occasion of war, the spark in fact which fired the powder. And it is fairly certain that even without this spark the explosion would have occurred: for the murder of a French priest, Chapdelaine, in Kwong Sai in July 1856 had already lit another fuse; and, in ignorance of the *Arrow* incident, indeed at the very moment when the *Arrow* incident occurred, the chancelleries of England and France were closely collaborating to demand redress.

In October 1856 the lorcha *Arrow*, Chinese-owned, registered as a Colonial vessel in Hong Kong, and flying the British flag, was suddenly boarded, while lying off the Dutch Folly in the Pearl river, by Chinese police; her crew of twelve Chinese arrested and marched off, and the British flag hauled down.

Immediate demands for an apology for the insult to the flag and for the restoration of the crew to the ship were made by the British Consul, Harry Parkes. The Commissioner Yeh refused, denying the flag was flying, denying the ship was British, protesting that she was harbouring a notorious pirate; and, though, before the sands ran out, he had yielded many points, the sands finally did run out before the demands were fully met.

Sir John Bowring, Harry Parkes, and Sir Michael Seymour, the senior naval officer, thereupon in close collaboration laid their plans for the enforcement of the full demands; and later, alleging that the present deadlock was due to the refusal of the Commissioner to admit British officials to the city for personal interviews, renewed the old, and crucial, demand for right of access to the city.

They first seized, by way of reprisal, an Imperial war-junk (or what appeared to be such) lying in the river; but Yeh blandly pointed out that it was a private merchantman. They trained their guns on the city. Yeh made no move. They threw in shells at intervals of ten minutes into his Yamen. They breached the city wall; landed a party of seamen and marines; marched through the deserted Yamen, thereby taking what had been refused—admission to the city. Yeh, true to type, placed a price upon all foreign heads. They then turned back and seized the Bogue forts; and, having done so, waited impatiently for Yeh to yield; Bowring himself even coming up to Canton to receive the submission. But Yeh continued to leave the next step to the other side. Clearly he did not know the rules of the game. Then, somehow, the factories caught fire and were burnt to the ground; and the fleet, beset or threatened by infernal machines, withdrew to the Macao fort across the river. And so the year ended in deadlock, while the factories and the western suburbs of Canton smouldered and the other foreigners withdrew protesting.

Early the following year the Commissioner hit back. A blockade was imposed upon Hong Kong in the hopes of starving the English out.[1] But while the Heung Shan district obediently refused supplies Tung Kwun and San On promptly rushed in to capture the market. And then in January an attempt at wholesale murder was made by seasoning the output of a Pottinger Street bakery with arsenic. This was also unsuccessful, for the would-be assassin, in an excess of zeal, overdid the dose; and though many Europeans, including

n. 3

[1] *Corr. rel. Operations*, 1857.

Lady Bowring, suffered inconvenience, none actually succumbed. The attempt, however, drew protests from the representatives of other foreign nations who pointed out that, as their nationals were also bread-eaters, unfortunate mistakes might result from this method of warfare. To which Yeh replied blandly regretting that his writ did not run in Hong Kong and hinting that if it was a question of barbarity there really was not much to choose between inserting arsenic pills into the loaves in Hong Kong and lobbing explosive shells into the populous streets of Canton.

The affair also created a great stir at home and led directly to the appointment of Lord Elgin as Envoy Extraordinary to China.

In May 1857 the Indian Mutiny broke out; and though it would no doubt be far-fetched to attribute it to the machinations of Yeh, it requires no stretch of imagination to believe that he had a considerable hand in the curious disturbances which broke out simultaneously among overseas Chinese at Singapore, Java, and elsewhere.

In May and June the British naval forces in China indulged in side-shows at Escape Creek and Fat Shan on the West river; with no very definite object in view, so far as can be seen, but presumably in continuation of the pressure against Yeh. But if this is so one cannot help feeling that they would have been more effective had they been a prelude to an attack upon Canton rather than an epilogue after a withdrawal from that disconcerting city. A naval print was, however, good business at this epoch, and in due course the action was faithfully n. 4 recorded in the form of an attractive coloured lithograph.

Lord Elgin reached Hong Kong on July 2nd only to find

that his French colleague, Baron de Gros, was not due for a month or two. But in October[1] 'de Gros arrived in the *Audacieuse*' and then 'after conferring with Lord Elgin took up his anchorage in Castle Peak Bay, Lantao island, where... the French fleet were at anchor'; and it was not until December 1857 that any active step was taken *vis-à-vis* the Chinese authorities.

It is easy to believe, therefore, that the year 1857 was a very anxious and uncomfortable one for the colony of Hong Kong, perhaps the most uncomfortable in its history. The poisoning attempt, for example, was followed by an attempt at arson, Duddell's bakery in Wantsai (to which presumably the foreign community had transferred its patronage) being selected. The incident is thus described by a Chinese agent whose private dispatches were intercepted:

n. 5

'I sent a man to Victoria to spy: he has returned with information that Duddell's store in the Ha-Wan, has been burned with upwards of 1,000 piculs of flour therein. The barracks to the left and the powder-magazine were guarded by several hundred devil soldiers ... the building burned was Duddell's store and not the great-devil building (Government House or the offices).'[2]

We may perhaps be justified, too, in deducing, from the absence of many of the customary statistics, an exceptional dislocation of the civil administration. It is certain that nerves were frayed and tempers strained; official accused official; libels were the order of the day; and every man's hand, or at least his tongue, was against his neighbour. The unhappy situation in due course filtered through to the offices of

[1] Oliphant, *Narrative of the Earl of Elgin's Mission*.
[2] *Corr. rel. Operations*, 1857.

The Times, which on March 15th, 1859, administered a severe reproof:

'... [Hong Kong] is always connected with some fatal pestilence, some doubtful war, or some discreditable internal squabble. So much so that the name of this noisy, bustling, quarrelsome, discontented and insalubrious little island may not inaptly be used for an euphonious synonym for a place not mentionable in polite society.'[1]

Trade, too, naturally suffered severely; but in this respect Hong Kong showed (as it has often shown since) a remarkable capacity, I do not say for profiting by the misfortunes of the adjoining continent, but for underwriting its own inevitable losses in times of disturbance. Thus when the ravages of the Tai Ping rebellion made life unbearable in China many Chinese flocked for security to Hong Kong, and when Hong Kong itself became unpleasant or unpopular as a residence it contrived to provide a gateway of hope to some fabulous 'Golden Hill' across the sea. In point of fact during 1857 and the next few years the coolie-emigration trade to San Francisco and Australia—the 'Old' and the 'New Gold Mountains'—not to mention British Guiana and Jamaica, reached such dimensions as to provide a valuable set-off to the dislocation of ordinary trade.

On December 10th, 1857, Bowring and Bourboulon, his French colleague, notified Yeh of the arrival of the Envoys extraordinary upon whom the conduct of affairs would thenceforward devolve, and delivered a joint ultimatum demanding within ten days, first, free entrance to the city, and second, compensation for losses thus far incurred; the island of Honam

n. 6

[1] Norton Kyshe, vol. i, p. 583.

to be held in pledge. To this Yeh replied briefly appealing to Elgin's sense of justice.

On December 28th the Anglo-French bombardment of the city began. A week later a British naval party, guided by Harry Parkes, found Yeh within the city and promptly made him prisoner.

He was in due course transported out of harm's way to Calcutta, where he died in exile a year later. But the difficulties of the allies did not vanish with the removal of an exasperating individual. Canton was now not merely at the mercy of their arms as it had been on several previous occasions but actually in their possession; and it now remained to govern the place. Nor is it necessary to remind the reader that, apart from being a city of upward of a million people, Canton is the administrative capital of a province of many millions.

The task was, however, faced. The Governor, Pik, was installed in the place of Yeh as Viceroy; a few hundred British and French troops garrisoned the city; and an allied Commission, of which Parkes was the life and soul, was set up in Canton and remained there—to 'soothe and comfort' Pik—for approximately three years.

Meantime Elgin in February announced his intention of going north; and together with Baron de Gros and other foreign envoys proceeded to the Peiho in April. On June 26th, 1858, the exact anniversary of the ratification of the Treaty of Nanking, the Treaty of Tientsin was signed. And on October 12th a tariff convention, which incidentally, almost casually, legalized the import of opium on payment of thirty taels a chest, was agreed to at Shanghai.

Meantime Bowring, out of the main current of stirring events, carried on the more prosaic task of governing Hong Kong. Public works of importance are associated with his governorship. One—the reclamation of the bay separating Morrison Hill from East Point—was named after him Bowrington; though the Chinese, emphasizing the canalization of the stream which drained the Wong Nei Chung valley, persisted (and still persist) in calling it 'Ngoh Keng'—the 'Goose's neck'.

n. 7

A more ambitious scheme of reclamation, extending the full length of the west and central districts of the city, was also fathered by Bowring, and was to a large extent carried through; but, as it meant the recovery by the Crown of a good many square feet of ground already surreptitiously won at their back-doors by the owners of premises backing on the sea, it was not universally popular; and Messrs. Dent and Lindsay in particular obstinately and successfully blocked it so far as their own important lots were concerned.

n. 8

To Bowring also falls the credit of a broadly conceived scheme for marketing fresh foodstuffs, a suite of retail markets—central, western, eastern, Tai Ping Shan, So Kon Po, and Wantsai—being built. The majority of these have long been superseded by more spacious buildings. But Wantsai market is, as I write, only just under sentence of demolition; while a vastly swollen So Kon Po is still served by the original market of Bowring.

Simultaneously with the erection of all these markets a Market Ordinance was passed, No. 9 of 1858, which continued to hold the field for nearly thirty years; while Ordinance 4 of 1856, validating Chinese wills made according to

Chinese law, remains (as Ordinance 1 of 1856) the law on the subject to this day. n. 9

In 1858, consequent, one presumes, on the legalization of the import of opium into China, an opium monopoly was reintroduced in Hong Kong for the first time since its abandonment in 1848. In March 1859 Lord Elgin, his work supposedly complete, left Hong Kong; the following month his younger brother, the Hon. Frederick Bruce (ex-Colonial Secretary under Sir John Davis), arrived to assume the duties of British minister to China; and on May 5th Bowring, reduced to a mere Colonial Governor, took his departure.

Although he had reached the age of sixty-two on appointment and sixty-seven on retirement, he contrived to survive for thirteen years longer, dying in 1872 at the respectable age of eighty.

CHAPTER XIII
SIR HERCULES ROBINSON

THE wheels of life among the foreign community in Hong Kong had once more developed considerable friction. It is true that the Chief Justice, who under an earlier régime had been suspended for excessive indulgence in intoxicating liquor, had returned to the bench; but the Attorney-General had now been dismissed for accusing the Registrar-General of associating with pirates: the Registrar-General in turn had hinted that the Captain Superintendent of Police had a financial interest in brothels; while the acting Colonial Secretary had been charged by a local editor with receiving a bribe in connexion with the opium monopoly; the Lieutenant-Governor with taking commission on the stall-rents at the Central Market; and the Governor himself had been pilloried in another newspaper for giving privileged treatment, in the matter of Government contracts, to a certain eminent firm.

Here indeed was material for scandal, but in the more prosaic spheres of official business there were complications too; for the Colonial Secretary, the acting Attorney-General, and the Surveyor-General had voted against the Government in a proposal for a reclamation of foreshore and caused the rejection of one of the Governor's most cherished schemes.

A man of tact and firmness was needed, and the choice fell on Sir Hercules Robinson, who thus was called on to play *vis-à-vis* Sir John Bowring much the same role as Sir Samuel Bonham had played with such success opposite Sir John Davis twelve years before.

There was, however, this subtle difference, that whereas Sir John Davis was frankly sent as a whip to control the 'free-traders' Sir John Bowring was the elect of the 'free-traders' themselves; or at least of a section led by Messrs. Jardine, Matheson. Bowring was, in fact, connected by the closest ties with the 'princely hong', his own son being a director; but the editor who, as noted above, jumped to the conclusion that the connexion was abused promptly found himself incarcerated in the local jail for libel. n. 1

Sir Hercules's task certainly looked a troublesome one, but he had at any rate one advantage over his predecessors in so far as he was relieved of all responsibility for affairs outside the boundaries of the Colony. He came out armed with a commission as Governor only, responsible to the Colonial Office only, the function of Trade Superintendent and plenipotentiary having been entrusted (as we have seen) to the Hon. Frederick Bruce, who had established himself in Shanghai.

He was thus plainly able to devote more attention than his predecessors to Colonial affairs. But it would be a mistake to imagine that the severance of the two functions automatically solved all problems. It avoided the difficult problem how one man could be in two places at the same time; but it created the new one how one country could be simultaneously represented at the other end of the world by two persons.

Whether this difficulty was fully appreciated at home may be doubted; but it is extremely improbable that Chinese officialdom failed to observe it, and to take full toll of its possibilities. In point of fact its first-fruits are of considerable interest to our story. The British consuls, unlike the representatives of other nations, had a responsibility under the treaty for collecting import duties from their nationals on behalf of the Chinese Customs; with the result that British importers were soon at a disadvantage as compared with those of other nations. A diplomatic protest was made, and the obvious step was taken: a British consul, Mr. Horatio Nelson Lay, was seconded to the Chinese Imperial Customs for the purpose of applying to all importing nations the same procedure which produced such delectable results when applied to Englishmen. It was the logical step; but it had this incidental result that it cut away the ground from that searing criticism of Sir Henry Pottinger that, in the absence of honest officials, the legalization of opium in China was the only reasonable course.

n. 2 Mr. Lay himself was superseded not long after his appointment by Robert Hart, another student interpreter, who was to make a great name for himself in China; but the effect was instantaneous, and nowhere was it felt more than in Hong Kong. For Hong Kong was ideally situated for smuggling; and the tide of its prosperity was at the flood. The smuggler, whether of opium or any other article on the tariff list, was brought up with a round turn, and the delighted customs officials of Canton took courage. The usual host of imitators became emboldened, too, and customs cruisers, official and self-styled, harassed the native shipping clearing from the Colony.

The British merchants of Hong Kong were angry, and, following the precedent of 1834, united in the face of this threat to their interests and formed a Chamber of Commerce in August 1861.[1] The Chamber's first act was to send a letter of protest to the British Minister; and thereafter for a decade

---

[1] Eitel, *Europe in China*, p. 384.

and more there ensued an interesting *parti* at which British Chamber, British Minister, British Governor, and British Inspector-General of the Imperial Chinese Customs played the hands.

The contest was protracted and hard-fought, and if in the end Robert Hart contrived in some measure to clip the wings of the merchants of Hong Kong, England need feel no discredit at the result.

Besides ceasing to be the seat of the British representative in China, Hong Kong became insulated from China in another important respect. It will be recalled that at the close of Bonham's régime[1] the legislative council of Hong Kong had ceased to make laws for the British residents of the Treaty ports, the machinery of 'China Orders in Council' having been evolved instead. The jurisdiction of the Supreme Court was now similarly restricted. With the cession of the island the Supreme Court of China, hitherto fixed at Canton, had been transferred to Hong Kong, certain limited judicial powers being conferred by ordinance on the Consuls at the Treaty ports. The Hong Kong Court, in consequence, besides dispensing justice for the residents of the Colony, became a Court of Appeal against the decisions of the Consuls. The arrangement—though it no doubt added something to the conception of extra-territoriality, had not proved an unqualified success, and Sir John Davis in particular had forcibly protested when, on a legal technicality (or so it seemed to him), Mr. Hulme, the Chief Justice, had upheld an appeal by a British merchant of Canton against the imposition upon him of a fine of $200 for instigating a riot which had threatened

[1] *Vide supra*, p. 169.

the safety of the 'factories' and resulted in the loss of Chinese lives.¹ The process was now once more reversed, and the seat of the Supreme Court for China removed to a Treaty port, the change being finally completed in 1863.

Sir Hercules Robinson reached Hong Kong on September 9th, 1859. Lord Elgin, Envoy extraordinary, had departed six months before, leaving to his younger brother, Frederick Bruce, the first British Minister to China, the formality of exchanging ratifications of the Treaty of Tientsin. But the task had proved anything but a formality; and in the course of the proceedings the British fleet had been severely defeated at the mouth of the Pei Ho. A settlement with Pekin, therefore, was as far away as ever; while at Canton an Allied Commission still sat in control.

The following February (1860) Sir Hope Grant arrived with an expeditionary force, which, after establishing its base at Hong Kong, proceeded once more to follow the customary procedure and occupy Chusan. In June Lord Elgin reappeared. In October Pekin was seized by the Anglo-French forces; the Summer Palace looted; the Tientsin Treaty at long last ratified; and a supplementary convention, the Convention of Pekin, added.

The Treaty itself affected Hong Kong little, but the Convention much. As we have seen, the peninsula of Kowloon had, from the earliest days of the Colony, looked alluring to Hong Kong residents, who contrasted its southern aspect and its comfortable recumbent spread with their own stiff and upright posture on the island's northern slopes; and it is not surprising to find that the possibility of securing a slice of this

---

¹ *Vide supra*, p. 144.

attractive-looking territory as part of the spoils of the second China war was frequently canvassed locally. But the first official suggestion seems to have come from the Royal Navy, whose concern was not so much to secure the peninsula as a site for residence, military or civil, as to neutralize it in the interests of the safety of shipping anchored in Hong Kong Bay. And the point of particular interest from the chronicler's viewpoint lies in the identity of the individual who advanced the suggestion;[1] for Captain Hall of H.M.S. *Calcutta*, who addressed the Admiralty on the subject in March 1858, is none other than Captain W. H. Hall of *Nemesis* who, as we know, had not only attended at the birth of Victoria seventeen years before but had been present also at the discovery, or rediscovery, of Hong Kong twenty-five years earlier still, a striking example of steadfast concern for the welfare of the young Colony.

The peninsula offered, too, a tempting camping-ground— perhaps the only possible camping-ground—for Hope Grant's expeditionary force; and Harry Parkes, then one of the Allied Commissioners in Canton, had little difficulty in persuading the Viceroy of that city to give him a lease; thereby affording covering authority for its occupation by British troops in February 1860. And now, by this Convention of Pekin, the ground covered by this lease was ceded in perpetuity to the British Crown 'with a view to the maintenance of law and order in and about the harbour of Hong Kong'. And on January 19th, 1861 (twenty years less one week since the first occupation of Hong Kong), delivery was taken with all formality by Lord Elgin.

It was Lord Elgin's last official act in China, for he left

n. 4

[1] Eitel, *Europe in China*, p. 357.

Hong Kong for England two days later. The following October the Allied Commission at Canton was 'wound up', the armed forces withdrawn, and the government restored to the Chinese authorities.

n. 5 With Sir Hercules Robinson came Mr. W. K. Adams, the new Attorney-General; but the latter stepped ashore to find himself forthwith elevated to the bench, the Chief Justice, Hulme, having gone on leave the previous April. As acting Chief Justice one of Mr. Adams's earliest duties was to hear the action[1] instituted by the Lieutenant-Governor, Caine, against one Tarrant, ex-civil servant and latterly editor of the *Friend of China*, for libel.[2]

The Court made short work of the case, the jury completely exonerating Caine, while Tarrant was sent for six months to Victoria jail.

Having got his verdict, Caine departed in peace; and with his departure Hong Kong lost a permanent official who had done more than any other to make the Colony. He had built the first mat-shed residence, and seen it blown about his ears by the first typhoon. He had built the first brick house. He had chosen the site and supervised the building of the original jail and magistracy; raised the original police force, estab-
n. 6 lished the original retail food market, and presided at the police court for the first five years of the Colony's existence.

[1] *Vide supra*, Chap. XIII, p. 186.
[2] Caine was on the eve of retirement on pension and the libel was a *réchauffée* of several years' standing; and the reader may wonder why he had left it unchallenged so long or alternatively why he could not leave it now for good and all. The reason may perhaps lie in the fact that this was the first opportunity that offered of getting a hearing before a judge other than Hulme, against whom he had found it necessary to give evidence which led to his suspension on grounds of insobriety in 1847.

He had seen the public revenues swell from nothing to six lacs of dollars a year; and the population from a mere handful to 120,000; and before he left 2,500 ships, representing nearly one and a half million tons, were entering and clearing the port in the course of a year.¹ In 1846 he had been promoted Colonial Secretary and in 1854 Lieutenant-Governor; and now, with the abolition of that office, consequent upon the severance of the Superintendency, he was automatically transferred to the retired list after nearly twenty years' service.

Sir Hercules proceeded forthwith to set up a Commission of Inquiry into Civil Service abuses, taking the chair in person. One of the main purposes of the Commission was to determine the quarrel between Mr. May, the Superintendent of Police, and Mr. D. R. Caldwell, the Registrar-General, over the body of one Ma Chow Wong who, besides making himself officially obnoxious to Mr. May by reason of his proclivities towards piracy, had placed Mr. Caldwell under a personal obligation by intervening to save his life on some past occasion. In the end, while Mr. May was exonerated, Mr. Caldwell's associations were regarded as unfitting him for Government service—an academic conclusion, for he had already severed his connexion. n. 7

Caldwell cuts a striking and somewhat tragic figure in the early history of Hong Kong, and it is perhaps possible to trace in him some at least of the features of Othello. His great qualification lay in his ability as a linguist. Besides English, he spoke Cantonese like a native and as such had proved extremely valuable to the Government of Hong Kong, which he had served successively as interpreter, interpreter and n. 8

¹ See Appendixes X and XI.

assistant superintendent of police, interpreter to the Supreme Court and Chief Magistrate, and acting superintendent of police and registrar-general; and finally registrar-general, protector of Chinese, and general interpreter to Government.

This last post he had been offered and had accepted shortly after tendering his resignation; the Government swallowing the unpalatable truth that, since the severance of the Consular from the Colonial service, his knowledge of the Chinese language made him virtually indispensable.

The possibility of this situation repeating itself no doubt occurred to Sir Hercules, and, bearing in mind that his predecessor had instituted for Consular officers a system of Student Interpreterships, he had wasted no time in putting forward a similar scheme for the Colony. In March 1861 a scheme of Cadetships was formulated; and in the following April the first three Cadets (C. C. Smith, W. M. Deane, and M. S. Tonnochy) were appointed; and, after devoting the next two years to the language, assumed their substantive duties. The post of Registrar-General, the official channel between the Chinese community and the Government, fell to Mr. Smith, subsequently to become Sir Cecil Clementi Smith; and the old system of *tei-po*, an embryonic form of self-government for the Chinese, was finally swept away.

n. 9

Sir Hercules proved a man of versatility; and besides thus laying a bridge giving to the Chinese community access to Government, he simultaneously devoted himself to the material comfort and convenience of residents as a whole. In 1860 the first water-works scheme, by which water was brought by conduit to the town from Pokfulam, was inaugurated; and the old system of oil-lamps for street-lighting was superseded

n. 10

Victoria Peak, Hong Kong

[*By permission of* "*Illustrated London News*"]

by a system of gas-lamps. Currency, too, received his attention, and it is noteworthy that the Government Estimates, hitherto expressed in £ s. d., were, for the first time, expressed in dollars in 1862. Silver had, in fact, won its way to acceptance as the currency of the Colony. But the rapid expansion of trade and the complications of exchange called for special measures; and the leading British merchants laying their heads together at this time sketched the first faint outline of an institution destined to make history—the Hong Kong and Shanghai Banking Corporation. n. 11

Education also saw important developments in this régime. A Board of Education was formed in June 1860 on the advice of Dr. Legge, and in 1861 the Government Central School, amalgamating three district schools, was established in Gough Street, the forerunner of Queen's College. At the same time, under the guidance of Bishop Raimondi, Roman Catholic educationalists redoubled their efforts, and besides supplying local offices with English-speaking Portuguese clerks provided for Chinese boys of the poorest class an industrial reformatory at West Point. n. 12

The year 1862 witnessed also the birth of the local Volunteer Corps, perhaps a by-product of the American Civil War which was then raging; while the possibilities of the Peak as a residential area were first seriously explored by Sir Hercules.

These things may be recorded as the signs of a progressive and enterprising régime. But Sir Hercules built soundly and, while showing a readiness to give a hearing to the Chinese, showed equally clearly that he did not intend to be dictated to or browbeaten by strikes. In 1860 the pawnbrokers shut their shops in protest against the Pawnbrokers Ordinance. In 1861 the cargo-coolies and in 1863 the chair-coolies in turn struck work in protest against the new rules requiring them to register. But each in turn found themselves met by unflinching firmness and each in turn accepted the situation.

Having cleared up the Civil Service abuses Sir Hercules proceeded to lay down salutary rules for the guidance of official members of the Legislative Council in relation to Government bills. Hitherto officials had voted according to their private views; and Sir Hercules, in frowning on the practice, was able to point out that in so doing he was merely applying to Hong Kong the orthodox procedure of Crown Colony government.

The subject, however, required a light touch, for the opposition, had it existed, might well have pointed out that, in the matter of municipal control, the parallel was far from exact; and we may be sure Sir Hercules, in consulting unofficials, stressed rather the value of the rule in checking the freedom of individual Government servants.

The insecurity in China, owing to the continued operations of the Tai Ping rebels and the presence once more of a substantial expeditionary force, combined to produce considerable material prosperity in the Colony, and the year 1862 appears to mark the climax of the munificence of the great British mercantile houses in adorning the town with public and semi-public buildings. In that year the Clock Tower at the top of Pedder Street (demolished in 1913), Dent's fountain outside the City Hall (demolished 1932), the City Hall itself (now fast disappearing), and the Sailors' Home at West Point (now under notice of demolition), all presented by

n. 13

private British citizens (with Robert Jardine heading the subscription-lists in princely style), were either built or building.

The period was a fruitful one, too, in the sphere of legislation; for by a series of ordinances which still remain on the statute-book, Ordinances 2–7 of 1865, Hong Kong consolidated its criminal law on the lines of the United Kingdom Acts of 1861.

Sir Hercules took his leave of Hong Kong on March 15th, 1865; and the following extract from his speech[1] delivered at the farewell dinner given in his honour by the British Community forms a fitting tail-piece to this chronicle:

'It will be six years since I received my appointment. Hong Kong at that time had the worst possible reputation in England, not only for unhealthiness but for being a place officially as well as socially ill-at-ease with itself. . . . My friend assured me that the state of things was perfectly appalling. The merchants, he said, appeared to be all smugglers and the officials either pirates or something worse.

'However I had not been out here long before I found that the place was by no means what it had been represented, and now, after more than 5 years' experience of it, I can honestly say I would rather live here than in any Colony with which I am acquainted.

'The healthfulness of the place is so improved that it is rapidly acquiring the reputation of being the Sanitarium of China. The mercantile community are proverbial not only for commercial integrity but for their boundless liberality and hospitality. And as regards the officials generally, I am glad to have this opportunity of acknowledging the very valuable support and cooperation which I have received at their hands. . . .

'The growth of the city of Victoria . . . [has] excited the wonder

[1] Norton Kyshe, vol. ii, p. 71.

of all who have returned to the Colony after a short absence. And the addition of the valuable dependency of Kowloon to the former limits of the Colony not only adds materially to the security of our town and harbour, but affords space and facilities for the further development of the Colony, both as a military station as well as a commercial entrepot. These circumstances have been recognised by the Home Government, and Her Majesty was graciously pleased when I was at home to direct that the Colony should be removed from the list of second class to that of first class Governorships.

'It would ill become me to enlarge here tonight upon the various changes and improvements which have been carried into effect during my term of office. Nor would any object be gained by my doing so: for such improvements as the Praya, the Public Gardens, gas, water, the new subsidiary currency, the mint in course of erection, the admirable scheme of public education—and such measures also as those adopted for improving the position of the Civil Servants, and for training up by means of Cadetships a body of gentlemen acquainted with the language and character of the people over whom they have to rule . . . these I say and numerous other measures remain to mark the course of my administration . . . and will be judged not by any words which I could speak in their praise tonight, but by the practical test of their failure or success.'

APPENDIXES

Appendix	I.	Elliot's Original Proclamation of February 2nd, 1841.
,,	II.	First Gazetteer and Census, May 15th, 1841.
,,	III.	Original Marine-lot Purchasers, June 14th, 1841.
,,	IV.	Extract from the *Canton Press*, February 1842.
,,	V.	The first Government House.
,,	VI.	Article III of the Treaty of Nanking.
,,	VII.	Pottinger's Proclamation.
,,	VIII.	Hong Kong Names: The derivation of street-names and place-names in early Hong Kong.
,,	IX.	A Short Glossary of Anglo-Oriental Terms.
,,	X.	Population 1841–1862.
,,	XI.	Ships entering and clearing 1841–1862.

APPENDIX I

ELLIOT'S ORIGINAL PROCLAMATION OF FEBRUARY 2ND, 1841

n. 1

By Charles Elliot, Esquire, a Captain in the Royal Navy, Chief Superintendent of the Trade of British Subjects in China, and holding full powers, under the Great Seal of the United Kingdom of Great Britain and Ireland, to execute the office of Her Majesty's Commissioner, Procurator and Plenipotentiary in China.

The island of Hong Kong having been ceded to the British Crown under the Seal of the Imperial Minister and High Commissioner Keshen, it has become necessary to provide for the government thereof, pending Her Majesty's further pleasure.

By virtue of the authority, therefore, in me vested, all Her Majesty's rights, royalties, and privileges of all kinds whatever, in and over the said island of Hong Kong whether to or over lands, harbours, property, or personal service, are hereby declared proclaimed and to Her Majesty fully reserved.

And I do hereby declare and proclaim, that, pending Her Majesty's further pleasure, the government of the said island shall devolve upon, and be exercised by, the person filling the office of Chief Superintendent of the Trade of British Subjects in China for the time being.

And I do hereby declare and proclaim, that, pending Her Majesty's further pleasure, the natives of the island of Hong Kong and all natives of China thereto resorting, shall be governed according to the laws and customs of China, every description of torture excepted.

And I do further declare and proclaim, that, pending Her Majesty's further pleasure, all offences committed in Hong Kong by Her Majesty's subjects, or other persons than natives of the island or of China thereto resorting, shall fall under the cognizance of the Criminal and Admiralty Jurisdiction presently existing in China.

And I do further declare and proclaim, that, pending Her Majesty's further pleasure, such rules and regulations as may be necessary from time to time for the government of Hong Kong shall be issued under the hand and seal of the person filling the office of Chief Superintendent of the Trade of British subjects in China for the time being.

And I do further declare and proclaim, that, pending Her Majesty's further pleasure, all British subjects and foreigners residing in, or resorting to, the island of Hong Kong, shall enjoy full security and protection, according to the principles and practice of British law, so long as they shall continue to conform to the authority of Her Majesty's Government in and over the island of Hong Kong, hereby duly constituted and proclaimed.

Given under my hand and seal of office, on board of Her Majesty's ship *Wellesley*, at anchor in Hong Kong bay, this Second day of February, in the year of our Lord 1841.

GOD SAVE THE QUEEN

CHARLES ELLIOT.

APPENDIX II
ORIGINAL GAZETTEER AND CENSUS, MAY 15TH, 1841   n. 1

		Population
Chek-Chu	The Capital, a large town	2,000
Heong Kong	A large fishing-village	200
Wong Nei Chung	An agricultural village	300
Kung-Lam[1]	Stone-quarry—poor village	200
Shek Lup[2]	do. do.	150
Soo-Ke-Wan	do. Large village	1,200
Tai Shek-ha	do. A hamlet	20
Kwan Tai-loo 群大路	Fishing-village	50
Soo-kon-poo	A hamlet	10
Hung-heong-loo	Hamlet	50
Sai Wan	Hamlet	30
Tai Long	Fishing hamlet	5
Too-te-wan	Stone-quarry, a hamlet	60
Tai Tam	Hamlet near Tytam bay	20
Soo-koo-wan	Hamlet	30
Shek-tong Chuy	Stone-quarry. Hamlet	25
Chun Hum	Deserted fishing-hamlet	00
Tseen Suy Wan	do.	00
Sum Suy Wan	do.	00
Shek-pae[3]	do.	00
		4,350
In the Bazaar		800
In the Boats		2,000
Labourers from Kowlung		300
Actual present population		7,450

[1] i.e. A Kung Ngam.   [2] i.e. Shek O.   [3] i.e. Aberdeen.

[204]

APPENDIX III
THE ORIGINAL MARINE-LOT PURCHASERS AT THE AUCTION OF JUNE 14TH, 1841[1]

n. 1

Lot Nos.	Purchasers	£	s.	d.
1–2	Gribble, Hughes & Co.	80		
2–3	Lindsay & Co.	80		
3–4	Dent & Co.	64		
4–5	do.	65	10	0
5–6	Dababhoy Rustonjee	50		
6–7	Hooker and Lane	43		
7–8	Prestonjee Cowasjee	50		
8–9	Dirom & Co.	57		
9–10	Reserved			
10–11	H. Rustonjee	52		
11–12	do.	52		
12–13	Halliday & Co.	38	10	0
13–14	W. & F. Gemmell & Co.	32	10	0
14–15	Ferguson, Leighton & Co.	21		
15–16	Robert Webster	20		
16–17				
17–18	Reserved			
18–19				
19–20				
20–21	D. Rustonjee	111		
21–22	James Fletcher & Co.	150		
22–23	W. & F. Gemmell & Co.	140		
23–24	Reserved			
24–25	H. Rustonjee	160		
25–26	Reserved			
26–27	J. Matheson & Co.	150		
27–28	do.	185		
28–29	do.	230		

Offered to be re-purchased.

[1] *Comm. Rel.*, 1847.

Lot Nos.	Purchasers	£.	s.	d.
29–30		—		
30–31	R. Gully	35		
32–33	Jamieson & How	60		
33–34	John Smith	57		
34–35	do.	67		
36–37	Famjee Jamsetjee	25		
38–39	Charles Hart	57		
40–41	MacVicar & Co.	75		
41–42	do.	95		
42–43	Fox, Rawson & Co.	100		
43–44	Turner & Co.	150		
44–45	Reserved			
45–46	do.			
46–47	Captain Larkins	265		
47–48	P. F. Robertson	250		
49–50	Not sold			
51	Captain Morgan	205		

APPENDIX IV
EXTRACT FROM THE *CANTON PRESS*
FEBRUARY 1842

... The projected town of Hong Kong extends along the shore of the bay in a direction almost due east to west about four miles, the last now occupied point to the east being the peninsula on which Messrs. Jardine Matheson & Co. are building, and to the west a barrack now occupied by the Bengal Volunteers. These two extreme points of the town are connected by a road, the cutting of which from the unequality of ground must have been a work of considerable labour, but which from the convenience it affords the settlers amply repays the trouble and expense. This road is so cut as to leave generally enough space between it and the water, for the erection of godowns, and this space has been parcelled out into water frontage lots of 100 feet frontage each, and many of them were last July disposed of to merchants at auction for a certain annual quitrent, while the Government reserved a great proportion for their own purposes.

Great bustle and preparation is at present observable on these water frontage lots; on five or six of them substantial godowns, built of brick, with a foundation of granite, which of a good quality abound everywhere on the island, have already been erected: whilst almost on all the others belonging to private individuals the ground is levelled, foundations for building are being laid, and piers of granite run out into the water for the greater convenience of landing goods. One of the largest warehouses as yet erected, has lately been purchased by Government. On one part of the road the space between it and the water is occupied by one of the Chinese bazaars which still chiefly consists of matsheds, but brick buildings are fast rising, and we doubt not that in a very short time no others will be seen there, since the great danger from fire will suggest to the occupants the greater economy of substantial buildings even were the authorities not to interfere.

APPENDIX IV

The ground immediately contiguous to the road on the other side away from the water is divided into what are called town lots, and their number and depth along the road varies according to the nature of the ground, which sometimes rises abruptly, not affording building room, whilst at other places buildings may be erected a considerable distance inland. On these town lots several dwelling houses have already been erected, and the applications for lots, particularly from the Chinese, are very numerous.

Two streets forming a bazaar built of brick houses are in a state of great forwardness; these houses, generally, we believe 15 feet street frontage and about 35 feet deep, pay an annual ground rent of five dollars each, and other town lots pay the same in proportion to their size. The prices realized for the water-frontage lots are much higher, and those apportioned since the public sale, are to pay quitrent in proportion to the prices realized at that sale.

Beyond the town lots, are the suburban lots; and these, we imagine, extend over the whole island; their value is much less, and will of course be governed by circumstances.

The Government buildings consist at present of a Magistracy, a large and convenient brick building, just finished; the post office, record and land office, the jail, and several other small brick buildings, some warehouses, and several barracks either finished or building.

. . . Its situation for mercantile purposes is admirable: it skirts along a magnificent bay, in which ships of all sizes and numbers may find shelter at all times, and although in July last year the typhoons did considerable damage all the ships that had paid due attention to the signs of the weather, and taken the necessary precautions escaped unhurt. . . .

Just now whilst the trade at Canton continues open and unmolested that carried on at Hong Kong is of little consequence, and chiefly confined to opium, and here and there a few manufactured goods may be disposed of, or a little tea and cassia purchased. The trade now carried on by the Chinese population is, with the exception of salt, of which already Hong Kong is said to have become a depot, chiefly confined to their immediate wants. This population, composed of mechanics, shopkeepers, and labourers has, we think been overrated at 15,000. We are aware that without a census it is almost impossible to arrive at numbers with any degree of correctness, yet we should think little more than half that number to be nearer the truth.

If however in a mercantile view the situation of Hong Kong be so very desirable, considering it as a place of residence, its locality offers many drawbacks to its other advantages. It stretches as before said along the bay from east to west with a southern [sic] aspect: it is consequently open to the piercing north wind in winter; whilst in summer the very high hills which rise abruptly immediately behind it and behind which the setting sun now disappears to the Hong Kongians before 4 o'clock preclude the possibility of its being cooled by the southerly winds, prevailing during the south west monsoon. It must therefore be very cold in winter, and almost insufferably hot in summer. We have hardly yet obtained sufficient experience to know whether this formation will be favourable to health or otherwise: the latter may be apprehended and indeed a good deal of fever prevailed during the warm season and till late last year, but there were several causes then besides the climate to account for its appearance. At the time of our visit the place was perfectly healthy. A great advantage is it being so well supplied with very fine water. Wherever wells have been dug water has been found of good quality at a small depth: and in a well lately dug behind the magistracy, although at a considerable elevation, water was found at the inconsiderable depth of 8 feet. Besides the wells there are numbers of rivulets which give a sufficient supply at all seasons.

The road running through the town of Hong Kong is continued all through the island to its southern coast, where it ends at Tytam bay, at the village of Chek Chuen [sic]. It is a work of great labor, for during its whole extent of about 8 or 9 miles it is cut into the sides of hills, or leads over ravines, and manifests considerable engineering skill, not however wholly ascribable to the English engineers as some part of it had already been made by the Chinese,

APPENDIX IV

and has only been improved and enlarged at present. The interior of the island presents scenes as wild as can be: it is with the exception of a few small valleys, from which the industrious Chinese reap scanty crops of rice and wheat, nothing but a wild jumble of hills, that generally seem to rise in an angle of about 45 degrees, and in many instances are even much steeper.

. . . It would therefore be a work of immense expense, if at all feasible, to make the road fit for carriages; at present with the exception of a few spots, gullies over which the bridges have not been completed, a horse may be rode to Tytam bay. This bay, near which and the village of Check Chuen there is plenty of ground for building a considerable town, is as far as regards climate, much more favorably situated than Hong Kong, it is sheltered from the north and open to the south winds, but unfortunately the bay, though capacious, is not sufficiently sheltered from the south winds to allow of ships anchoring there during the south west monsoon. Another place, Checkpewan, to the southwest of the Island is said to offer a situation for a settlement more favorable than either Hong Kong or Tytam bay: but the shortness of our visit did not permit us to go there. At Checkpewan one barrack for 36 men, and an officer's house is already completed, and the foundation for another barrack of the same sizure laid down.

NOTE. *This survey was supplemented in the same issue by the remarks of an anonymous 'Idler in Hong Kong' who confines himself to the barracks and fortifications:—*

Beginning east of our projected town you will find a Fort now building on Kellett's island which was intended but certainly does not command the Lei Moon passage. . . . A casual observer would say that this fort was specially constructed to protect the magnificent establishment of an eminent firm which is proposed to be erected on the point immediately contiguous. To resume, going westwards we encounter a half moon battery or platform which is to mount some half dozen heavy guns on carriages. This work is in front of the barracks now occupied by the 37th native Infantry and a similar one is constructing at the extreme west of the town to protect the barracks there, and at which are stationed the Bengal Volunteers. . . . The barracks on the other side of the island are situated at Check Chuen and seem admirably adapted to the purpose. . . .'

APPENDIX V

THE FIRST GOVERNMENT HOUSE n. 1

THE earliest Government House seems to have disappeared without trace. And yet the evidence, pieced together little by little, provides a solution as conclusive as it is interesting. The retrospect of January 1842 already quoted from the *Canton Press* speaks of 'Government Hill' on which 'a public office to serve as a temporary residence for the head of the Government is just finished'. The *Canton Press* again, in February 1842, says, 'Next in importance and pretension is Government House (which has changed its name to the "Record Office" since the late acting (?) governor has been metamorphosed into a Lieutenant Governor).' The acting governor at the time was, of course, Mr. A. R. Johnston; and Dr. Legge, in his lecture delivered in 1872 on Hong Kong in 1843, speaks of 'the house of Mr. Johnston, who had been administrator of the island on its first occupancy', which 'rose as conspicuous as are now Messrs. Heard and Co's. offices which were manufactured out of it'. Now Messrs. Augustine Heard's offices are easily traced to the site close to St. John's Cathedral now occupied by the Missions Étrangères building; while if we pursue the other clue we reach the same result no less easily, for Lieutenant Collinson's map of Victoria in 1844 signed by Major Aldrich, R.E., in 1845 (and now in the survey office of the P.W.D.) marks Government House a little east of Murray Battery; and a site-plan of the centre of the town made in connexion with the land sale of July 1844 calls the same site 'Mr. Johnston's'. The first Government House in fact stood where the Missions Étrangères building stands to-day; and a curious corroboration of this may be found in the fact that the milestones on the road from town to Aberdeen (and also, I fancy, on the bridle-track to Stanley) start from this terminus.

My next reference adds, I admit, little to my brief. It is a sepia drawing of an unimposing house entitled 'Sir Henry Pottinger's' to be found in the Chater Collection of prints and pictures. This, I am willing to believe, portrays the site and Mr. Johnston's house upon it.

But Captain Cunynghame, in his *A.D.C.'s Recollections* [1844], is a little disconcerting, for he speaks of Government House as being not only a poor building, much more humble than Jardine Matheson's (which no doubt it was), but also as on comparatively level ground. True, he adds that if it were anywhere but Hong Kong you would not call it level; but for a house which, as we know, stands on a sharp bluff it seems a very inapt description, and one is almost tempted to suppose an even earlier governmental abode (somewhere near the Cheero Club, maybe) which housed Pottinger in 1842 while 'Johnston's' was being built (and which at any rate was a step in advance on 'the pitched tent' which housed him in August 1841).

However that may be, it is certain that all the arrangements were temporary. Even the site was unsettled, and Bernard in his *Voyage of the Nemesis*, referring to 1843, tells us that North Point had its advocates, among whom no doubt was a certain 'eminent firm'.

The *Chinese Repository* for 1845 carries the story a step farther with three references. The first speaks of 'a review of the troops which took place on Queen's Road in front of Government House' —fixing the position clearly on the sea front. The second, describing the military section, speaks of 'a line of commissariate buildings' which 'filled up the space to the streamlet descending from the East side of Government House'—fixing it just as clearly, just west of the stream which, now trained, has assumed the name of Albany Nullah, and obviously some distance up its course. But the third reference throws a flood of light on the matter, for speaking of what we now know as Murray Parade Ground the writer says: 'the post office is on the south'—it was at or near the present Cathedral site —'and the Governor's private residence on the west of the parade ground. Further westward and higher up the hill is Government House.' The house 'higher up the hill' I identify unhesitatingly with the Albany, or Civil Officers' Quarters, a familiar and conspicuous landmark overlooking the Botanical Gardens which has just been demolished as I write. This building, said by Dr. Legge to have been fashioned out of an earlier range of barracks, served (like 'Johnston's') the double purpose of offices and quarters before the present Government offices—the Colonial Secretariat—were completed, and thus vied with 'Johnston's' for the title of 'Government House'. In point of fact the Governor neither resided there nor had his office there; the early Governor's office being a separate building within the area of the present gardens (and doubtless within convenient range of the Albany) which Legge thus describes—'beyond the site of the present [1872] Government House was a small bungalow where Sir Henry Pottinger and Sir John Davis after him held their court'.

Sir John Davis's residence we know exactly, for the *Friend of China* (p. 1168) tells us, 'The Governor, if he has not built a palace, pays for one', and we are in no doubt which house he rented, for, giving evidence in 1847 before the Parliamentary Commission on Commercial Relations, Mr. Alexander Matheson says, 'There is no Government House. The Governor lives in a rented house', and, later, 'with regard to forts I forgot to mention that there is a saluting battery'—Murray Battery—'erected at Hong Kong close to the Governor's house'; while another witness states, 'notwithstanding the large sums of money expended the Governor is now obliged to hire a residence which belongs to the late deputy-governor Mr. Johnston'. The estimates for 1847–8 confirm it with this item: 'rent of Governor's residence . . . £625'; while Davis, in a dispatch to Earl Grey in March 1846 forwarding the Blue Book, says, 'The works already in progress . . . comprise all that are required except . . . a Government House which I have left to the last.'

How long Sir John remained at 'Johnston's' is not certain, for two widely separate sources seem to point to a move up the hill to Major Caine's house in Caine Road. I refer first to the lithographed panorama, of which there are copies in the Council Chamber and the Hong Kong Club, which calls Caine's House 'Government House', and secondly to a woodcut in the *Illustrated London News* of 1857 of the same house described in the letter-press as 'late the residence of Governor Sir J. F. Davis, Bart.'[1]

At this point Mr. Robert Fortune steps in to introduce complications, for in his *Tea Districts of India and China*, published in 1852, he tells how 'many of the inhabitants have taken up the matter [of gardening] with great spirit and have planted all the ground near their houses. . . . I may instance those of His Excellency the Governor at "Spring Gardens" etc.'

This is the first and only evidence that any Governor ever lived at Spring Gardens, and we ask ourselves what year Mr. Fortune refers to. The answer is something of a curiosity, for no sooner had Mr. Fortune published *Tea Districts* than he was asked to publish an abridged edition embodying this work and an earlier work on China issued in 1843; and in the abridged edition, while we find no reference at all to His Excellency or 'Spring Gardens', we find in the preface a statement by the author that he has 'struck out many things which experience has taught me to improve'. This, however, does not necessarily mean that Fortune admits that he was romancing in consigning His Excellency to 'Spring Gardens' in *Tea Districts*. The truth is that, while *Tea Districts* describes Hong Kong in 1848, the abridged edition entitled *Tea Countries* describes Hong Kong in 1843, and Fortune, however confusing, may be a veracious witness; in which case the solution seems to be that Davis's successor Bonham, who arrived in March 1848, preferred to rent premises (pending the completion of the new Government House) on the delectable sea front at Wan Tsai.

[1] See the illustration facing p. 195.

APPENDIX VI
TREATY OF NANKING
Article III

IT being obviously necessary and desirable that British subjects should have some port whereat they may careen and refit their ships when required and keep stores for the purpose, His Majesty the Emperor of China cedes to Her Majesty the Queen of Great Britain etc. the island of Hong Kong to be possessed in perpetuity by Her Britannic Majesty, her heirs and successors and to be governed by such laws and regulations as Her Majesty the Queen of Great Britain etc. shall see fit to direct.

APPENDIX VII

POTTINGER'S PROCLAMATION OF JUNE 26TH, 1843

THE treaty of peace, ratified under the Signs Manual, and seals of the respective sovereigns, between her majesty the Queen of the United Kingdom of Great Britain and Ireland &c. and his imperial majesty the Emperor of China, having been this day formally exchanged, the annexed royal charter and commission, under the great seal of state, are hereby proclaimed and published for general information, obedience, and guidance.

His Excellency, Sir Henry Pottinger, Bart., G.C.B., etc., has this day taken the oaths of office and assumed charge of the Government of the Colony of Hong Kong, and its dependencies.

In obedience to the gracious commands of her majesty as intimated in the royal charter the Island and its dependencies will be designated and known as 'The Colony of Hong Kong'; and his excellency the Governor, is further pleased to direct, that the present city, on the northern side of the island, shall be distinguished by her majesty's name, and that all public communications, archives, etc., etc., shall be henceforward dated 'Victoria'.

GOD SAVE THE QUEEN

HENRY POTTINGER.

Dated at the Government House,
at Victoria on 26th day of June 1843.

APPENDIX VIII

HONG KONG NAMES

n. 1

THE DERIVATION OF STREET-NAMES AND PLACE-NAMES IN EARLY HONG KONG

CAPTAIN ELLIOT has no memorial in Hong Kong; but the two first Governors, Pottinger and Davis, the first naval Commander-in-Chief and his rear-admiral, Parker and Cochran, and the first General Officer Commanding, Gough, have all lent their names to mountain peaks, while Gough's successor D'Aguilar bespoke a cape.

The early naval surveyors—Belcher in *Sulphur*, Kellet in *Starling*, Collinson in *Plover*, and the early engineers, Aldrich and Collinson, contrived to leave their mark broadcast on many natural features.

As for street-names, besides Pottinger himself and Caine and Pedder, many of the smaller fry of the early civil service are commemorated, such as Gutzlaff (Chinese Secretary), Staunton (Colonial Chaplain), Hillier (Assistant Magistrate), Cleverly (Assistant Surveyor), and Bridges (acting Attorney-General). Governor Bonham and his G.O.C. Jervois gave their names to Bonham Strand and Jervois Street, and Bonham's successor, Bowring, gave his to Bowrington. Cochran and Gough and D'Aguilar (though already awarded natural features) were given streets as well. Stanley and Aberdeen—Secretaries of State for Foreign Affairs and the Colonies—secured streets in addition to the familiar villages on the south side of the island. But Sir Robert Peel, Premier, and Lord Lyndhurst, Foreign Secretary, and Elgin, Plenipotentiary Extraordinary, were awarded streets only. Black's Link perhaps commemorates a G.O.C. of a somewhat later date—General Black. The Master-General of Ordnance receives *in absentia* his full share of recognition in Murray Battery, Murray Parade Ground, Murray Barracks, and Murray Pier. Wellington needs no introduction. But who was Waglan and who Wyndham? Who was Gage, and who or what was Hollywood?

APPENDIX IX

n. 1   A SHORT GLOSSARY OF ANGLO-ORIENTAL TERMS

THE words fall into several well-defined categories. First the purely English words used on the China coast with a special meaning: the *country ship*, which means the merchantman trading in Far Eastern waters, notably between India and China, as distinct from the East Indiaman which hailed from the port of London; *boy*, the foreigner's Chinese servant, valet and butler combined, whose age may range from the callow youth of 17 to the grandfather of 70; *squeeze*, the gentle but steady pressure which, when applied to a suitable object, induces it painlessly and imperceptibly to yield up a drop or two of its substance, with special reference to the propensity of 'boys' and other Chinese servants who, without spoken word, adopt the method to reimburse themselves for services (frequently quite real) rendered to their foreign masters; *pigeon* or *pidgin*—familiar in the expression of 'pidgin English'—a mere mispronunciation for 'business'.

The next category is the Anglo-Indian; under which head I shall put *shroff*, though *saraf*, a bank clerk, appears strictly to be Persian; and *godown*, which derives from the Malay 'godong', a warehouse. *Punkah* surely needs no explanation, though electric fans have driven it from Hong Kong. *Tiffin*, for lunch, still hovers on, but *chota hazri*, for early breakfast, is no longer heard. *Sycee*, silver, survives, and *lac* (for 100,000) is far too useful to be lost. *Tael*, an ounce, is Anglo-Indian; and so, too, are *chunam* (lime), *bungalow* (a single-storied house), *veranda*, and *bazaar* (a retail shopping centre).

Then come the Portuguese words: the *ladrones* (pirates); *comprador* (the provider); *mandarin* or *mandarim* (the giver of mandates); *praya* (the water-front parade); *joss* (dios, the Divinity); *amah* (a native nurse); and *lorcha* (the junk-rigged sloop with foreign hull).

Japan provides two familiar words at least: *cheese-eye*, a small

APPENDIX IX

child, from *chüsai* = small; and *jinricksha*, 'the man's strength cart', or (as we should say) 'the one-man-power car'.

Lastly there are the Chinese words divisible by dialects. Amoy gives us *tea* which we have adopted; *junk*, a sailing-ship; and (I suspect) *maskee*, the equivalent of Cantonese *m'shai* ('don't bother').

Canton supplies *hong*, a factory, literally a double row of shops—the Chinese 'bazaar'; *chop-chop* (k'ap k'ap), quickly; *chop-boat* (chap-chiu), a registered boat (obsolete); *chow*, food, apparently a mistranslation of 'tsau', wine (cf. *Tsau tim*, a hotel, which means literally a 'wine-house' rather than a 'food-house'); *chit*, a small note (chi-tsai, a little piece of paper); *tai pan*, the big manager.

Consoo (used in the expression 'Consoo fund' of the factory days) is, I suspect, a corruption of 'Kung Sz' (a company) or perhaps 'Kung Soh' (the company office). *Cumshaw*, though still familiar for a tip, is still of uncertain origin. Some attribute it to the Pekingese 'Kan hsieh' ('thank you') which, for a Cantonese practice, seems far-fetched. Others make it a corruption of 'kam sha', 'gold-dust', thereby relating it to that other form of 'squeeze' which the Cantonese would call 'li kam' (gift-gold) but which is far better known to Europeans by its Pekingese name 'li-kin'.

APPENDIX X

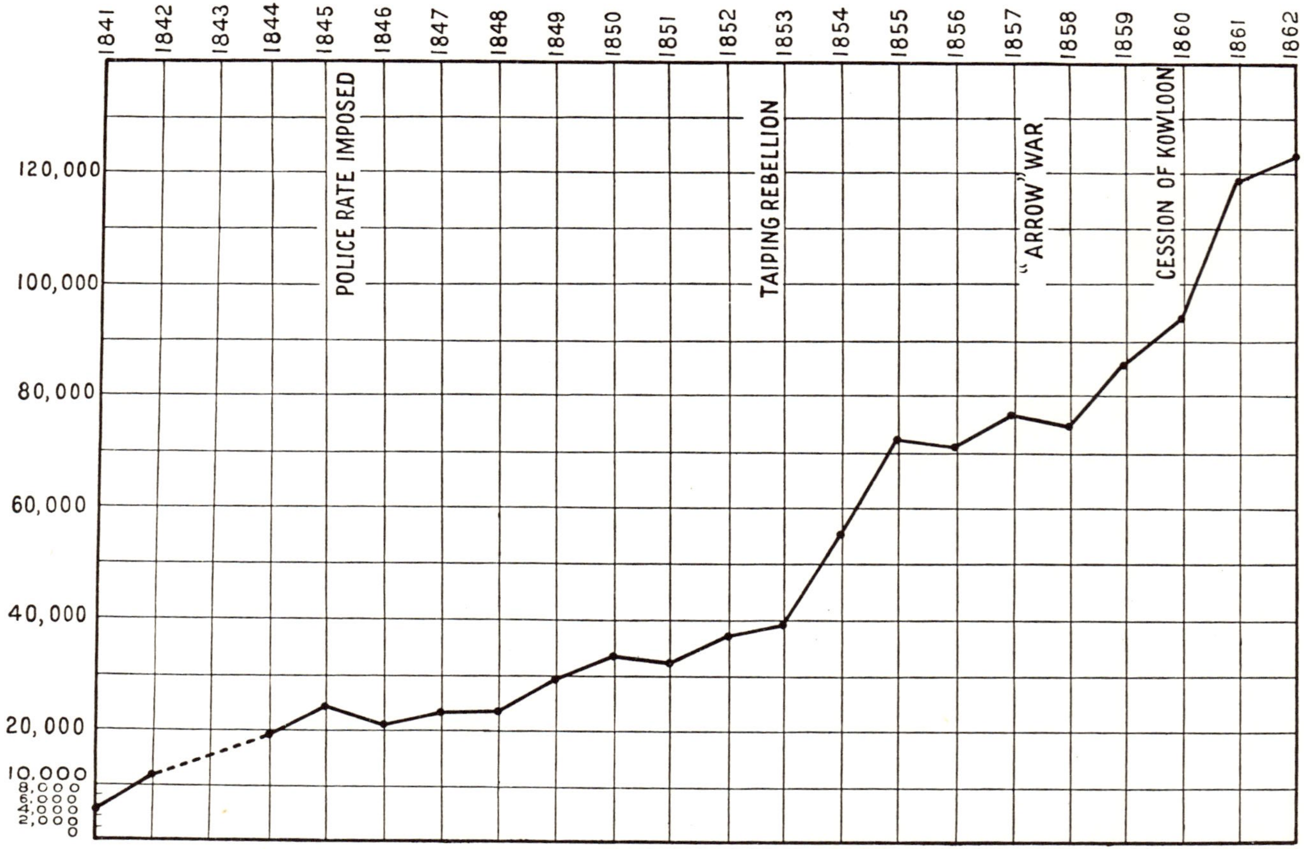

POPULATION OF HONG KONG 1841-62

Based on *Historical and Statistical Abstract 1841-1930*, published by the Hong Kong Government.

APPENDIX XI

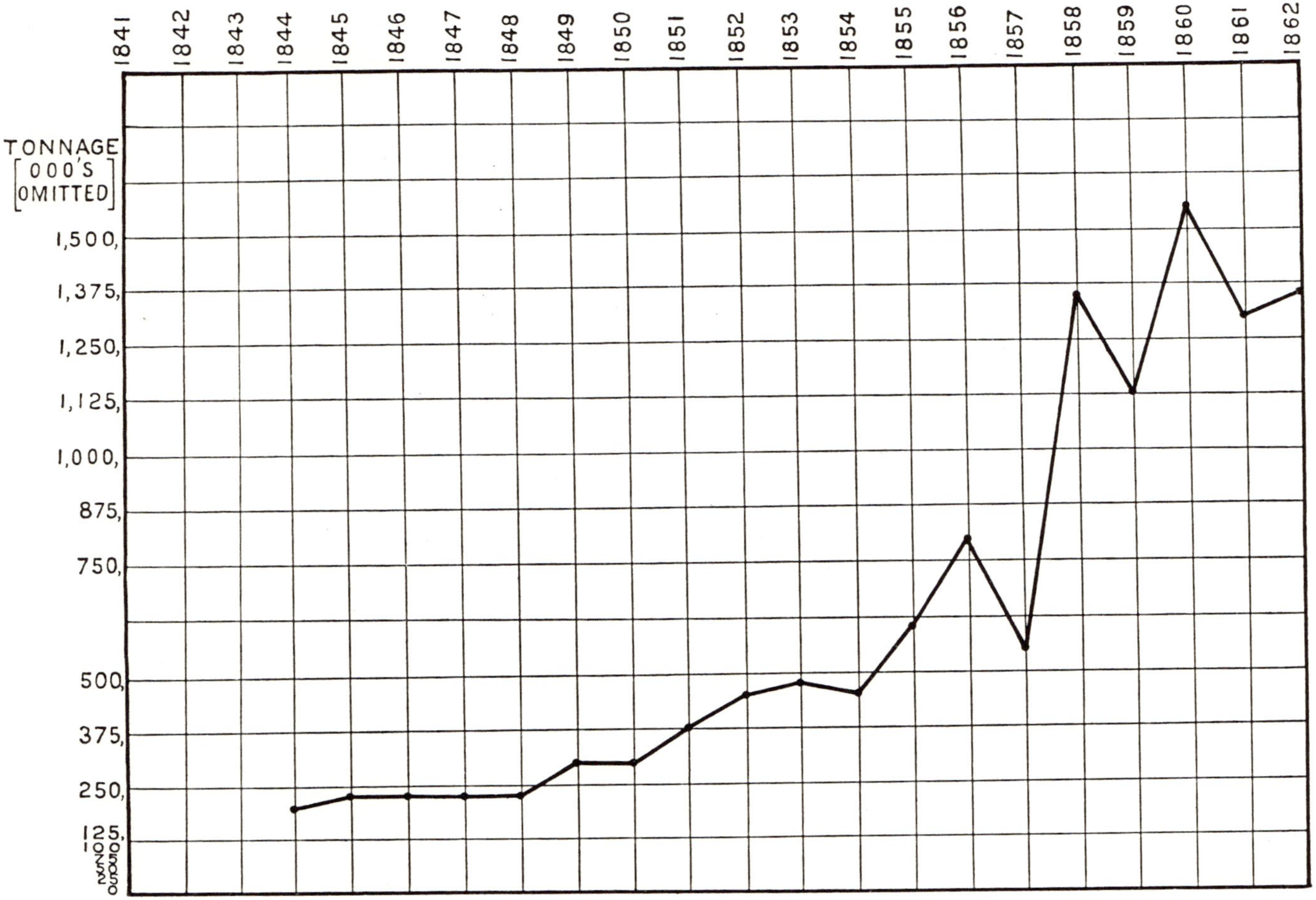

[221]

SHIPS ENTERING (from 1857 onwards ENTERING AND CLEARING) HONG KONG HARBOUR 1841–62

Expressed in tonnage to the nearest 25,000 tons: based on *Historical and Statistical Abstract 1841–1930*, published by the Hong Kong Government.

MAP OF THE
CANTON DELTA
1850
Miles

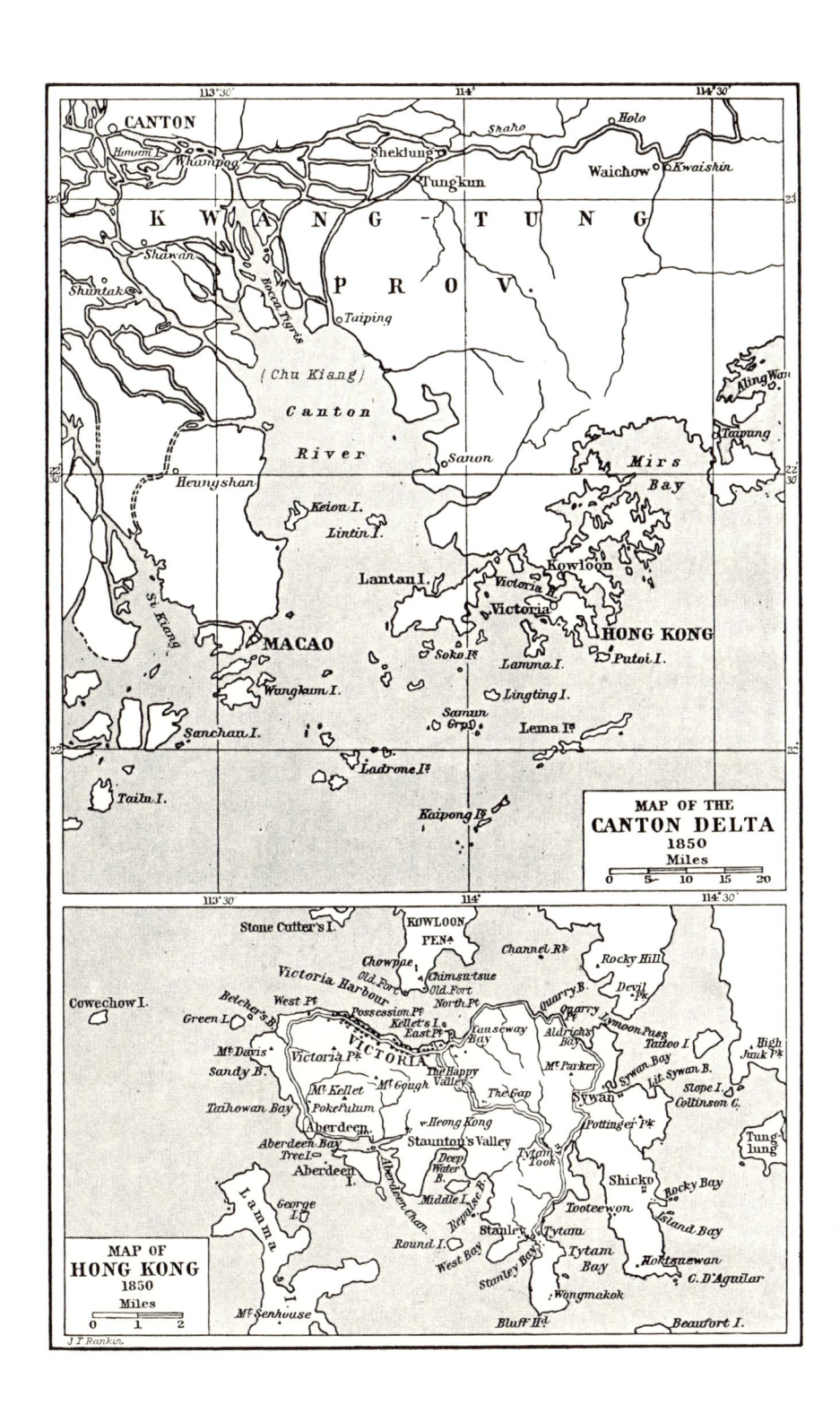

MAP OF
HONG KONG
1850
Miles

INDEX

Page numbers in this Index refer only to the original text

Abel, Dr. Clarke, author of *Narrative of a Journey*, 26.
Aberdeen, Lord, Foreign Secretary, 158.
Aberdeen, place-name (Chuk-Pi-Wan), 22, 101; (Shek Pae Wan), 121; (Check Pe Wan), App. IV, 209.
Adams, W. K., Attorney-General, 192.
Albany Godowns, 111.
Albany, civil officers' quarters, 134, 151.
Alceste, H.M.S., 24.
Alcock, Rutherford, Consul in Shanghai, 164.
Aldrich, Major R. E., 136.
Amoy, 10, 71.
Andromache, H.M.S., 35, 39–41.
Anglo-Oriental Terms, App. IX.
Anstruther, Captain, captured at Tinghai, 71.
Argyle, merchantman, 45.
Ariel, 68.
Arrow, lorcha (the *Arrow* incident), 177, 178.
Artillery Barracks, 99, 134, 151, 154.
Atalanta, H.C.'s steamer, 89.

Bantam, Java, 9.
Baptist Chapel, Shuck's, 127, 154.
Belcher, Captain Sir E., of *Sulphur*, records the occupation of Hong Kong Island, 93.
Belcher's Battery, 98.
Bengal Volunteers, 120.
Bernard, W. D., author of *Voyage of the Nemesis*, 76.
Bilbaino, Spanish brig, 60.
Bingham, J. E., Commander, author of *Expedition to China*, quoted, 95, 100, 101.
Bogue, forts, 2; Napier enters, 36; Weddell 1637, 41; Elliot enters, 54; Bocca Tigris, 60, 67; assaulted Jan. 1841, 74; assaulted Feb. 1841, 81; Bonham meets Hsu at, 165; second interview, 166; seized 1856–7, 179.
Bonham, Sir Samuel George, Bt., Governor and Superintendent, XI *passim*.
Bonham Strand, 171.
Borget, Auguste, author of *La Chine et les Chinois*, 33.
Bourboulon, A. de, French Envoy, 182.
Bowring, Dr. John, Governor, Consul-General at Canton, 169; acting Superintendent, 169; knighted, 190, XII *passim*.
Bremer, Sir James John Gordon, Kt., C.B., K.C.B., Commodore, arrives, 69; reward offered, 81; goes to Calcutta, 83; returns from Calcutta, 87; takes possession of Hong Kong, 93; issues proclamation jointly with Elliot, 94.
Bruce, the Hon. Frederick W. A., first British Minister to China, 185; establishes himself in Shanghai, 187.

Cadet Service founded, 194.
Caine, William, appointed magistrate, 103; original residence, 118; imposes curfew, 131; confirmed as Chief Magistrate, 135; M.L.C., M.Ex.Co., 135; administers the Government, 175 *n.*; Lieut.-Governor, 175; 'Senior Member of Legislative Council', 176; libel action, 194; review of career, 192.
Caldwell, D. R., Registrar-General, 193, 194.
Calliope, H.M.S., 82.
Cambridge, merchantman, renamed *Chesapeake*, 82.
Canton Bazaar, 152.
Cantonment Hill, 99, 100, 101, 117, 120.
Cap Shui Mun, *see* Kap Sing Mun.
Carolina, merchantman, 21.

Q

226 INDEX

Castle Peak Bay, 181.
Cathedral, St. John's, stone laid, 153; Supreme Court used pending completion, 171; opened, 172.
Cemetery, 117.
Centurion, H.M.S., 22.
Chamber of Commerce, founded in Canton, 40; founded in Hong Kong, 188.
Chapdelaine, Père Auguste, 178.
Chapel of the Conception consecrated, 132.
Chekchu, Stanley, 90, 121; sickness at, 128.
Chuenpei, 62; first battle of, 64; second battle, 74.
Churchill, Lord John, Commander of *Druid*, dies, 68.
Chusan, the pledge, 70; to be exchanged for Hong Kong, 75.
City Hall, 196.
Clarendon, Lord, Foreign Secretary, 175.
Cleverly, Charles St. G., Acting Surveyor-General, App. VIII, 217.
Clock Tower, 196.
Cochran, Sir Thomas, Rear-Admiral, 157.
Co-Hong, 11, 98.
Colledge, Dr., 40.
Colonial Church (Chapel), 134, 152.
Colonial Secretariat, 153; opened, 171.
Columbine, H.M.S., 75.
Commissariat, 152.
Conventions: Tariff Convention of Oct. 1858, 183; of Pekin, 190.
Cornwall, merchantman, 30.
Court, Criminal and Admiralty, vested in Superintendency, 34; transferred from Canton to Hong Kong, 131; re-transferred to Shanghai, 190.
Cricket Club, established, 172.
Cunynghame, Captain, author of *An A.D.C.'s Recollections*, 22.
Currency, 195.

D'Aguilar, G. C., Major-General, G.O.C., arrives, 140; delivers *coup-de-main* against Canton, 150; erects barracks, &c., 154.
Davis, John Francis, Governor and Superintendent, with Amherst 1816, 29; member of Commission, 35; Superintendent, 43; lies low, 44; succeeds Pottinger, 141, X *passim*.
Deane, W. M., first Cadet, 194.
Defence, merchantman, 11, 21.
Dent, L., partner in Dent & Co., 49; seized, 54; petitions Home Govt., 68; $50,000 reward for, 86; builds 'Green Bank', 110; inquiries *re* Macao, 116; blocks Praya reclamation scheme, 184.
Dent's fountain, 196.
Discovery, H.C.'s survey-ship, 26.
Douglas, Lieutenant, captured in *Kite*, 71.
Douglas, Master of *Cambridge*, 82.
Druid, H.M.S., arrives at Tong Kwu, 68.
Duddell's bakery, burnt down, 181.

East Battery, 99; a small battery, 120.
East India Company, 9, 10, 11, 12, 25, 30.
East Point, 99, 121, 184, App. IV, 206.
Edger, Joseph Frost, first unofficial member of Legislative Council, 171.
Education, Central School established, 195; Bishop Raimondi, 195.
Eitel, Dr., author of *Europe in China*, 91.
Elepoo, Viceroy of Chekiang, 75.
Elgin, Lord, Envoy Extraordinary, 180; reaches Hong Kong, 180; goes north, 183; leaves for home, 185; returns, 190; finally leaves, 192.
Elliot, Charles, Captain, R.N., Superintendent, VI, VII *passim*; Master Attendant, 35; Third Supt., 44; *Argyle* incident, 45; Second Supt., 48; Superintendent, VI; junior plenipotentiary, 69; announces Admiral Elliot's resignation, 73; $50,000 on his head, 81; $100,000 on his head, 86; shipwrecked, 88; superseded, 89; returns home, 89; issues proclamations at Hong Kong, 94.

INDEX

Elliot, the Hon. George, Rear-Admiral, 69; resigns, 72.
Ellis, Sir Henry, member of Amherst's embassy, 24, 25.
Embassies, Macartney 1793, 13; Amherst 1816, 13, 24.
Escape Creek, naval action, 180.
Executive Council, created, 135.

Factories at Canton, 11, 83–5.
Falcon, merchantman, 32.
Flagstaff House, 'the General's quarters', 152, 154.
Fu Mun (Hoo Mun-Chai), *see under* Bogue.

Gazetteer and Census (first Gazetteer), App. II.
General Hewitt, merchantman, 24.
Gibb, Livingstone, office, 133.
Gillespie, C. V., builder of Albany Godowns, 114, 120.
Gough, Sir Hugh, Lieutenant-General, arrives, 69; attacks Canton, 85.
Government Hill, 120.
Government House: the first Government House, App. V.
Grant, Sir Hope, General, arrives, 190.
Gribble of *Royal Saxon*, captured at Tong Kwu, 67.
de Gros, Baron, French Envoy Extraordinary, 181.
Gutzlaff, Rev. C., Chinese Secretary, 31, 45.

Hall, Captain, W. H., midshipman on *Lyra*, 30; Commander of *Nemesis*, 73; urges cession of Kowloon Point, 191.
Harbour Master's house, 134, 152, 154.
Hart, Robert, seconded to Chinese Customs, 188.
Head-quarters House, *see* Flagstaff House.
Health, 127; Committee of, 136, 137; suggestion to abandon Hong Kong, 138; improving, 154; improved, 197.

Hillier, Charles Batten, Assistant Magistrate, App. VIII, 217.
Hong Kong Club, opened, 153.
Hong Kong Wai, 29.
Hsu Kwong Tsin, acting High Commissioner at Canton, 165; rewarded, 167.
Hulme, J. W., First Chief Justice, 143.
Hyacinth, H.M.S., 64; enters Macao, 68.

Ice-house, 152.
Imogene, H.M.S., 37, 40, 41.
Innes, James, 46; and opium, 53; opium again, 56; dies in Macao, 56 *n*.
Interpretation: Lord Amherst's Embassy, 26; Dr. Gutzlaff, 31; Robert Morrison, 35; Paou Chung, 78; Thom, R., 86; J. R. Morrison, 137; linguists, 150; D. R. Caldwell, 193; Cadets, 194.
Investigator, H.C.'s survey-ship, 26.

Jail, nearing completion, 116, 120, 126 *n*., 133; App. IV, 207.
Jameson, How & Co., premises, 133.
Jardine, William, 14, 37, 40, 43, 49; ordered to leave, 50; leaves, 54; member of deputation at F.O., 80.
Jardine, David, first unofficial member of Legislative Council, 171.
Jardine, Matheson, Messrs., select East Point, 99; acquire lots at first land sale, 111; closely connected with Bowring, 187.
Jardine, Robert, subscribes to Sailors' Home, 197.
Jervois, William, Major-General, G.O.C., administers, 174.
Jervois Street, 133, 171.
Johnston, A. R., Deputy Superintendent, takes charge of Hong Kong, 87, 112; Postmaster in addition, 118; again left in charge, 127; Registrar to the Supt., 134; Member of Legislative Council, Member of Executive Council, 135.

INDEX

'Johnston's', *see* App. V (the first Government House).

Kap Sing (or Shui) Mun, 23, 32; fleet removes to, 68.
Keshen, Viceroy of Chihli, Imperial Commissioner at Canton: interview with Elliot at Pei Ho, 71; appointed Commissioner, 73; interview with Elliot at the Second Bar, 77.
Keying, Imperial Commissioner, Canton, ratification of Treaty, 132; meets Pottinger and Davis at the Bogue, 145.
Kite, armed brig, wrecked, 71.
Kowloon (Cow Loon), 93, 94–8; ceded, 190–1.
Kum Sing Mun, 159.
Kwan, Admiral of the Bogue, 91.
Kwan Tai Lo, Hong Kong, 90, 120, 122.

Ladrone Islands, 2, 27; fleet arrives at, 70.
Lamma island, 25, 93.
Land Committee 1842, 125; Second Land Committee 1843, 137.
Land Office, 117; retrenchment in, 126, App. IV, 207.
Land Sales: first land sale, 109–11; second, 140.
Lantao, 3; alias Backelow, 21; 31, 32, 46.
Larne, H.M.S., 54.
Lay, Horatio Nelson, seconded to Chinese Customs, 188.
Legge, Rev. James, quoted, 101; description of the town, 133–4; Legge and education, 195.
Legislative Council, created, 135; active, 140; dual functions, 145; dual functions end, 169; two unofficials added, 170; Sir Hercules Robinson guides official members, 196.
Lemma (Lema), 25, 28.
Lin Tin Island, 2, 12, 31, 46, 55.
Lin Tse Sü, Imperial Commissioner at Canton, arrives, 53; tours the British factories, 57; offers rewards, 71.

Lin Wei Hi, loses his life at Tsim Sha Tsuy, 57.
Lindsay & Co., merchants: offices, 134; block Praya reclamation scheme, 184.
Louisa, cutter, 35, 40; at Lin Tin, 47; 51; Elliot embarks, 88; meets a typhoon and is wrecked, 88.
Lung Wan, colleague of Yik Shan, 'pacificator', 79.
Lyemun, 30, 31, 32; App. IV, 209.
Lyra, H.M.'s brig, 24.

Ma Liu Ho (Waterfall Bay), 25.
Macao, 2, 10, 11; Napier reaches, 35; Elliot waits at, 49; Elliot retires to, 52; Elliot discusses, 56; *Hyacinth* enters, 68; *Druid* enters, 71; Elliot remains at, 87, 112; Pottinger transfers from, 123.
Magistracy, nearing completion, 117; completed, 120, 133, App. IV, 207.
Maitland, Rear-Admiral, 52.
Malcolm, Major, member of Land Committee, 125; returns with treaty ratified, 131; officiating Col. Sec., 135.
Markets: 'Malcolm's' or 'Canton Bazaar', 125; Central, 207; suite of retail markets, 184.
Martin, R. Montgomery, Colonial Treasurer, 144; resigns, 161.
Matheson, Alexander, 99; builds first stone house, 122.
Matheson, James, leaves China, 123; founded press in China, 124.
Maxwell, Capt. Murray, of H.M.S. *Alceste*, 24, 27.
May, Charles, Superintendent of Police, 193.
M'Leod, John, author of *Voyage of the Alceste*, 26.
Meik, Captain, 49th foot, member of Land Committee, 125.
Mercer, W. T., Colonial Treasurer: Col. Sec., 175.

INDEX

Military Hospital, 151; *see* Wellington Barracks.
Military Lands, define limit of Cantonments, 125, 135.
Modeste, H.M.S., 95, 100.
Morgan, Captain, purchaser of M.L. 51, App. III.
Morrison, J. R., $50,000 reward for, 81; Chinese Secretary, 135; Member of Legisl. Council, Member of Exec. Council, 135; dies, 137.
Morrison, Rev. Robert, interpreter to Napier, 35; death, 37.
Morrison Hill, 127.
Murray Barracks, three buildings are being erected, 151, 154.
Murray Battery, a guard house, 120.
Mylius, Captain Jno. F., Land Officer, 117 *n*.

Names: Hong Kong Villages, App. II; Hong Kong Street-names, &c., App. VIII.
Namoa, opium station, 158.
Nanking, Treaty of, *see under* Treaties.
Napier, William John, eighth Lord, V *passim*; death, 41.
Navy Bay, 98.
Nemesis, H.C.'s iron steamer, arrives, 73; appears at Canton, 83; Elliot steams round Hong Kong, 94.
Ningpo, 71.
Noble, Mrs., captured in *Kite*, 71.

Opium: pre-Napier, 12, 13; Sir G. Robinson, 47; expansion of traffic, 50; Lin Tse Sü and, 53; delivery of by Elliot, 55; store-ships in Hong Kong, 61; situation in Pottinger's time, 129–30; situation in Davis's time, 155–60; Bonham and opium, 172; legalized by tariff convention of 1858, 184.
Orlando, H.M.S., 27.
Ouchterlony, Lieutenant, author of *The Chinese War*, quoted, 96, 101.

Palmerston, Lord, Foreign Secretary, 34.
Paou Chung, interpreter, 78.
Parker, Sir William, K.C.B., Commander-in-Chief, arrives, 89.
Parkes, Sir Harry, Consul at Canton, 178; an Allied Commissioner, 191.
Pascoe, J., member of Land Committee, 125.
Pedder, William, Lieutenant of *Nemesis*, 8; gazetted Harbour Master, 112; confirmed, 135.
Pedder Street, 113.
Pedder's Hill, 113, 134; Harbour Master's house, 152, 154.
Pekin Convention, *see under* Conventions.
Phlegethon, H.C.'s steamer, 89.
Pik, Governor of Canton, installed as Viceroy, 183.
Plover, H.M.S., 24.
Plowden, William Chichely, member of Trade Superintendency, 35.
Population, estimate for 1841, 119, 122; growth 1837–47, 154; growth 1841–62, App. X.
Possession Point, Possession Mount, 93, 94.
Post Office, nearing completion, 116, 134, 152, App. IV, 207.
Pottinger, Sir Henry, Bt., IX *passim*; arrives at Macao, 89.
Proclamations: Bremer and Elliot jointly, 94; Elliot's, App. I; Pottinger's, App. VII.

Queen's Road, 113, 116, 124, 127, 133, App. IV, 206.

Raimondi, R.C. Bishop 1862, 195.
Regiments stationed at Hong Kong, *see* Troops.
Robinson, Sir George Best, Bt., Superintendent, member of Commission, 35; Superintendent, 45; discusses opium, 47; post abolished, 48.
Robinson, Sir Hercules, Governor, XIII *passim*.

230 INDEX

Royal Saxon, merchantman, enters the Bogue, 67.
Russell & Co., 82.

Sai Wan, 101.
Sai Ying Pun, 99.
Sailors' Home, West Point, 99, 196.
Sarah, merchantman, 14.
Sargent, Ensign, member of Land Committee, 1842, 125.
Senhouse, Sir Humphrey Le Fleming, Commodore, R.N., 85; dies, 87.
Seymour, Sir Michael, Admiral, 178.
Shek Pai Wan, Chuk-Pi-Wan (Aberdeen), 22, 101, 121, App. IV, 209.
Ships:
  H.M. ships:
    Alceste (frigate).
    Andromache.
    Blenheim [72].
    Calliope [26].
    Centurion.
    Columbine [16].
    Druid [44].
    Herald [26].
    Hyacinth [18].
    Imogene.
    Jupiter.
    Kite (brig).
    Larne [18].
    Louisa (cutter).
    Lyra (brig).
    Melville [72].
    Modeste [18].
    Orlando.
    Plover.
    Samarang [26].
    Starling.
    Sulphur [8].
    Volage [18].
    Wellesley [72].
    Young Hebe (cutter).
  H.C.'s ships:
    Steamers:
      Atalanta.
      Enterprise.
      Madagascar.
      Nemesis.
      Phlegethon.
      Queen.
    Survey-ships:
      Discovery.
      Investigator.
  Merchantmen:
    Argyle.
    Ariel.
    Arrow.
    Bilbaino (Spanish).
    Cambridge (later *Chesapeake*).
    Carolina.
    Cornwall.
    Defence.
    Falcon.
    General Hewitt.
    Royal Saxon.
    Sarah.
    Thomas Coutts.
    Thomas Grenville.
Shipping, 1841–62, App. XI.
Shuck, Rev. J. L., Minister of American Baptist Chapel, 127.
Smith, Captain of *Volage*, 59; ordered to prevent entrance of British shipping to Whampoa, 63; opens fire at Chuen Pei, 64; anchors at Kwoon Chung, 69 *n*.; at Macao, 68; transferred to *Druid*, 71.
Smith, Cecil Clementi: first Cadet 1862, 194; Registrar-General, 194.
'Spring Gardens', on lots 41–3, 111; occupied by the Governor, App. V, 214.
Stanley, Lord, Secretary of State for the Colonies, 101.
Stanley (Chekchu), place-name, 101, 121; sickness at, 128, App. IV, 208.
Stanton, Rev. V., captured at Macao, 71; released, 74; First Colonial Chaplain, 140.
Staunton, Sir George, 24, 173.

INDEX

'Staunton's Valley', 30.
Starling, H.M.S., 24.
Stewart, Charles, first Treasurer, 135.
Sulphur, H.M.S., 93.
Supreme Court, established, 146; opened, 171; used as a church, 171; jurisdiction restricted, 189.
Sung Wong T'oi, 5.

Tai Ping rebellion, 168; Tai Pings occupy Nanking, 170; still raging, 176, 182, 196.
Tai Po Hoü, 24.
Tai Tam, 24, 121, App. IV, 208.
Tai Tat Tei, Possession Point, 94.
Tang Ting Ching, Viceroy of Canton, 32, 49, 50; transferred, 68.
Tarrant, W., editor of *Friend of China*, 192.
Thom, R., interpreter, $50,000 reward for, 86.
Thomas Coutts, merchantman, passing the Bogue, 62.
Thomas Grenville, merchantman, 25.
Tientsin, Treaty of, *see under* Treaties.
Tinghai, port of Chusan, 71, 103; free port, 123.
Tong Kwu, 23; Urmston's harbour, 32; British shipping removed there from Hong Kong, 65; Mr. Gribble captured at, 67; *Druid* at, 68; *Wellesley* at, 70; *Nemesis* at, 73; native bazaar removes to Hong Kong, 100.
Tonnochy, M. S., first Cadet 1862, 194.
Treaties: Nanking, 127, App. VI; ratifications exchanged, 132.
   Supplementary of the Bogue, ratified, 138; published, 145.
   Tientsin, signed, 183; ratified, 190.
Treaty Ports: Canton, Amoy, Fuchow, Ningpo, Shanghai, 128.
Troops stationed at Hong Kong:
   Bengal Volunteers, 70, 101, 120, App. IV.

26th (Cameronians) Regiment of Foot, 70, 103, 128.
18th Regiment (Royal Irish), 70.
49th Regiment of Foot, 70, 125.
55th Regiment of Foot, 120, 128 *n*., 133, 137.
98th Regiment of Foot, 128 and *n*.
37th Madras Native Infantry, 101, 120; stationed at Aberdeen, 122.
41st Madras Infantry, 128 *n*.; headquarters, 133.
Madras Artillery, 70.
Tsim Sha Tsui (Kowloon Point), receiving vessels proceed to, 32, 51; affray at, 57; fort erected at, 65, 90; proposal to exchange Hong Kong for, 98.
Typa (Taipa), Macao, 30, 56.
Typhoons, 88, 114, 115.
Tytam Bay, 119; Tai Tam, 121.

Urmston's Harbour, 32; *see* Tong Kwu.

Victoria, City, birth of, VIII *passim*; growth, 124, 151.
Victoria Barracks, *see* Artillery Barracks.
Victoria Fort, 95.
Volage, H.M.S., 59, 60, 66.
Volunteer Corps founded, 195.

Wantsai Road, constructed, 171.
Waterfall Bay, 25, 26, 27.
Waterworks, 194.
Weddell, Captain (1647), 10, 41.
Wellesley, H.M.S., 52, 70, 74, 94.
Wellington Barracks, 99, 154.
West Point Barracks, 99, 101, App. IV.
West Point Battery, 99.
Whampoa, 11; in 1820, 12, 14; 30; Napier reaches, 35; opium-craft at, 53; foreign shipping returns to, 84; opium trade, 1843, 157.
Wong Kwu Fan, 5.
Wong Nei Chung, 91; Wiang La Chung, 153.

Woosnam, W., Member of Land Committee 1842, 125, 136.

Yang Fang, colleague of Yik Shan, 79.
Yeh Ming Chin, Governor of Canton and High Commissioner: Governor of Canton, 165; rewarded, 167; High Commissioner, 174, 175; refuses to yield, 179; replies to ultimatum, 183; made prisoner, 183.
Yik Shan, 'pacificator of the rebellious', 79, 109, 114; reaches Canton, 84; reports to the Emperor, 87.
Young Hebe, cutter, 88.

ADDITIONAL NOTES

CHAPTER I

p. 2
1. The Bogue forts here were the Chinese batteries which guarded the entrance to the river, the Bocca Tigris, or Tiger's Mouth 虎門.

2. More recent geological studies date the oldest rocks in Hong Kong as being 225 million years old. The geographical features show that Hong Kong is a drowned portion of a mountain range, followed more recently by a gradual movement upward. See P. M. Allen and E. A. Stephens, *Report on the geological survey of Hong Kong 1967–1969*, Hong Kong, Govt. Printer, 1971, p. 2.

CHAPTER II

p. 5
1. Studies by the Hong Kong Archaeological Society indicate that areas of Hong Kong were probably inhabited by approximately 4000 B.C. Tun Mun 屯門 in the New Territories was visited by Han Yu 韓愈, the famous Confucian scholar, in the T'ang dynasty and possibly during one of the voyages of Ch'eng Ho 鄭和 in the Ming dynasty. 'Ta hsi shan', which stood for Hong Kong island, appeared in the map used by Cheng Ho. Also 'T'un men post' was marked in the Staunton map. See J. V. G. Mills (ed.), *Ma Huan, Ying-yai sheng-lan. 'The overall survey of the ocean's shores'*, Cambridge, Cambridge University Press, 1970, pp. 271, 350 and 351. It was also a trading area of the Portugese in the sixteenth century. See Balfour, *Hong Kong before the British* and Lo, *Hong Kong and its external communications before 1842*.

2. Further information on the Sung Wong T'oi 宋王臺 can be found in a note by J. L. Cranmer-Byng in *JHKBRAS* 2(1962) 126, and Jen Yu-wen, on pages 26–29 of his article on the 'Travelling Palace of Southern Sung in Kowloon' in *JHKBRAS* 7 (1967) 21–38. The inscription 'Sung Wong T'oi' was made during the Yüan period shortly after the fall of the Sung dynasty (according to Jen, who further states that it was re-carved in 1807). When the planning of the new runway at Kai Tak was in progress, the part with the inscription '宋王臺' was placed in a public park off Olympic Way very close to its original site.

p. 6
3. There is a confusion here between Tang Yuk 鄧旭 and his two wives (who are all buried at Tsun Wan), and the Sung princess ('the Emperor's aunt') who was married to Tang Wai-kap 鄧惟汲 of Kam Tin 錦田. In fact, the princess was not buried in Hong Kong at all, but in Tung Koon 東莞 county to the north. See

ADDITIONAL NOTES, Chapters I-III

the general note, 'The Tang 鄧 clan in the New Territories and its oldest graves' in *JHKBRAS* 17 (1977) 180–185. Dr J. W. Haye's assistance is gratefully acknowledged.

4. Eitel, *Europe in China*, p. 132–133, states 'the scattered remnants of the Ming army ... took refuge on the Island of Hongkong (about A.D. 1650)', and makes no mention of 'forests'.

p. 7 5. Sayer's account of the history of British trading to China in this chapter sometimes differs in dates and other details from other sources such as Morse, *The chronicles of the East India Company trading to China, 1635–1834;* Morse, *The international relations of the Chinese empire*.

6. Overland trading contacts have been traced back to the time of the Roman empire and the Arabs had established a thriving sea trade and trading community in Canton by the ninth century A.D.

p. 9 7. Framed copies in Latin and English of this letter from Queen Elizabeth I to the Emperor Wanli were finally delivered in Peking, 382 years later on 8 August 1978, by the British Trade Minister, Mr Edmund Dell, to the Chinese Foreign Trade Minister, Mr Li Chiang, at an embassy dinner (*South China Morning Post*, 9 August 1978).

CHAPTER III

p. 17 1. Lin refers to Lin Tse-hsü 林則徐 and Yeh to Yeh Ming-chen 葉名琛.

2. Keshen is the Manchu name for Ch'i-shan 琦善, Keying for Ch'i-ying 耆英, and Eleepoo for I-li-pu 伊里布. For their biographies, see Hummel, *Eminent Chinese of the Ch'ing period*.

3. Howqua (Hao-kuan) 浩官 was the name known to Westerners for the successive leaders of the Hong merchant family named Wu 伍 (Ng in Cantonese). Howqua I was Wu Kuo-ying 伍國瑩, but the name How came from the pet-name Ah Ho 亞浩 of his eldest son Wu Ping-chien 伍秉鑑 (Howqua II). Their firm was named I-ho 怡和 (Ewo in Cantonese), which was also adopted by Jardine, Matheson & Co. Ng I Wo 伍怡和 whom Sayer refers to on p. 18 was Wu Ping-chien (Howqua II). See under Wu Ping-chien and Wu Ch'ung-yüeh in Hummel, *Eminent Chinese of the Ch'ing period*.

Mowqua (Mao-kuan) 茂官 was also a title taken from a familiar name for the Hong merchant Lu Chi-kuang 盧繼光 who was the head of the Kuang-li hang 廣利行. See Hummel, *Eminent Chinese of the Ch'ing period*, p. 512.

ADDITIONAL NOTES, Chapter III

Hing Tai (Hengtae) 興泰行, also known as Sunshing, was the firm established by Yen Ke-chang (Yen Ch'i-chang) 嚴啓昌 in 1829 as one of the new firms admitted to the Co-hong in Canton. See Morse, *The international relations of the Chinese empire*, vol. 1, p. 162.

Puankiqua or Puankhequa (P'an Ch'i-kuan) 潘啓官 was the name used for the Hong merchant P'an Ch'i 潘啓 or P'an Chen-cheng 潘振承, his son P'an Yu-tu 潘有度 and his son's nephew P'an Cheng-wei 潘正煒. See under P'an Chen-cheng in Hummel, *Eminent Chinese of the Ch'ing period*.

Shykinqua or Gonqua refers to Shih Chung-wo 石中和 of the firm Yi-i 而益行.

Further details of the Co-hong and the merchant are given in 梁嘉彬 (Liang Chia-pin), 廣東十三行考 (The thirteen Hongs of Canton) and in 'History of the Hong and their difficulties', *The Canton Press*, 1 July 1837.

4. The character for 'kwan' (kuan) is 官.

5. The character for 'chi' (Cantonese 'kei') is 記. However, the explanation given for Puankiqua is not correct. The characters are 潘啓官, not 潘記官.

p. 18　6. This explanation for Hing Tai is doubtful. The company's name was Hing T'ai 興泰 and seems to have no connection with the similarly pronounced Hing Tai 兄弟—'brothers'. See also note 3 above.

7. Heung Kong 香港 is now generally thought to indicate not 'fragant lagoon' or 'fragant harbour' but 'incense harbour' and to derive from the transport of fragrant teas or incense. See Lo, *Hong Kong and its external communications before 1842*, p. 84, and also 'Notes and queries' in *JHKBRAS* 7 (1967) 162.

Further information on place-names in Hong Kong can be obtained from *A gazetteer of places names in Hong Kong, Kowloon and the New Territories*, Hong Kong, Hong Kong Government Printer, 1969.

8. The characters are 粉嶺 (Fan-ling), 北京 (Pekin, now Beijing).

9. The characters are 深水灣 (Shum Shui Wan) and 深水埗 (Shum Shui Po).

p. 19　10. The Pinyin spelling (in this case Beijing) is now being generally accepted for Chinese place-names.

11. Hamun 廈門; Swatow 汕頭; Swabue 汕尾; O Mun 澳門; Pok Liu Chow 博寮洲; Tai Yu Shan 大嶼山.

Chapter IV

p. 25   1. Lemma (Lema) Islands or Li-ma Ch'un-tao 利馬群島 is a group of islands lying about fifteen miles south of Hong Kong Island.

        2. The old name for Waterfall Bay, Ma Liu Ho 馬尿河, is no longer used.

p. 26   3. The flow of water at Waterfall Bay had probably been substantially diminished even in Sayer's day as a result of the construction of the Pokfulam Reservoir. But it is still recognizable as that which Clarke Abel depicted and is now the Urban Council Waterfall Bay Park 瀑布灣公園.

p. 30   4. Staunton's Valley has now disappeared as a topographical feature. The tidal stream which meandered down it was full of boats on the muddy banks in the 1950s. It has now been canalized and the land reclaimed largely covered by the Wongchukhang industrial estate. Hong Kong Wai 香港圍 now is used as the name of that part of the valley north of Island Road.

p. 31   5. Now Lei Yu Mun 鯉魚門.

        6. The Viceroy was Tang Ting-ching 鄧廷楨.

p. 32   7. The island of Lin Tin is about five miles north of Tong Kwu. Orange, in his *The Chater Collection*, pp. 145–151, gives a description of the places along and near the Canton River. Toon Kwu or Tong Kwu is an island lying west of Castle Peak and is now known as Lung Kwu Chau 龍鼓洲. Kap Shui Mun 汲水門 (Kap Shing Mun), 'fast water channel', is the strait between the northern end of Lantau Island and Ma Wan Island 馬灣.

Chapter VI

p. 53   1. James Innes, who arrived in China about 1825, was chieftain of the clan of Innes of Dunkinty. He was one of the most intractable of the opium traders and his persistence in smuggling opium (and being caught) was an important precipitating factor in the onset of hostilities. For further information, see a note in *JHKBRAS* 4 (1964) 40.

p. 62   2. Ch'uan Pi 穿鼻 was also romanized from Cantonese as Chuenpee, Chuenpi, or Chuen Pei.

Chapter VII

p. 68   1. Henry John Spencer Churchill's tombstone in Macao gives the date of his death as 2 June 1840.

ADDITIONAL NOTES, Chapters VII-VIII

2. J. Elliot Bingham's book is titled *Narrative of the expedition to China, from the commencement of the war to its termination in 1842*. The quotation appears on p. 183 of the book.

p. 83   3. 'Broadway or Inner or Macao Passage led direct from Macao to Canton; it had been only used by native boats and believed by the Chinese to be inaccessible to foreigners owing to the shallowness and intricacy of the channels and to the defences on the banks.' (Orange, *The Chater Collection*, p. 148).

p. 86   4. Casa Branca, 'White House', is the name given to Tsin Shan 前山, a small town in Heung Shan 香山 near Macao, by the Portuguese after the colour of the Chinese yamen there.

p. 87   5. The advertisement by Elliot is dated Macao, 7 June 1841 and was published in the Hong Kong Gazette. It was reproduced in *The Canton Register*, 8 June 1841, p. 140 and *The Canton Press*, 12 June 1841. The sale was first advertized for 12 June 1841 but postponed to 14 June 1841. The results of the land sale are given in Appendix III.

p. 88   6. Dumbbell Island is an obsolete name for Cheung Chau 長洲, an island lying off the eastern side of Lantao.

Chapter VIII

p. 91   1. At the time of writing (1979), only one may still be *in situ* along the road to Aberdeen near the Wah Fu housing estate. There has been much inconclusive speculation on the meaning of the term Kwan Tai Lo (see 'Notes and queries' in *JHKBRAS* 7 (1967) 161 and 162, and Sayer's further references on pp. 120 and 122 below).

p. 94   2. The recreation area, Tai Tat Tei 大笪地, on a hill at the side of Possession Street, still existed, until a few years ago when the whole area was redeveloped. It contained in the central part a restaurant, various small stores and a well.

3. The Chinese version of the 1 February 1841 'manifesto' gives precedence to Elliot. See Additional Note to Appendix I.

p. 96   4. The Treaty or Convention of Chuenpi 穿鼻條約 is said not to have been signed, in spite of Elliot's Proclamation of 2 February 1841 (see Appendix I and its Additional Note). Eitel, *Europe in China*, p. 122 says that the Treaty was agreed on 20 February 1841 and lists the four preliminary proposals, which include dismantling of the Chinese batteries at Tsimshatsui. The agreement is also confirmed by a reference of *The Canton Register*, 16 February 1841, p. 31.

ADDITIONAL NOTES, Chapter VIII

p. 97   5. Sayer's discussion of the Kowloon forts at Tsimshatsui does not mention Eitel's inclusion of the dismantling of these Chinese batteries as part of the first of the 'four preliminary propositions of the Treaty of Chuenpei' (Eitel, *Europe in China*, p. 122). Sayer rightly points out (p. 96) that Elliot himself did not include this reference to the Tsimshatsui forts in his public circular of 20 January 1841 which was published in *The Chinese Repository, The Canton Press* and *The Canton Register*. Elliot's Circular was as follow:

CIRCULAR.

TO HER BRITANNIC MAJESTY'S SUBJECTS.

Macao, 20th January, 1841.

Her majesty's plenipotentiary has now to announce the conclusion of preliminary arrangements between the imperial commissioner and himself, involving the following conditions.

1. The cession of the island and harbour of *Hongkong* to the British crown. All just charges and duties to the empire upon the commerce carried on there to be paid, as if the trade were conducted at Whampoa.

2. An indemnity to the British government of six millions of dollars, one million payable at once and the remainder in equal annual instalments, ending in 1846.

3. Direct official intercourse between the two countries upon an equal footing.

4. The trade of the port of Canton to be opened within ten days after the Chinese new year, and to be carried on at Whampoa, till further arrangements are practicable at the new settlement:—details remain matter of negociation.

The plenipotentiary seizes the earliest occasion to declare that her majesty's government has sought for no privilege in China exclusively for the advantage of British ships and merchants; and he is only performing his duty in offering the protection of the British flag to the subjects, citizens, and ships of foreign powers that may resort to her majesty's possession.

Pending her majesty's further pleasure, there will be no port or other charges to the British government.

The plenipotentiary now permits himself to make a few general observations.

The oblivion of past and redressed injuries will follow naturally from the right feeling of the queen's subjects. Indeed, it should be remembered that no extent of modification resulting only from political intervention can be efficacious in the steady improvement of our condition, unless it be systematically seconded by conciliatory treatment of the people, and a becoming deference for the institutions and government of the country, upon the threshold of which we are about to be established.

The plenipotentiary can only presume to advert very briefly to the zeal and, wisdom of the commander in chief of the expedition to China, and to that rare union of ardour, patience, and forbearance which has distinguished the officers and forces of all arms, at all points of occupation and operation.

He is well assured that the British community will sympathize cordially with him in those sentiments of lasting respect for his excellency and the whole force, which he is ashamed to express in such inadequate language.

He cannot conclude without declaring that next to these causes, the peaceful adjustment of difficulties must be ascribed to the scrupulous good faith and enlarged opinions of the very eminent person with whom negotiations are still pending.

(Signed)   CHARLES ELLIOT,
Her Majesty's Plenipotentiary in China.

p. 99   6. St Peter's church was erected by Bishop Alford who secured from the Trustees of Sailors Home a portion of their ground at West Point for the purpose and raised money from England and the local public. The Church was opened on 14 January 1872. The Church came to an end in 1933 when the Government resumed the site. See Eitel, *Europe in China*, p. 467; Endacott and She, *The diocese of Victoria, Hong Kong*, pp. 43, 141–143.

7. The erection of the Sailor's Home was financed by Jardine, Matheson & Co. and public subscriptions. The site of the Sailor's Home at West Point was resumed by Government in 1924 and the present Western Police Station was built on it to replace the former No. 7 Police Station which was established in 1858 at the junction of Queen's Road and Pokfulam Road. The new Police Station opened in 1955. For more information on the Sailor's Home, see Eitel, *Europe in China*, p. 402.

8. The name 'Seven-and-sixpenny Hill', whatever its origin, has long been obsolete. It was the former eastern entrance to the Barracks from Queensway. The Barracks have now been handed over to the Government of Hong Kong.

9. The 'old Reformatory Building' stood on the site of the present St Louis School in Third Street, a site which has a history of educational use since 1864 when the Catholic-run 'reformatory' (really more of a training institute than a reformatory in the more modern sense) was moved from its home in Wellington Street.

10. 'West Point' was originally a spur of land to the west of Possession Point.

11. Belcher's Battery is the present Belcher Gardens, a housing estate for civil servants.

12. The Wellington Barracks lay very close to the western end of the present Royal Hong Kong Police Force Headquarters in Arsenal Street.

13. Sayer is mistaken here and his error has subsequently been perpetuated by those who have used him as a source of information. The site was taken by Jardine, Matheson & Co. in February 1841 without authority and upon which they had by their own admission commenced building at that time (see Alexander Matheson's reply to question 2260 in 'Minutes of Evidence' in *Report of the Select Committee on Commercial Relations with China, 1847* and Evans, 'Jardine, Matheson & Co's first site in Hong Kong', in *JHKBRAS* 8 (1968) 149–153). This site lay on Queensway on what was then the shore opposite the site upon which Flagstaff House (see Additional Note 18 to this chapter) was to be built. The land was put up for auction on 14 June 1841 as lots 26, 27 and 28 and the firm bid successfully for them (though Tarrant, *Hong Kong, 1839–1844*, p. 14, suggests that no one bid against them). After the boundaries of the military cantonment had been determined, these lots (and the site of Flagstaff House) were compulsorily purchased from the firm in February 1842 and they were allowed to choose two new lots elsewhere (for which see Additional Note 29 to this chapter below). East Point only became Jardine, Matheson & Co's headquarters after they were forced to surrender their central location. The lot which was to become known as 'East Point' had been purchased at the same auction by William Morgan, their Hong Kong manager at the time (the firm did not move their headquarters from Macao until 1844), and it was later leased to Alexander Matheson in 1844 as Marine Lot 52.

p. 100   14. The Central Market originated as a public market in 1842 on the site now occupied by the modern Central Market.

15. 'Scandal Point' is now no more than a half-forgotten name. It denoted a high spur which still comes down to the line of the old Queen's Road East on Queensway. The site of the Canton Bazaar is discernible also, lying as a recess between that spur and the site upon which Flagstaff House stands to the west. Flagstaff House served from 1846 (then known as Headquarters House) until 1978 as the residence of the Commander of British Forces but has now been handed to the Government of Hong Kong with the remainder of Victoria Barracks.

16. There is some considerable doubt as to the truth of this suggestion that the settlement at Hong Kong 'flitted', but certainly Bingham, Sayer's source for this, undoubtedly stated that it did happen (see also the reference in *The Canton Press* quoted on p. 105). Tarrant (op. cit., pp. 10–11) on the other hand, quotes the following report from *The Canton Press* on movement of British shipping in 1839: 'The departure of H.M.'s S. *Hyacinthe* seemed to cause some alarm among the merchant vessels [i.e., those lying in the Bay of Hong Kong], as they followed by the dozens.... This is the third or fourth "flitting" by the British.' This was a reference to Elliot's insistence that the merchant vessels move from Hong Kong to the anchorage at Saw Chu or Sha Chau 沙洲, between Castle Peak and Tong Kwu or Lung Kwu Chau 龍鼓洲 where they would be better protected by the Navy. If the Chinese traders who provisioned the Navy and the merchant vessels did move, it is likely either that they set up on the mainland shore opposite Tong Kwu or that they too were afloat. But Sayer's interpretation is possibly doubtful. There was, however, no civil settlement until Elliot set up the machinery for it later in 1841.

17. The Treaty of Nanking was *signed* on 29 August 1842 and ratifications were exchanged in Hong Kong on 26 June 1843.

18. Sayer is here confusing two separate developments. It is clear that a temporary structure was erected where now a service reservoir stands in the Botanical Gardens, see Evans, 'Hong Kong's first Government House', *JHKBRAS* 8 (1968) 157; Mattock, *This is Hong Kong: the story of Government House*, Hong Kong, 1978; 'Notices of Hong Kong' in *The Chinese Repository*. XIV (1845), p. 295, and Appendix V to this work, p. 211 below. But he confuses this with Legge's mistaken recollection of 'The Albany' as a range of barracks (see Additional Note 19 to this chapter).

19. The lecture by Dr James Legge from which Sayer quotes was delivered, as he says, almost thirty years after the event and is not entirely reliable. The lecture was published in the *China*

Review 3 (1874) 163–176, and reprinted in *JHKBRAS* 11 (1971) 172–193. 'The Albany' was in fact erected by the Government as a row of four houses for rent to senior civil servants at a rent of $400 p.a. each (see Minutes of the Executive Council, 14.8.1844 in *Colonial Office Records,* hereafter referred as CO, 131/1). The Home Government disapproved, however, of the provision of housing for civil servants even at a rent and it was only later that 'The Albany' became quarters for military officers. It passed into private ownership in 1862. The present block of the same name lies on the opposite side of Albany Road, see also p. 151.

p. 103 20. Captain Elliot's Proclamation of 2 February 1841 (see Appendix I on p. 201 and Sayer's reference to it on p. 94) and the terms of his warrant to Captain Caine gave rise to the widespread opinion held for many years that the Crown, through Captain Elliot, had promised to leave undisturbed Chinese custom, thereby creating a dual system of law with the introduction of English Law by the Supreme Court Ordinance of 1844 (No. 15 of 1844); see, for example, the speech of Hon. Dr P. C. Woo in the Legislative Council on 7 May 1969, in which he referred to the Elliot and Bremer Proclamation of 1 February 1841 and the Elliot Proclamation of 2 February 1841 and concluded that the wording of the Supreme Court Ordinance, taken with those two proclamations, clearly showed that there were two systems of laws in Hong Kong, 'one applicable to the Chinese and the other applicable to other inhabitants' (*Hong Kong Hansard,* 1969, pp. 270–272). The reality lay somewhere in between but this is not the place in which to enter into dispute on the matter.

p. 104 21. There is apparently no extant copy of the first issue of the *Hong Kong Gazette,* though it is referred to and extensively quoted in *The Canton Press, The Canton Register* and *The Chinese Repository.* Later issues of the *Hong Kong Gazette* appeared, until 1854, as a section of a number of Hong Kong newspapers, commencing with the *Friend of China* in its second issue on 24 March 1842. The notice to which Sayer refers was reproduced in the Appendix to the *Report of the Select Committee on Commercial Relations with China, 1847,* p. 374, and in *The Canton Register,* 4 May 1841. It appeared over the signature of Captain Elliot and he did not state the capacity in which he was acting in this regard. (Other Public Notices in this first issue of the *Hong Kong Gazette* describe him as 'H.M. Plenipotentiary, Charged with the government of the island of Hong Kong'.) Since it is a document which proved vital to the founding of the infant Colony, it is reproduced here. It should be read in conjunction with Sayer's account of the sale on p. 110 and Appendix III. The Public Notice and Declaration reads as follows:

PUBLIC NOTICE AND DECLARATION.

The following Notice is published for general information; but the necessary particulars not having yet been obtained regarding the portions of land already surveyed, the blanks relating to the number and extent of allotments, and period of sale, cannot yet be filled up.

Arrangements having been made for the permanent occupation of the island of Hong Kong, it has become necessary to declare the principles and conditions upon which allotments of land will be made, pending Her Majesty's further pleasure.

With a view to the reservation to the Crown of as extensive a control over the lands as may be compatible with the immediate progress of the establishment, it is now declared, that the number of allotments to be disposed of from time to time, will be regulated with due regard to the actual public wants.

It will be a condition of each title, that a building of a certain value, hereafter to be fixed, must be erected within a reasonable period of time, on the allotments; and there will be a general reservation of all Her Majesty's rights.

Pending Her Majesty's further pleasure, the lands will be allotted according to the principles and practice of British law, upon the tenure of quit-rent to the Crown.

Each allotment to be put up at a public auction, at a certain upset rate of quit rent, and to be disposed of to the highest bidder. But it is engaged, upon the part of Her Majesty's Government, that persons taking land upon these terms, shall have the privilege of purchasing in freehold (if that tenure shall hereafter be offered by Her Majesty's Government), or of continuing to hold upon the original quit-rent, if that condition be better liked.

All arrangements with natives for the cession of lands in cultivation, or substantially built upon, to be made only through an officer deputed by the government of the island; and no title will be valid and no occupancy respected, unless the person claiming shall hold under an instrument granted by the government of the island, of which due registry must be made in the government office.

It is distinctly to be understood, that all natives in the actual occupancy of lands in cultivation or substantially built upon, will

ADDITIONAL NOTES, Chapter VIII

be constrained to establish their rights to the satisfaction of the land officer, and to take out titles, and have the same duly registered.

In order to accelerate the establishment, notice is hereby given that a sale of ... town allotments, having a water frontage of ... yards, and running ... back yards, will take place at Macao on the ... instant, by which time it is hoped plans exhibiting the water front of the town will be prepared.

Persons purchasing town lots, will be entitled to purchase suburban or county lots, of ... square acres each, and will be permitted for the present to choose their own sites, subject to the approval of the government of the island.

No run of water to be diverted from its course without permission of the government.

Macao, 1 May 1841.   (signed) *Charles Elliot.*
(True copy.)
(signed) *J. Robert Morrison,*
Macao, 1 May 1841.   Acting Secretary and Treasurer to Superintendents.

p. 105 22. Wang Tung is a small and barren island lying just inside the Bocca Tigris. The reason for its selection for the purpose of mocking Hong Kong is obvious.

p. 107 23. A reference to Captain Caine.

p. 109 24. This may be a reference to Alexander Robert Johnston, Deputy Superintendent of Trade, to whom, though young (he was then less than thirty years of age), Elliot entrusted a good deal of the day-to-day-business. It may equally be a reference to J. R. Morrison whom Sayer has already mentioned. But there was no little force in some of the satirical criticism contained in the 'Wang Tung Argus'.

p. 110 25. For more information about the reclamation, see Hudson, 'Land reclamation in Hong Kong', Ph.D thesis, University of Hong Kong, 1970.

        26. The first lot actually sold on the day was Marine Lot 15, knocked down to an English merchant, Robert Webster; see Appendix III, p. 204. It lay to the west of the Central Market.

        27. The original Marine Lot 1 lay to the east of the present Ice House Street and, after its purchasers, Gribble, Hughes & Co., did not take it up, the Government resumed the lot and the number was re-used for a marine lot in the Lower Bazaar.

p. 111 28. The Canton Bazaar lay, in fact, on the landward side of Queen's Road.

ADDITIONAL NOTES, Chapter VIII

29. Lots 72 and 73 lay, not at West Point, but at the northwestern end of the Wongneichung Valley (at the foot of what was then Morrison Hill) and were never taken up by the firm. See also Additional Note 13 to this chapter. The erection of the Sailors' Home in Western District was financed by Jardine, Matheson & Co. and public subscriptions (see Additional Note 7 to this chapter).

30. It is not clear when the name Spring Gardens became attached to the locality rather than to a particular house, but Murdoch Bruce's lithograph of 1846 certainly uses it to indicate a locality. The house which bore the name was originally built by the firm of Turner & Co. and it was used as a residence for a time by two Governors, Sir John Davis and Sir George Bonham (see *Friend of China*, 3 April 1852). Why it was so called is something of a mystery, though it did have a well of good water in its ground and a stream still runs through the area. There may also be connections with an area which lay in front of the Admiralty Arch in London which was known as Spring Gardens, a fashionable residential district for a long time which only disappeared with the construction of Admiralty Arch and the adjoining government offices (see Walford, *Old and new London,* vol IV, London, Cassell, 1873–1878 and 'Trafalgar Square and neighbourhood', *Survey of London,* vol. XX, pp. 58–68). There was also, however, a 'Spring Gardens' in the business district of Manchester, England with which British merchants in Hong Kong might have been familiar.

31. Marine Lot 44 was sold at auction on July 7, 1844 to Augustus Carter who developed it as a residence and godown. It occupied the entire area between Turner & Co.'s Marine Lot 43 and Thomas Larkins' Marine Lot 46. Marine Lot 45 did not in fact exist on the day of the sale and the number was used for a different lot which lay elsewhere.

32. The Albany Godowns were erected on Marine Lot 47. See also Additional Note 36 to this chapter. The confusion may have arisen because the first advertisement for the Albany Godowns gave their address as '46 Victoria Road, Ha Wan'. Thomas Larkins' godown lay on Marine Lot 46. The error is repeated on p. 114.

p. 112 33. Lieutenant Pedder was First Officer of H.E.I.C. *Nemesis.*

p. 113 34. 'Tai Chung Lau' 大鐘樓 (Great Clock Tower) as a name for Pedder Street has not been used for many years, as the memory of the Clock Tower has faded. On the other hand, Pedder Street was known over 100 years ago as 'Pi Ta Kai 畢打街. The Clock Tower stood at the junction of Queen's Road and Pedder Street.

p. 114 35. It is strange that Sayer, with access to records now lost, should not have known more about Gillespie. Charles Vanbruggen

ADDITIONAL NOTES, Chapters VIII-IX

Gillespie was an American from New York and it is possible that the Albany Godowns were named after the capital of New York State. Gillespie operated the godowns possibly on his own account by renting them from the partnership which had bought the land at the first land auction (the partnership consisted of P. F. Robertson, Alexander McCulloch and Samuel Rawson). Tarrant, op. cit., p. 41, described Gillespie as a 'vendor of everything from a sheet anchor to a skupper nail—from a penny whistle to a German flute'. Gillespie found himself in difficulties over his handling of agency business for the American firm of Wetmore & Co. of Macao, and Pottinger interdicted him from leaving Hong Kong until he settled his affairs and he was only allowed to sell his property for the benefit of his creditors. He eventually left Hong Kong but remained in business in Macao and Canton for some years.

36. The mistake about the location of the Albany Godowns is repeated here. See Additional Note 32 to this chapter.

p. 115 37. There is little direct evidence that 'Hong Kong fever' was *exclusively* malaria. It is true that the role of the anopheles mosquito in carrying the disease was to remain unknown for many years after the founding of Hong Kong but the symptoms, amply described by medical practitioners of the day, may be equally consistent with a virus infection to which newcomers had no resistance—perhaps the first appearance of 'Asian 'flu'! See, for example, the analysis of Dr Frederick Dill, Colonial Surgeon, in a paper read before the China Medico-Chirurgical Society in 1845 which was quoted in Tarrant, op. cit., p. 65. See also a paper by Drs Tucker (a naval surgeon) and Dill which was published in *The Chinese Repository* in March 1846.

CHAPTER IX

p. 117 1. St Francis Square is now St Francis Yard.

p. 118 2. Lan Kwai Fong 蘭桂坊 still exists today. The bungalow 'was constructed entirely by Chinese mechanics' and 'assumed very much of form of a Chinese house' (Bernard, *Narrative of the voyages and services of the Nemesis*, vol. II, p. 83).

3. The wooden houses were in fact built; see p. 122 below.

p. 120 4. Sayer confuses the Lower Bazaar situated in the area of the present Bonham Strand with the Central Market. It is likely that *The Canton Press* was referring to the former.

5. A hospital under the supervision of Dr Alexander Anderson, Colonial Surgeon for a short time, stood on the site opposite Mr Gillespie's residence until it was taken over by the Royal Navy in

ADDITIONAL NOTES, Chapter IX

1873 as a Naval Hospital. The buildings then erected, with additions, now form the Ruttonjee Sanatorium.

6. The Magistracy and Prison is now the Victoria Reception Centre and Central Magistracy.

7. The Central Government Offices (West Wing) now stands on this site of Murray Battery.

8. The magazine is no longer in existence.

9. The battery is no longer in existence.

p. 121 10. The name Gap Road has fallen out of use and Gap Road is now the eastern end of Queen's Road East. East Point no longer exists as a geographical feature and the name is obsolete. The tip of the Point was approximately where the World Trade Centre and the Excelsior Hotel now stand.

p. 124 11. The dateline 'Government Hill' first appeared in October 1841.

p. 125 12. Woosnam's name was Richard W. Woosnam and he was of Huguenot extraction from Montgomeryshire. He was originally assistant surgeon to Pottinger as Plenipotentiary and officiated as Deputy to Colonel Malcolm, Colonial Secretary and acted as personal secretary to Pottinger with whom he left Hong Kong. His family retained his successful Hong Kong land investment until 1920.

13. The reference here is to the Central Market on Queen's Road Central. Malcolm's (Canton) Bazaar lay on Inland Lot 74 on the southern side of the present Queensway. There is also confusion in the reference on p. 126 to Flagstaff House and the confusion arose probably because of Malcolm's involvement on the one hand in the establishment of the Central Market and on the other hand in a private venture with Richard Woosnam (see Additional Note 12 to this chapter) in the building of the Canton Bazaar as a private speculation. The Bazaar was built for Malcolm and Woosnam by William Morgan of Jardine, Matheson & Co. at a cost of $12,000 and was said to have been a paying investment at the time (Tarrant, op.cit., p. 41). When they sold the Bazaar to George Duddell in 1858, they received only $5,000.

p. 128 14. One of the least-known ironies of the Opium War was that the son of Thomas de Quincy, author of *Confessions of an English opium eater*, died at Stanley at this time.

p. 131 15. John Prendergast's employment in the Land Office must have been brief. He first appeared in *The Chinese Repository*'s list of foreign residents in 1844 where he is also found listed as a 'draughtsman' in the Land Office. He is shown as 'absent' in the list for 1845 and his name does not appear thereafter. Only two of Prendergast's aquatints (engraved by E. Duncan and published by S. & J. Fuller, London, 1844) are now known. They are finely depicted views and both are reproduced in colour in Orange, *The Chater Collection*, pp. 384–385. They both show East Point and Kellett's Island (now the Royal Hong Kong Yacht Club) with Burrell's newly built battery on it.

p. 133   16. See Additional Note 19 to chapter VIII.

17. Kau U Fong 九如坊 still exists today.

p. 134   18. The plot of land referred to (Inland Lot 80) was apparently granted for use as a site for a dispensary but the dispensary was not in fact built there but instead it was established on the corner of D'Aguilar Street and Queen's Road Central and later became the still extant firm of A.S. Watson & Co. For an account of the uses to which the site was put, see *Friend of China*, 2 November 1850 and Tarrant, op.cit., p. 42.

19. Sayer is mistaken here and his error has been copied by later writers. 'Green Bank' stood between the upper part of D'Aguilar Street and Lan Kwai Fong and Legge's siting of the building is, therefore, correct. Dent & Co. offered to sell the entire property to the Government in 1850—the house to be the Governor's residence and the excellent gardens as Botanical Gardens. The offer was refused in somewhat peremptory terms (see Bonham to Earl Grey, 25 October 1850 in CO129/34).

p. 135   20. Another reason for the revocation of the commission and one to which Sayer does not refer was the limitation of the functions of the newly appointed Justices of the Peace: their oath required them to swear that they would 'well and truly, according to the best of my ability, skill and understanding, and without fear, favour or affection, do and fulfil the duties and powers of a Justice of the Peace, over and towards all subjects of Her said Majesty presently or hereafter residing within or resorting to the Dominions of the Emperor of China.' Since Hong Kong was no longer part of those Dominions, their oath gave them no powers or duties in Hong Kong! (See *Hong Kong Gazette Extraordinary* in *Friend of China*, 30 June 1843).

21. It is not correct to describe Johnston as a 'merchant'. He was the son of Sir Alexander Johnston, a distinguished civil servant and judge, and Alexander the younger was born in Colombo in 1812. He entered the Colonial Civil Service in Mauritius in 1828 and accompanied his cousin, Lord Napier, Britain's first Superintendent of Trade, to China in 1834. He received the appointment of Third Superintendent in Macao and Canton and became Deputy Superintendent in 1837. He remained as Deputy Superintendent after the foundation of Hong Kong and much of the early development of the colony during Pottinger's absence

in 1841 and early 1842 is attributable to his zeal. He was elected a Fellow of the Royal Society for his contribution to the natural history of China. He retired from the service somewhat dissatisfied in 1853 and went to live at Yoxford in Suffolk where he adopted the description 'sometime acting Governor of Hong Kong'. He died in Californa in 1888. John Robert Morrison, second son of Rev. Robert Morrison, was the son of a missionary but was not himself one. He was, perhaps, the first of the missionaries' sons who, because of their upbringing in China, obtained an acquaintance with the language and were thus invaluable in the early years of diplomatic contact with Chinese officials. It was in this capacity in which he was appointed to serve the Superintendency. He was a man of great promise whose premature death came within a few days of his appointment to the Legislative Council. Sayer refers to his death on p. 137.

p. 137 22. The membership of the Land Committee raised a general feeling of resentment and anger amongst the merchants whose title to their landholding was thus called into question. The *Friend of China* had reported (on 20 July 1843) a general feeling of relief at the appointment of the Committee, though not of satisfaction, since at least the suspense over land title would be attenuated. The Committee consisted of Richard Burgass, a lawyer acquaintance of Sir Henry Pottinger who was serving as his legal adviser and clerk to the Councils, A. T. Gordon, the Land Officer, C. St. G. Cleverly, his assistant and C. E. Stewart, the Colonial Treasurer. Their report, which was not unreasonable in its terms, was presented to Pottinger on 13 January 1844 (and will be found in the Appendix to the *Report of the Select Committee on Commercial Relations with China, 1847* (p. 398). The furore which was to break out very shortly was largely concerned with the terms upon which land was offered on Crown leases of only 75 years duration. Sayer turns to this on p. 148.

23. Equally calamitous in the eyes of the contemporary press was the death at the same time from the same cause of Pottinger's younger brother, Eldred, who was widely respected and even thought of as a possible successor to Pottinger. His involvement in the Afghan campaign had earned him the soubriquet 'the hero of Herat and Cabul [sic]' (see Tarrant, op.cit., p. 60).

p. 140 24. The sale was held on 22 January 1844.

25. The Ordinance was disallowed somewhat peremptorily by the Home Government on the grounds that the Imperial enactments were quite sufficient to cope with any problems which Hong Kong might have. But the fact that the 'mui tsai' 妹仔 problem of

18 ADDITIONAL NOTES, Chapters IX-X

effective young female servitude was to remain a problem in Hong Kong right until towards the end of Sayer's service in Hong Kong perhaps suggests the opposite.

26. With minor recent amendments, this Ordinance 3 of 1844 is still in force.

Chapter X

p. 144 1. The origin of this animosity between Davis and Hulme is said to have been Hulme's insistence that he took precedence over Davis since he, Hulme, already had his commission as Chief Justice whereas he maintained that Davis had no rank until he was sworn as Governor.

p. 151 2. The auction was held on 9 July 1844.

3. Sayer quotes Legge (p. 101) as describing 'The Albany' as barracks for the military.

4. The reference to the 'ruins of a market' would appear to refer to what was known for a short time as 'Meik's Bazaar'. A plot of land had been granted to a Captain Meik to enable him to erect a bazaar adjacent to the cantonment. Before completion of the building, he sold the lot (Town Lot 77) to two merchants, Webster and Kinsley, but Pottinger directed that the lot be forfeited, even though the sale had been notified to the Land Officer, on the ground that Meik had not fulfilled the conditions of grant. Webster pursued the matter over a number of years and it was not until 1849 that the Secretary of State, Earl Grey, accepted Bonham's recommendation that the land be leased to Webster. What Legge appears to have been describing was the abandoned uncompleted building. Part of the lot was granted to Webster as Inland Lot 77 and became known as 'Webster's Crescent' and another part must have been treated as granted to Kinsley as the Government re-entered in 1853 for nonpayment of Crown Rent. The land concerned lay in the corner of 'Death Bend' which has now been eliminated by the construction of the present Queensway.

5. The hospital was near the present headquarters of the Royal Hong Kong Police Force in Arsenal Street.

p. 152 6. This is a reference to what was first known as 'Headquarters House' and now, as Flagstaff House, is still standing (one of the two oldest European buildings standing in Hong Kong, the other being Murray House, referred to by Legge in the following paragraph as a building being erected for officers). The house

ADDITIONAL NOTES, Chapter X

occupied by Lord Saltoun had originated as a residence built on Town Lot 42 by Jardine, Matheson & Co. directly above the godowns which they were building on their Marine Lots; see Additional Note 13 to chapter VIII. The building was requisitioned early in 1842.

7. Part of the old matshed Church may have been sketched by George Chinnery in 1845. The Toyo Bunko in Tokyo has a Chinnery sketch with the title 'Hong Kong Club' added later but this is obviously inaccurate. What the sketch in fact depicts is Murray House from the west with Flagstaff House showing faintly on the hill behind it. Another building is shown in part in the foreground and, judging from its position relative to Murray House, it must have been the matshed church. It is possible that part of the building also shows in Bruce's lithograph of Murray House looking towards the west.

8. This is a reference to a report by Gordon, the Land Officer, which he sent to the Colonial Secretary, on 6 July 1844 (in CO129/2). He not only envisaged the construction of a waterfront praya, a dream which was not to become a fully practical reality until the completion of the great Central Praya Reclamation scheme in the early years of this century and the Wanchai Reclamation in the 1920s (and even then only imperfectly so). Gordon's scheme for the 'construction of a canal to enable goods to be water-borne into the town' was in fact a plan to develop the Wongneichung Valley as the principal site of the mercantile settlement and involved a careful separation of the Chinese and European sections of the town. Gordon's ambitious plan might, he thought, be financed either by a grant from the Government and the income from letting out lots thus formed or by letting the land to a company which could be formed for the purpose. However, the Government had no intention of embarking on public investment on this scale and no merchant was interested in a long-term investment of this nature when the principal object of trade in China was short-term profit.

p. 153
9. The term 'lorcha' appears in Appendix IX, p. 218.

10. 'Kum-sing-mun' lies a few miles to the north of Macao on the western side of the Pearl River estuary. For many years opium receiving ships under European masters lay there and, in contravention of the Treaty of Nanking, there was a shore establishment which catered for their needs also. See also p. 159.

p. 154
11. The land auction on 1 October 1846 was preceded by no fewer than eight auctions of Crown land: they took place on 14 June 1841, 22 January 1844, 9 July 1844, 2 December 1844, 24

December 1844, 12 December 1845, 2 March 1846 and 1 July 1846. The first land sale took place, of course, before formal cession.

12. Sayer gives here the correct location of the Canton Bazaar.

p. 157   13. Sir Thomas's surname is correctly spelled 'Cochrane'.

Chapter XI

p. 171   1. David Jardine had first come to China in 1838 and became a partner in Jardine, Matheson & Co. in 1843 and remained in the firm until his death in 1856. Joseph Frost Edger had been a partner in Jamieson, How & Co. and its successor, Jamieson, Edger & Co.

2. Tei Po 地保 is the leader in the traditional system of local administration; see also p. 194 below.

3. The reclamation of what had formerly been the 'Lower Bazaar' had been necessitated by the disastrous fire of December 1851 which razed much of the area to the ground. Since, as the Lower Bazaar, it had always been the heart of the Chinese business district, its rebuilding in a new form on reclaimed land enabled it to continue in this role and, even today, Wing Lok Street and Bonham Strand is almost exclusively an area of Chinese business.

4. The old Supreme Court building was located partly on Marine Lot 7 and partly on Marine Lot 61 and the site (and more) is now occupied by the new China Building. Sayer's identification of its site with that of the former Queen's Theatre is not wholly accurate.

Chapter XII

p. 174   1. Sayer refers to this building on pp. 152 and 154 as 'Flagstaff House', the name by which it is known today. In Sayer's index, at the entry 'Headquarters House', the reader is referred to 'Flagstaff House' but there is no reference to p. 174 under that heading.

2. For further discussion of Spring Gardens and Government House, see also Additional Note 30 to chapter VIII and Appendix V, p. 214.

p. 179   3. The bakery in question was situated in Queen's Road East; see Additional Note 5 to this chapter.

p. 180   4. The lithograph referred to is 'The action at Fatshan Creek, 1857', listed in Orange, *The Chater Collection*, Section IV, 'China Wars', no. 38 and illustrated on p. 134 of that book.

ADDITIONAL NOTES, Chapters XII-XIII

p. 181   5. Duddell had in fact bought the bakery premises (on Inland Lot 269A and part of Inland Lot 315) at a public auction on 10 July 1857. The sale was ordered by the Sheriff to enable Cheong Alum, the owner who was suspected of having poisoned the bread, to meet his creditors' claims before he left Hong Kong. A curiosity is the fact that Duddell had previously had dealings with Cheong, having sold bakery machinery to him.

p. 182   6. The Chinese called the goldmines in California Old Gold Mountains 舊金山 and those in Australia New Gold Mountains 新金山.

p. 184   7. 'Goose neck' 鵝頸 is no longer current in English but is still used in Chinese.

        8. Lindsay & Co. and Dent & Co. held the Marine Lots between the existing Ice House Street and Pedder Street and it can thus be seen that their opposition was central to the implementation of the whole scheme.

p. 185   9. The modern law is now found in the Wills Ordinance (cap. 30, Laws of Hong Kong, 1964 ed.). This replaced the earlier legislation to which Sayer refers (see in particular s.5(2) which replaced the 1856 provision). Until the enactment of the present Wills Ordinance in 1970, Hong Kong's law of testamentary succession was largely governed by the English Wills Act 1837 and it was the provisions of that Act, with the Wills Act Amendment Act 1852 which was thought to necessitate the enactment of the Ordinance referred to as No. 1 of 1856.

CHAPTER XIII

p. 187   1. John Charles Bowring first became an assistant in Jardine, Matheson & Co. in 1843—though the firm's 'official' centenary commemorative history states incorrectly that he first came to China in 1848 (Steuart, *Jardine, Matheson & Co., 1832-1932*, Hong Kong, privately printed, 1932, p. 59).

p. 188   2. The Imperial Maritime Customs Service originated in 1854 with an agreement between the consuls for Great Britain, United States of America and France with the Taotai of Shanghai which resulted in the appointment of three inspectors, one from each of the above countries, whose task was to oversee the observation of treaty and custom-house regulations both to attempt to minimize smuggling and to eliminate irregularities in procedure. The first British inspector was Thomas (later Sir Thomas) Wade but he was replaced by Lay within about a year. Lay took his duties very seriously (which apparently the other inspectors did

ADDITIONAL NOTES, Chapter XIII

not) and, in 1861, was given the title of 'Inspector General of Customs' in a new service organized after the Convention of Peking and which was put under the direct control of the Imperial government. Lay was forced to retreat to England in 1862 because of ill-health following a wound and his office was temporarily filled by Hart and G. H. Fitzroy. Hart had first come to Hong Kong as Supernumary in the Superintendency of Trade and worked subsequently in the consular service before appointment as Deputy Commissioner of Customs at Canton. Whilst in England, Lay was commissioned to purchase and fit out a number of vessels to serve as a navy for the Chinese Government. He threw himself into this task with great enthusiasm but he was a man of uncertain temperament and, it is said, almost universally disliked. He mishandled the 'navy question' and he was dismissed, his successor in the Customs Service being Hart. Hart was knighted in 1882 and, throughout a long and distinguished career in China, exercised a great deal of influence over the course of events and China's foreign relations. He died in office in 1911. For an account of his career and the Imperial Maritime Customs generally, see Morse, *The international relations of the Chinese empire*, vols. II and III, *passim*.

p. 190 3. Frederick William Bruce had succeeded J. R. Morrison as Colonial Secretary of Hong Kong in 1843 but left in 1846 to take up a position as Lieutenant-Governor of Newfoundland.

p. 191 4. Sir Harry Parkes had first come to Hong Kong at the age of 14 in 1842 and, after studying Chinese, was appointed interpreter in the consular service in 1844. He was put in charge of the consulate in Canton in 1853 and, after having been involved in the negotiations with the King of Siam, was given the task of 'taking home' the Treaty with that King concluded by Sir John Bowring in 1855. For an account of his role in the 'Arrow War' and his subsequent diplomatic career in China, see Lane-Poole, *Sir Harry Parkes in China*, London, Methuen & Co., 1901. He died, at the relatively early age of 57 whilst British Minister in Peking in 1885.

p. 192 5. This should read W. H. Adams—his full name was William Henry Adams.

6. This is a somewhat doubtful claim as the Central Market as such was organized by Colonel Malcolm; see Evans, 'The origins of Hong Kong's Central Market and the Tarrant Affair', *JHKBRAS* 12 (1972) 150–160 and Malcolm's own evidence given to the Select Committee on Commercial Relations with China (answer to Q.4633, pp. 347–348). But see *supra*, pp. 117–118, where Sayer

ADDITIONAL NOTES, Chapter XIII

sets out a price list in the market which he says was organized by Caine before Pottinger's arrival.

p. 193   7. Robinson's stinging report was presented to the House of Commons and was printed but unfortunately without the minutes of evidence which accompanied it.

8. Caldwell always was and remained until his death something of an enigma. For a general account of his life, see Endacott, *A biographical sketchbook of early Hong Kong*, Singapore, Donald Moore for Eastern Universities Press Ltd., 1962, pp. 95–99. The account there given of his early career does not tally with the details which emerged during the 'Anstey Inquiry' of 1858 which probed Caldwell's association with known criminals. He first came to Macao in 1834 and worked for a number of employers before being forced to return to Singapore for reasons of health. He then returned to China with the expeditionary force in 1840. He married a Chinese woman, Chun Ayow (also known as Mary Ayow Caldwell) and his brother Henry Charles established himself as a solicitor to whom his son, Daniel Edmund, was articled and for whom Mary Ayow acted for many years as interpreter. Caldwell himself, though out of official favour, remained an important figure and a link between the colonial government and the Chinese community. He died in 1875.

p. 194   9. Sayer did not include '*tei-po*' [sic] 地保 in his index but there is a brief reference to them on pp. 146 (Chinese Peace Officers) and 171. For a consideration of the history of this institution, see Evans, 'Common law in a Chinese setting', *Hong Kong Law Journal* 1 (1971) 17–20.

10. The idea of a supply of water from Pokfulam was initiated in 1860 when a civilian engineer with the Royal Engineers, Samuel Bartlett Rawling won a public competition for a waterworks scheme with his plan for a reservoir at Pokfulam. Supply commenced in 1862 but the original scheme rapidly proved too inadequate and a new dam impounding considerably more water was built above Rawling's original dam (which can still be seen).

p. 195   11. Before 1846, no paper currency was used in Hong Kong. The only gold coins legally current were those of the United Kingdom, and the East India Company's gold mohur which equalled £1-9-2. The silver coins in use, besides those of the United Kingdom, were the dollars of Spain, Mexico and the South American States, each equivalent to 4/2 sterling, and the East India Company's rupees equivalent to 1/10 sterling. The copper coins of Great Britain, from a penny to a half farthing, and the copper 'cash' of China which equalled 1/6 of a farthing, were also in use.

ADDITIONAL NOTES, Chapter XIII & Appendix I

A branch of the Oriental Bank was established in Hong Kong in 1846 and from it notes for various amounts from 5 to 1000 dollars were issued. As the bank was not yet chartered, the notes were not recognized by the Government. The Oriental Bank Corp. was chartered in 1852 and consequently its notes were the only recognized paper currency in Hong Kong. From 1 July 1862, the accounts of the Government which were formerly kept in sterling were kept in Hong Kong dollars according to instructions from the Secretary of States for the Colonies.

Paper currencies were issued by several other banks, including the Chartered Mercantile Bank of India, London and China in 1859, and The Hongkong and Shanghai Banking Corp. in 1865. See *Hong Kong Blue Book,* 1842–1865.

12. Dr James Legge, D.D. of the London Missionary Society.

p. 196 13. See the Index to Sayer, *Hong Kong 1862–1919* for the Clock Tower, Dent's fountain, City Hall and the Sailors' Home, and the illustrations between pp. 82 and 83 of that book.

APPENDIX I

1. Elliot's proclamation in English is dated 29 January 1841 by both *The Canton Press* (13 July 1841) and *The Chinese Repository* X, January 1841, pp. 63–64. *The Canton Press* also says that it (as well as Elliot and Bremer's Proclamation of 1 February 1841) was not made public in Macao until 7 February 1841. The Proclamation of 1 February 1841 was given in the following Chinese and English versions:

大英公使大臣住中華領事義律，軍師統帥水師總兵伯麥示，爲曉諭事：
照得本公使大臣奉命爲英國善定事宜，現經與欽差大臣爵閣部堂琦議定諸事，將香港等處全島地方，讓給英國寄居主掌，已有文據在案，是爾香港等處居民，現係歸屬大英國主之子民，故自應恭順樂服國主派來之官，其官亦必保護爾等安堵，不致一人致（受）害。至爾居民，向來所有田畝房舍產業家私，概必如舊，斷不輕動。凡有禮儀所關，鄉約律例，率准仍舊，亦無絲毫更改之議。且未奉國主另降諭旨之先，擬應大清律例規矩之治，居民除不拷訊研鞫外，其餘稍無所改。凡有長老治理鄉里者，仍聽如舊。惟須稟明英官治理可也。倘有英民及外國人等，致（致）害居民，准爾即赴附近官前稟明，定即爲爾查辦。自所有各省商船，來往貿易，均准任意買賣，所有稅餉船鈔掛號等規費，輸納大英國帑。儻嗣後有應示事，即派來官憲，隨時曉諭，責成鄉里長老，轉轄小民，使其從順。毋違特示。一千八百四十一年二月初一日（道光二十一年正月初十日）

(中國史學會 (Chung-kuo shih hsueh hui) 主編，鴉片戰爭 (Ya p'ien chan ch'eng) 上海，神州國光社, 1954, vol. 4, pp. 241–242)

PROCLAMATION

Bremer, Commander-in-chief, and Elliot, Plenipotentiary, &c. &c., by this Proclamation make known to the inhabitants of the Island of Hongkong, that that Island has now become part of the Dominions of the Queen of England by clear public agreement between the high officers of the Celestial and British Courts; and all native persons residing therein must understand, that they are now subjects of the Queen of England, to whom and to whose officers they must pay duty and obedience.

The Inhabitants are hereby promised protection, in Her Majesty's gracious name, against all enemies whatever; and they are further secured in the free exercise of their religious rites, ceremonies, and social customs; and in the enjoyment of their lawful private property and interests. They will be governed, pending Her Majesty's further pleasure, according to the laws, customs, and usages of the Chinese (every description of torture excepted), by the Elders of Villages, subject to the control of a British Magistrate; and any person having complaint to prefer of ill-usage or injustice against any Englishman or Foreigner, will quietly make report to the nearest officer, to the end that full justice may be done.

Chinese ships and merchants resorting to the Port of Hongkong for purposes of Trade are hereby exempted, in the name of the Queen of England, from charge or duty of any kind to the British Government. The Pleasure of the Government will be declared from time to time by further proclamation; and all heads of Villages are held responsible that the commands are duly respected and observed.

Given under Seal of office, this 1st day of Feb. 1841.

(*The Canton Press*, 13 July 1841)

Appendix II

1. *The Chinese Repository*, X (May 1841) pp. 288–289 quotes the same list from the *Hong Kong Gazette*, no. 2 (15 May 1841), but includes Chinese characters for all the place names and also adds that the 'Isthmus of Kowlung, or Tresemshatsuy [sic] 尖沙嘴 contains about 800 people. Kowlung 九龍, Taipang 大鵬, and Lye moon 鯉魚門, are villages and places near the isthmus.' Eitel, *Europe in China*, p. 171, also refers to this first census and disputes the figure of 2,000 as the population for Stanley 赤柱 (Chekchu) and its description as 'the capital, a large town'.

Appendix III

1. Sayer describes the list in this Appendix as the 'authentic list of the results of the auction', but his source was J. R. Morrison's list reproduced in Appendix I to the *Report of the Select Committee on Commercial Relations*

with China, 1847 (abbreviated as *Com. Rel.*), p. 376. A later and more detailed list is also reproduced in the same Appendix on pp. 407–408, and includes later grants up to 26 June 1843, covering marine lots 1–73, but without the dimensions and the price of each lot. However, Morrison's original list is also extracted from the *Hong Kong Gazette*, where it first appeared, by *The Chinese Repository* X (June 1844), *The Canton Press* (3 July 1841) and *The Canton Register* (29 June 1841). Further details about the arrangements and conditions of this first land sale were also given by Morrison in the *Hong Kong Gazette* as an introduction to his list. Both *The Canton Press* and *The Canton Register* comment on this sale on more than one occasion.

APPENDIX V

1. The whole question has now been explored in detail and Sayer's investigation, though interesting, is now entirely superceded by Katherine Mattock's *This is Hong Kong: the story of Government House* (Hong Kong, Government Printer, 1978). Sayer's biggest error was to belittle the notion that a Governor ever lived at Spring Gardens; see also Add. Note 30 to chapter VIII, and it does, perhaps highlight Sayer's reliance on secondary sources for much of his work. The house in which Governor Bonham lived was referred to as 'Old Government House' when its owners, Turner & Co., advertised it for sale in the *Friend of China* on 3 April 1852.

The French Missions Étrangeres de Paris building (p. 211) was assigned to the Government in 1952 and was used by the Education Department and then the Victoria District Court, but now *pro tempore,* the Supreme Court.

APPENDIX VIII

1. This Appendix has a number of errors: Elliot has no direct memorial in Hong Kong. Glenealy was once known as 'Elliot's Vale' but this name was superceded as the house called 'Glenealy' (which stood incidentally on the site of the house built by Caine and rented for a time as a residence for Governor Davis, see pp. 213–214) gave its name to the locality both above and below its site. The Roman Catholic Cathedral now occupies the site of 'Glenealy'. Elliot is now barely remembered in the name of the Elliot Filter Beds, themselves named after the Elliot Battery which lay directly above Belcher's Battery (see Add. Note 11 to chapter VIII). Elliot Block in Wongneichung Road is used as Royal Naval married quarters and there is a private road named Elliot's Crescent off Robinson Road in the Mid-Levels.

In referring to the early naval surveyors, he might also have referred to Hebe Haven, named after the *Young Hebe,* a surveying vessel.

Staunton Street is named after Sir George Leonard Staunton who accompanied Lord Macartney to Peking in the 1790s, or after his son Sir George Thomas Staunton. The Colonial Chaplain was Rev. Vincent J. Stanton (misspelt as Staunton on pp. 71, 74 and 140 of the text).

Bridges Street is something of a puzzle. It is possible that it was named after W. T. Bridges since the lots lying either side of it did come into existence during his sojourn in Hong Kong. But it is also possible that it was named after James Bridges Endicott, an American, who had property in the area.

Governor Bowring's mark—Bowrington—has dropped out of use since Sayer's day. It described the area on either side of Canal Roads East and West. There is now a Bowring Street in Kowloon.

Lord Lyndhurst after whom Lyndhurst Terrace was named was a Lord Chancellor and, incidentally, a critic of Hong Kong as a British colony.

Black's Link was named after Major General Wilsone Black, sometime Commander of British Forces.

As for Sayer's queries, the most interesting relates to Hollywood. 'Who or what was Hollywood?' asks Sayer. The answer is quite simple: Sir John Davis's country mansion at Westbury-on-Trym in Gloucestershire was named 'Hollywood Towers'. This information could have been available to Sayer as one of Davis's own copies of one of his works about China is in the Hankow Club Collection (transferred to the University of Hong Kong in 1932). That volume bears Davis's signature followed by his address.

Appendix IX

1. This Appendix is itself a piece of history now as many of the expressions have dropped out of common use.

   Sayer's definition of 'country ship' is not entirely accurate; it simply referred to non-Company ships which would not, by virtue of the nature of the Company's monopoly, be allowed to trade to London but which were licensed by the Company to trade to China.

   'Boy' is commonly held to be a corruption of the Hindu *bahi* and is found in the Anglo-Indian 'sepoy'. It simply means a person.

   Some of his other expressions are now obsolete: 'shroff' is still current as is 'godown,' though only the latter retains its proper meaning. 'Punkahs' are remembered more today from novels about life in nineteenth-century India and 'tiffin' has all but disappeared—some clubs in Hong Kong still so describe their luncheons. 'Sycee' and 'tael' may have been too useful to be lost in Sayer's day but are rarely heard today (except that the latter is a standard measure for the sale of gold in Hong Kong), likewise 'Lac'. We still use 'chunam' (it has become a verb by now) but 'bazaar' really only lives on in street names (e.g. Gilman's and Jardine's Bazaars).

'Comprador' is still with us but only in a much-devalued sense of a universal provider of food and other provisions. We think of a 'praya' only in terms of Macao, and 'joss' we normally only hear in connection with joss sticks. 'Amah' surely meant more than 'native nurse' even in Sayer's day. Few boating enthusiasts today would be able to describe the nature of a 'lorcha' but the expression does occur.

Of the Japanese words cited, 'rickshaw' is still in current use but the rickshaw pullers are literally a dying breed as no new pulling licenses have been issued for a number of years now.

The Chinese loan words, if Chinese they be, are far more common in English as a whole. 'Maskee' is a peculiarity not really heard today but 'Hong' has acquired what seems to be a wider connotation from that which it may have had in Sayer's day. 'Taipan' is, of course, familiar to all as the managing director or chairman of the larger 'Hongs'. We still use 'chit' but Sayer's derivation of it from 'chi-tsai' is doubtful as the *Oxford English dictionary* indicates that the word is an abbreviation of an Anglo-Indian word 'chitty', derived from the Hindi meaning a letter, a note or pass given to a servant. This seems more plausible than Sayer's derivation. Sayer mentions the now obsolete 'chop boat' and 'chop-chop' but he does not mention 'chop' in the sense of an official seal or stamp, a sense in which the expression is still in current use in Hong Kong—on many official forms, a space is provided for the stamping of the official company chop. This word, again, seems more likely to have been derived from Anglo-Indian usage, stemming from the Hindi word 'chhāp', meaning an official impress or stamp. It is interesting that the extended meaning of the expression, as in 'chop boat' or in 'chop' for a hulk, has now diminished and the word is used simply in its original sense. 'Consoo' has disappeared and 'cumshaw' has given way to more mundane descriptive expressions.